D1159741

MEDIA AND NATION BUILDING

Asia Pacific Studies

The Asia Pacific is the most economically dynamic region of the world. It can boast large numbers of new economic and political groupings that extend from the Russian Far East in the north to Australia and New Zealand in the south. The forces of globalization are producing new population, cultural and information flows throughout the region. At the same time, the past continues to cast a long shadow and newer issues are fuelling regional tensions.

This series provides an outlet for cutting edge academic research on Asia Pacific studies. The major focus will be the politics, histories, societies, and cultures of individual countries together with overviews of major regional trends and developments.

Series Editors:

J. S. Eades, *Professor of Asia Pacific Studies, Ritsumeikan Asian Pacific University*

David Askew, *Associate Professor (Legal Studies), Ritsumeikan Asian Pacific University*

Volume 1
Media and Nation Building: How the Iban Became Malaysian
John Postill

MEDIA AND NATION BUILDING

How the Iban Became Malaysian

John Postill

Berghahn Books
New York • Oxford

302.2309595
P85m

First published in 2006 by
Berghahn Books
www.berghahnbooks.com

©2006 John Postill

Library of Congress Cataloging-in-Publication Data
Postill, John, 1965-
    Media and nation buildings : how the Iban became Malaysian / John Postill.
    p. cm.
    Includes bibliographical references and index.
    ISBN 1-84545-132-5 (alk. paper) – ISBN 1-84545-135-X (pbk. : alk. paper)
    1. Mass media policy–Malaysia.   2. Nationalism–Malaysia.
3. Iban (Bornean people)–Malaysia–Politics and government.   I. Title.

P95.82.M4P67 2006
302.2309595–dc22

                                                2005056785

British Library Cataloguing in Publication Data
A catalogue record for this book is available from the British Library
Printed in the United States on acid-free paper

ISBN 1-84545-132-5 hardback

For Vandon

CONTENTS

LIST OF FIGURES

LIST OF TABLES

LIST OF APPENDIXES

ACKNOWLEDGEMENTS

I wish to thank Marion Berghahn for her support and encouragement throughout the process of publication. Andrew Beatty read the entire manuscript and made very useful comments on it. Mark Stanton was very helpful with the technical aspects, as was Nicki Averill who drew the maps.

Quite a few years ago now, Mark Hobart, of the School of Oriental and African Studies (SOAS), University of London, was a most supportive MA tutor. It was at SOAS that I discovered the work of Benedict Sandin, the Iban ethnohistorian, and reread Derek Freeman's classic Iban work. The present book grew out of a doctoral thesis at University College London (UCL) presented in 1999. I would like to thank Simon Strickland and Chris Tilley, my supervisors, for all their advice and faith in the project. Research for the thesis was generously supported by the Anthropology Department at UCL, the Graduate School at UCL, the Central Research Fund of London University, and the Evans Fund of the Anthropology Department, Cambridge University. My postdoctoral research at the Staatlichen Hochschule für Gestalrung, in Karlsruhe, was supported by the German Research Foundation (DFG).

In Sarawak I was attached to Majlis Adat Istiadat (Council for Customary Law) and the Sarawak Museum. I was also assisted by staff from the State Planning Unit, Tun Jugah Foundation, Bahagian Teknologi Pendidikan, the Iban Section of RTM in Kuching and Sri Aman, and CATS Radio. The State Government of Sarawak kindly allowed me to undertake research in Sarawak and facilitated my work there.

There are so many people in Sarawak who helped me along the way that I can only name but a few here in alphabetical order. My warmest thanks to Indai Amoi, Edward J. anak Alban, TR Baling and family, Nicholas Bawin Anggat, Dr Madeline Berma, Alfred Buma, Chai Soong Yee and family, TR Jabu anak Chaong, Dr Sandy Craig and Kirsten A. Edey, Dr Ipoi Datan, Mary Sian anak Dugat and family, Alfred Dass, TK Dayan F. Dunggie, D.O. Gani, TR Garan, Henry Gerijih, Stevenson anak Ingkon, Tan Sri (Dr) Alfred Jabu, Dr Jayum anak Jawan, TR Layang anak Jelian, Datuk Amar (Dr) Linggi Jugah, Father Jugah, TR Randi anak Julak and family, Dr Peter Kedit, Roland D. Klabu, Thomas T. Laka, Empani Lang, Nichol R. Lang, Jayl Langub, the

Rt. Rev. Datuk Made Katib, Dr James Masing, Luta anak Nalang, Janet R. Noel, Mr Pulin, Penghulu Thomas Dundang anak Ringgie, Robert Menua Saleh, Laja Sanggin, Datuk Chris Sim and family, Sim Kwang Yang, Dr Otto Steinmayer, Prof Vinson Sutlive, Jimbun Tawai, Edward Untie, and Datin Tra Zehnder. In particular, I am extremely grateful to all the residents of Entanak and Nanga Tebat Longhouses for inviting me to live among them and for their generosity during my stay. *Aku tu, Bujang Rengayong, deka meri tabi enggau besai terima kasih ngagai kita semua. Arap ka kita semua gerai nyamai, lantang senang baka ka selama.*

During my UCL years (1995 to 2000) I benefited greatly from the comments and encouragement of Adam Drazin, Michelle Lee, Daniel Miller, Alex Pillen, Chris Pinney, Mike Polterack, Sarah Posey, Andrew Skuse, Elena Yalouri and other staff and doctoral students, as well as from the advice of Terry King and Roger Silverstone, my thesis examiners who wrote a very detailed report. I also wish to thank Dorle Drackle and all other staff, volunteers and students at the memorable summer school in media anthropology held at the University of Hamburg in 1999. In Bucharest, Vintila Mihailescu, Iulia Hasdeu, Urban Larssen and my students at the National School of Political Science and Administration (SNSPA) adopted me into a thriving anthropological scene. At the Staatlichen Hochschule für Gestaltung, in Karlsruhe, I have to thank my colleagues Hans Belting, Martin Schultz, Birgit Mersmann and all the *Bildanthropologie* doctoral researchers for their interest in my postdoctoral work on Iban visual media (2001 to 2002). In Heidelberg, Olli Hinkelbein and Julia Schunck were very welcoming, as were Jürg Wassmann and everyone at the Anthropology Department.

More recently, as a sessional lecturer at SOAS, the City Literary Institute in London and Loughborough University, I have been fortunate to teach outstanding students who have asked difficult questions about some of the materials presented here. In preparing this book over the years I have also derived much inspiration from friends and colleagues at other institutions, especially Shamsul A. Baharuddin, Véronique Béguet, Cora Bender, Clare Boulanger, Alex Drace-Francis, Jens Franz, Jack Goody, Eric Hirsch, Ron Inden, Tim Ingold, Mercedes López Invarato, Ken Nakata-Steffensen, Filipe Reis, Anthony Richards, Jeff Roberts and Reed Wadley.

Special thanks to all those who have read and commented on earlier versions of parts of this book: Fausto Barlocco, Maurice Bloch, Nick Couldry, Mike Crang, Faye Ginsburg, Eric Kaufmann, Samuel Onn, Mark A. Peterson, Annalisa Piñas Postill, Carlos Piñas Postill, Gini Ras, Clifford Sather, as well as all participants in the 4th EASA Media Anthropology Network e-Seminar, 19–26 April 2005 (www.philbu.net/media-anthropology/workingpapers.htm) and several anonymous readers for the *Borneo Research Bulletin, Time & Society,* and *Social Anthropology.* These publications also deserve my gratitude for allowing me to use revised versions of previously published articles in a number of chapters, namely chapter 3, 'Propagating the State, Phase I' (Postill 2001), chapter 4, 'Propagating the State, Phase II' (Postill 2002a), chapter 6, 'Writing Media' (Postill 2003) and chapter 8, 'Clock Time' (Postill 2002b).

Finally, I have to thank my scattered friends and family for keeping in touch all along. I am most grateful to my parents, Francisco and Jennifer, for supporting my early encounters with anthropology, and to my partner, Sarah Pink, for persuading me to write this book knowing what it would entail.

1

INTRODUCTION:
MEDIA ANTHROPOLOGY IN
A WORLD OF STATES

The present world is a world of states, neither a world of tribes nor a world of empires, though the remnants of such forms are still present and occupy part of our thinking.

Nicholas Tarling (1998)

We live in a world of states. We have lived in such a world since the dismantling of the British and French empires after the Second World War. The remnants of both empires are still present, but the influence of Britain and France has waned as steadily as that of the United States, China, India and other large states has grown. In the 1990s, the now global inter-state system penetrated deep into the former Soviet bloc (the last European empire) and into non-aligned Yugoslavia. The result was a host of post-socialist states, some of which have joined the European Union – a curious entity at odds with the statist logic of the global system (Tønnesson 2004). By 2004 the misleadingly named United Nations had recruited a record number of 191 member states. Together with other global institutions, the UN actively supports the present state system. By the same logic, these institutions and the powers that bolster them strongly discourage secessionism. Thus between 1944 and 1991 only two territories around the world – Singapore and Bangladesh – managed to secede from recognised states and join the United Nations (Smith 1994: 292). Many other secessionist attempts were thwarted during that same period, as they still are to this day.

This book examines a neglected aspect in the study of this world of states: how states use modern media to 'build' nations within their allocated territories. The case study is Malaysia, a state created in 1963 as part of a third, Afro-Asian wave of modern state formation. The first wave broke upon the Americas in the nineteenth century, the second across Europe in the

1

twentieth century, and we have recently experienced a fourth, post-Soviet wave (O'Leary 1998: 60).

The Federation of Malaysia was initially an amalgam of four British colonies: Malaya, Singapore, Sarawak and North Borneo (Sabah). Whilst Singapore seceded in 1965, the other three territories have remained united, and further separations seem highly unlikely. Malaysia's birth was inauspicious: it had inherited an economy wholly dependent on export commodities and a deeply divided multiethnic population. The new country faced the immediate threats of civil war, a belligerent Indonesia, and Filipino claims over Sabah. As I write these lines in mid-2005, Malaysia is a stable polity with a prosperous economy, a quasi-democracy, negligible levels of inter-ethnic violence, and amicable relations with neighbouring states. In an era of 'failed states' and ethnic massacres, how can we explain Malaysia's undoubted success? What are the domestic and external factors that have contributed to Malaysia's survival and prosperity?

A comprehensive account of all the possible contributing factors is beyond the scope of this book. Instead, the present study concentrates on a single domain of state intervention – the media – and on a single Malaysian people – the Iban of Sarawak, on the island of Borneo. What we lose in scope, we gain in focus: by studying in detail Iban uses of state media over time, we can

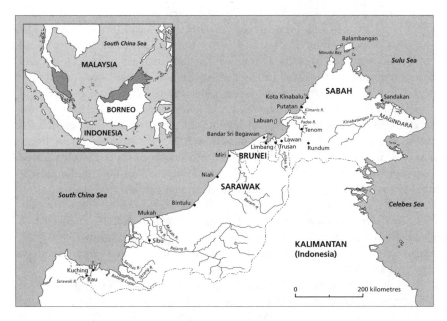

Figure 1.1.   Sarawak, Sabah and Peninsular Malaysia.

Source: adapted from Andaya and Andaya (1982).

2

gain an appreciation of analogous processes in other parts of Malaysia and elsewhere.[1] I argue that state-led media efforts have been amply rewarded, for the Iban of Sarawak have become thoroughly 'Malaysianised'. I also suggest that the Iban experience has important implications not only for anthropologists, development experts and indigenous activists, but also for our understanding of media in a world of states. I study four foundational media forms common to modern states virtually everywhere, namely state propaganda, writing (literacy), television, and clock-and-calendar time. In the developed North it is easy to forget that even the latest media technologies rely on earlier – but by no means superseded – media. For instance, both email and mobile telephone messaging depend on writing and clock-and-calendar time. New media rarely replace old media; the two usually co-exist.

This chapter provides a theoretical background to the book. In the following section I clarify my usage of terms such as state, nation, nation-state, nation building, and nation making, and suggest that 'nation building' is still a concept with social scientific validity. I then define this study as an *ethnological* contribution to a research area known as 'media anthropology'. My approach is ethnological in that it tracks the intertwined fates of the Iban and other Malaysian peoples (*ethnos*) across time and space through concepts such as diffusion, appropriation, cultural form, media form and culture area. In this respect, it differs from social anthropological (ethno*graphic*) studies centred on the embedded sociality of contemporary groups. I suggest that Malaysia is becoming a 'thick' culture area in its own right, distinct from both the Indonesian and Singaporean culture areas, and that the consolidation of Malaysian variants of global media forms is central to this process. This consolidation entails what I call 'sustainable propaganda', i.e., state propaganda fully assimilated into the life and institutions of a population. The chapter ends with an outline of the book.

Nation Building

There is broad agreement amongst scholars on the meaning of the term 'state'. In the contemporary world system, a state is an independent territory recognised by the United Nations, e.g., East Timor, Germany, or Canada. It is 'the major political unit in world politics' (Connor 2004: 39). In this book I use the term state interchangeably with the more colloquial 'country'.

Defining the term 'nation' is far more problematic. A vast literature has been devoted to this problem, which has acquired renewed urgency with the demise of the Soviet Union and the expansion of the European Union. As is often the case, no consensus has been reached on the matter. The debate is closely linked to the inter-disciplinary study of nationalism. Two broad camps have formed on the question of origins: those who argue that nations are modern creations arising from the Enlightenment and industrialisation and those who trace the roots of nations to Antiquity or even further back.

The first position – modernism – is commonly associated with Ernest Gellner (1983), the Czech-Jewish philosopher and anthropologist. Other influential modernists, also known as 'constructivists', are Anderson (1991 and below) and Hobsbawm and Ranger (1983). For Gellner (1983: 140–143), the ideology of nationalism was the result of the economic modernisation of nineteenth century Europe. Industrialisation demanded a realignment of culture and state. The new economy could only develop if the population learnt to communicate fluently across ethno-linguistic divides, both face-to-face and through abstract media. The driving principle was 'one state, one culture'. Under these circumstances, most European states developed national languages and mass educational systems. The aim was to create a 'literate sophisticated high culture' that could cope with the demands of economic modernisation. As a result of these changes, some ethnic groups began to feel excluded from their polities and to demand autonomy in their 'own' homelands. The simple doctrine of self-determination became a rallying call across Europe and eventually the whole planet. This doctrine demanded that the governing and the governed be co-nationals (O'Leary 1998).

The second position has a strong advocate in A.D. Smith (1986, 2001, 2004), a proponent of the 'ethno-symbolist' theory of nationalism. A nation, for Smith, is a

> named human population which shares myths and memories, a mass public culture, a designated homeland, economic unity and equal rights and duties for all members (Smith 1995: 56–57).

Smith contends that although many of the ideals of nationalism are indeed modern, the roots of nations such as England, France or Japan can be traced to ancient times. Nations are not built out of thin air; they have solid ethnic foundations, myths of ethnic origin and election, and symbols of territory and community (Guibernau and Hutchinson 2004). They are patterned on, and often have evolved from, dominant *ethnies*, or ethnic communities. Yet the obdurate 'presentism' of modernist scholars, says Smith (2004), leads them to focus on elite manipulation, downplaying processes of national formation over the *longue durée*.

One criticism levelled at Smith is of special relevance to the present study. Connor (2004: 41) takes exception to Smith's questioning of the nation as a mass phenomenon, a questioning that contradicts Smith's own definition of the nation just quoted. To Connor, the notion of nation must necessarily imply 'a single group consciousness' that unites the elites and the masses. Such a consciousness cannot arise overnight; it requires many generations to spread from the elites to the masses. This poses a formidable methodological challenge for historians of nationalism, adds Connor, for illiterate masses are invariably 'silent'. It is here, I would suggest, that an ethnological approach can make a lasting contribution, in that it combines ethnographic and historical research. Thus the present work springs from a direct fieldwork engagement with, and historical work on, both the Iban 'masses' and the elites.

Both Smith's and Gellner's theories suffer from weaknesses, but they also have much to recommend them. Gellner's linking of nationalism with modernisation is highly pertinent to Southeast Asia, a different region and historical period from those central to his thesis. As I explore in chapters 3 and 4, Iban and other Malaysian elites have used media to 'modernise' the Iban through cultural standardisation under conditions of rapid economic growth. Smith's definition of the nation, on the other hand, captures succinctly the aspirations of Malaysia's nation builders, including most rural Iban leaders, teachers and schoolchildren. These varied social agents all hope that Malaysia will achieve full nationhood by the year 2020. There is an important caveat, though: there is no provision as yet for Malaysia's ethnic Chinese and Indians to be given rights equal to those enjoyed by the Malays – the dominant *ethnie* (see chapter 5 and conclusion).

The notion of 'nation building' is no less problematic than that of nation. This term has long been marginalised from serious Western social theory for its association with modernisation theory (Smith 2004: 195, cf. Deutsch and Foltz 1963, Deutsch 1966). The latter had its heyday in the 1950s and 1960s, as the U.S. government recruited scores of social scientists in its efforts to win the 'hearts and minds' of Third World populations in rivalry with the Soviet Union and China. Modernisation became an elastic notion used by U.S. academics and policy-makers to explain the persistence of traditional 'mind-sets' and ease the transition to market-driven, 'democratic' regimes in the postcolonial world. In other words, it was used to promote a form of nation building modelled on an idealised United States (Latham and Gaddis 2000). In Vietnam, 'the other war', the propaganda war over hearts and minds, was fought and lost by American social scientists who failed to agree on a nation building strategy for that country (Marquis 2000). At present, the term is often used in the Anglophone media and popular scholarship with reference to America's half-hearted attempts at 'reconstruction' in occupied countries such as Afghanistan or Iraq (e.g., Ignatieff 2003).

Given its pedigree, it is little wonder that anthropologists and other social scientists are wary of the term 'nation building'. One recent search for an alternative term has been Foster's (1997, 2002) work on media and 'nation making' in Papua New Guinea (PNG). In his monograph *Materializing the Nation*, Foster (2002) argues that although PNG inherited a weak state from the Australian colonists, the making of a PNG nation is well under way. Foster's notion of nation making differs from that of nation building in that it does not privilege state-led processes of change. In addition to the state, this notion directs our attention to the private sector and the wider population. Foster finds compelling evidence that PNG, independent only since 1975, is already far more than an 'imagined' political community (Anderson 1991). He analyses Coca-Cola advertising, law and order campaigns, letters to the English-language press, millennial cults, betel nut chewing and other practices, and reports the emergence of a distinctly PNG public culture. Foster follows Billig (1995) in stressing the significance of banal everyday practices in the maintenance of a national public culture, whether they be reading the PNG weather forecast or viewing street hoardings in *Tok Pisin*, the national language.

There are good reasons, PNG notwithstanding, to retain the term 'nation building'. First, in contrast to PNG, Malaysia inherited a strong state from its colonial rulers. Efforts to create a Malaysian nation began in the early 1960s and are still given priority by the government. The state was, and remains, the most powerful agent of social and cultural change in Malaysia – as in many other countries. Second, Malaysian state propaganda on security, development and national integration soon percolated even into remote rural areas and began to shape people's worldviews, as I show in chapters 3 and 4. Today official nation-building propaganda is hardly distinguishable from the views of Iban from all walks of life. Third, the term nation building is still widely used by the 'beneficiaries' of America's Cold War largesse: the elites and middle classes of postcolonial states around the globe. It is also routinely used by inter-state organisations (the UN, World Bank, Commonwealth, etc.) and the media in relation to ongoing development strategies for East Timor, Afghanistan, Iraq, South Africa, and so on. The term captures the *built* nature of modern state and nation formation (Kolstø 2000). The close relationship between metaphors of development and building is clearly seen in the etymology of the Malay and Indonesian word *pembangunan* (development), derived from the term *bangunan* (building, structure). In the contemporary world, there is the universal expectation that a built infrastructure consisting of roads, airports, schools, hospitals, etc., will be put in place. Without such an infrastructure, not only is a country deemed underdeveloped, it cannot possibly operate in a capitalist world economy (Tønnesson 2004). A concomitant requirement is the existence of a mass workforce; a nomadic band of fifty hunters and gatherers can build neither a state nor a nation (Diamond 1999). In sum, the term nation building both reflects and produces socio-economic realities. It has tangible effects on the world, often unintended ones, but far-reaching all the same. All this lends the term enormous practical and theoretical importance in a world of states. Whilst not denying that the concept of nation making has great analytical potential, in this study I deal primarily with state media interventions that fall under the rubric of 'nation building'.

A final word on the term 'nation-state'. Strictly speaking, a nation-state is 'that relatively rare situation in which the borders of a state and a nation closely coincide; a state with an ethnically homogeneous population' (Connor

2004: 39). The term should be used sparingly when referring to present-day countries, but it is worth remembering that the nation-state as an *ideal* is still well entrenched in many corridors of knowledge and power, not least amongst politicians and social activists in Malaysia.

Media Anthropology

This book is intended as a contribution to a research area known as 'media anthropology', the anthropological study of contemporary media (Askew and Wilk 2002, Ginsburg et al. 2002).[2] Like the study of nation building, the early history of media anthropology is tightly bound up with American foreign policy. Early functionalist fieldwork on media in small town America gave way during the Second World War to the study of enemy and allied media as part of the war effort (Mead and Métraux 2000). Some of the world's leading anthropologists, including Gregory Bateson, Margaret Mead and Ruth Benedict, studied national cultures 'at a distance' through films, novels and other media produced in enemy countries they could not visit owing to the war. After the war, interest in the media diminished as anthropologists returned to field research. There was scant anthropological interest in the media until the late 1980s, which saw the onset of a rapid growth in the number of studies that has continued unabated into the early years of this century (Peterson 2003).

Just as post-war anthropologists lost interest in the media, mass communications researchers in the U.S. became increasingly concerned with the effects of media (Morley 1992: 45). Their approach was often behaviourist. It assumed that mass media could 'inject' a positive ideology directly into the populace – the so-called 'hypodermic needle' model. This optimistic model, like its pessimistic precursor from the Frankfurt School, presumed a passive, atomised audience unable to resist the allure of the mass media. The model proved popular with modernisation theorists working on nation building projects within America's sphere of influence in the Third World (Peterson 2003: 44). It sustained the modernist ideology of the early Cold War through well-funded research and journals prone to scientistic jargon. At the same time, it failed to address critically questions of power, knowledge or economy (Lull 1990: 15). But a reaction against this mass communications 'dominant paradigm' was already under way in the 1960s. It came to be known as 'uses research'. If effects research had asked 'what media do to people', uses research asked 'what people do to media'. Its theoretical orientation was structural-functionalist. People were seen as active participants in the selection of media contents, not as passive recipients, seeking to meet their societal needs (Morley 1992: 52).

In Britain, media research followed its own paths. Like the old Frankfurt School, British cultural studies scholars in the early 1970s were keenly interested in media power. They shifted, however, the analytical focus from production to reception. Influenced by Gramsci and Foucault, they held the view that media producers have no monopoly of power; this is always shared with consumers (Askew 2002: 5). Although Raymond Williams, the Cambridge don, was the founding father, Birmingham remained the centre of British cultural and media studies through the 1970s and 1980s. For many years, Stuart Hall was the leading figure of a network of scholars who kept their distance from America's media effects researchers. They had an explicitly leftist agenda: to fight capitalism, racism and patriarchy (Lull 1990). Most practitioners followed Hall in his rejection both of economic determinism and of the structuralist stress on the autonomy of media discourses, i.e., the idea of texts as the sole producers of meaning. Instead they emphasised creativity and social experience, placing media and other practices within the 'complex expressive totality' of a society (Curran et al. 1987: 76–77). Hall argued persuasively that although media producers shape the future 'decoding' of their texts by encoding what he called 'preferred readings', they hold no ultimate control over their audiences' interpretations (Askew 2002). Most audiences actively appropriate media contents, turning them to their own uses, but within the constraints imposed by both medium and message.

The bulk of media research down the decades has been carried out in North America and Western Europe. Media anthropologists, who are relative latecomers, have helped to extend the geographical reach of media research beyond its North Atlantic heartland. In theoretical terms, however, they remain resolutely North Atlantic, yet they are far more influenced by Williams, Hall and other British cultural studies luminaries than they are by American media effects research. These anthropological studies share a careful attention to ethnographic detail and theoretical sophistication. There is a general rejection of the top-down 'positivism' of the American tradition, and a selective use of Hall's model of media reception. Media users are presented not as the passive recipients of powerful messages but rather as skilled interpreters (within bounds) of media texts (Askew 2002, Ginsburg et al. 2002).

Hall (1973) distinguished three types of audience positioning with regard to mass media ideology: 'dominant', 'oppositional' and 'negotiated'. Media consumers who adopt a dominant position accept wholesale the broadcast ideology; oppositional consumers challenge it; whilst the latter resist some elements of it. Most anthropologists working on media have regarded their informants' positioning as being 'negotiated'. For instance, Mankekar (1999) describes urban television viewers in India enjoying epic dramas yet being able to 'read through' to the encoded nationalist propaganda. My findings in rural Sarawak (chapter 5) suggest a very different positioning there. Most rural Iban have adopted a dominant position, that is, their interpretations of official broadcasts are fully in line with the state ideology. In 1997, for instance, when the region went through a series of alarming crises, Malaysia's propagandists succeeded in assuaging the rural population's fears. By contrast, the urban middle classes were more doubtful, as they had access to non-governmental sources of information and critique. These citizens 'negotiated' mainstream reports throughout the crises. Finally, members or sympathisers of opposition parties in urban Sarawak adopted, not surprisingly, oppositional stances. This suggests that media anthropologists may have been too hasty in elevating marginal viewers to interpretive parity with the intelligentsia (e.g., Abu-Lughod 1997). As Morley (1980) has shown for Britain and Caldarola (1993) for Indonesian Borneo, media consumers' interpretive competence roughly correlates with their levels of formal education. It also suggests that Hall's model has stood the test of time.

Recent anthropological research into state-controlled media can be grouped into three categories. Coincidentally, these three categories overlap with the three types of political formation distinguished by Tarling in the quotation that opened this chapter, namely tribes, states and empires. First, there are media ethnographies on the relationship between indigenous groups ('tribes') and the state in white-settler countries (e.g., Turner 1992, Ginsburg 1993, Perrot 1992). Second, there are ethnographies of low-income urban groups and their 'negotiated' consumption of official propaganda in non-Western countries (e.g., Abu-Lughod 1997, Mankekar 1999, Rofel 1994). Third, there are studies of Western propaganda across state borders, for example 1990s British propaganda in Afghanistan (Skuse 1999) and Kazakhstan (Mandel 2002) – i.e., contact zones between two former empires (Britain and Russia) reluctantly demoted to mere statehood.

One key subject-matter sidelined in these studies (but see Spitulnik below) is the uses of media in the making of modern states. Instead, we encounter ethnic minorities or the urban poor engaging with a fully formed state; both people and state are ethnographic givens. The chief reason for this neglect is anthropology's over-reliance on ethnographic research at the expense of historical research. In the present study I seek to redress the balance by adopting an ethnological approach as defined earlier; an approach centred on the comparative history and geography of peoples (*ethnos*) (Seymour-Smith 1986). Another common feature of much media anthropology (and indeed media studies) is the focus on a single medium, often television or film. In later chapters I study a range of media, from radio and television to karaoke videos, including understudied media such as clocks, wristwatches and public-address systems. I also ignore the unhelpful division of labour between the study of literacy and that of media (chapter 6). This broad take on media allows me to investigate how different media were used in the latter half of the twentieth century to crystallise a new set of ethnic and national identities in Sarawak, notably 'Iban', 'Dayak' and 'Malaysian'.

Finally, in the present study I borrow from both the U.S. and British traditions, as I see no reason to jettison the notion of media effects. For example, as I show in chapter 8, television has had a huge effect on rural Iban sociality. Prior to the advent of this technology in the 1980s, the main site of social interaction in Iban longhouses ('villages under one roof') was the public gallery (*ruai*), a manner of village street (Freeman 1992 [1955]). By the 1990s, most *ruai* were deserted at night, as longhouse residents 'migrated' *en masse* to the semi-private family rooms to watch television. In stark contrast, television sets have had no comparable effect on the Iban exchange system (chapter 7). Rather, they have been smoothly assimilated into a pre-existing system of gift-giving and monetary exchanges that cuts across divides of residence, occupation, ethnicity, and even life and death.

Media Research in Malaysia

In Malaysia, media research has followed developments in the United States. Mohd. Hamdan bin Adnan (1990) reported in 1990 that 66 out of 74 faculty members working on media surveyed were trained in the U.S., three each in the Philippines and Malaysia, and only one each in Britain and Indonesia. Lent (1994: 74) found among Malaysian scholars uncritical 'enthusiasm and devotion' concerning their American counterparts. Over the years, a worthy attempt at publishing Malay-language media textbooks has been made. However, in

> almost all cases, textbook translations are from books from the U.S., and the methods of selecting books for translation seem to be based on concepts of old boy networks (favorite U.S. professors of Malaysian lecturers or those who meander through the region occasionally), important guru, or politically safe topics … No better example of these pitfalls exists than the book, *Four Theories of the Press* [Siebert et al. 1963], translated and published in Malaysia in recent years. Conceived and written in the Cold War mid-1950s, *Four Theories of the Press* sets up a dichotomy of good (U.S. and Western Europe) and bad (Soviet Union) press systems, ignores what has since become the Third World, and labels all Communist systems under Soviet Communist. Although the book has had a number of reprintings, not a word has been changed (1994: 78).

Besides the influence of mainstream, often dated, American works, governmental constraints on media research have stunted the growth of 'critical' media studies in Malaysia.[3] One much neglected region is East Malaysia (Borneo), the setting of the present study.[4]

The implications of this Americanisation go beyond Malaysia's academia. As we shall see in chapters 3 and 4, the hypodermic needle and other models of media effects have also strongly influenced the work of media professionals in Sarawak. Another social legacy of modernisation theory is the notion of 'mind-set', a term originally used by radio and press propagandists which has entered everyday Malaysian English. It is commonly employed to refer to the purportedly conservative mentality of rural residents (chapter 4).

The Uneven Diffusion of Media Forms

In recent decades, many social theorists have sought ways out of a perceived bias towards static social structures. In their search for theoretical models that can accommodate human agency, some have outlined theories of social practice as 'structured improvisation' (Bourdieu 1998), others have allowed non-human 'actants' into actor-network theories (Latour and Woolgar 1979), devised scenarios where social agents and 'patients' interact (Gell 1998), or called for the analytical blending of structure and action by way of 'structuration theory' (Giddens 1984). More recently, Mark Peterson (2003: 15) has intriguingly claimed that anthropologists

> have always recognised the tension between cultural representations (myth, ritual, media) and social formations (families, communities, polities). But they have also significantly focused on systems of exchange as the third leg of a theoretical triad.

This dynamic anthropological model, adds Peterson,

> differs from a transmission or producer/consumer model [of media]. Exchanges may be of many types – exchanges of spouses, linguistic exchanges, sharing of food. Exchanges may take place in markets, involve redistribution, or be organized by forms of reciprocity. *Anthropological models have traditionally examined cultural representation, exchange, and social formation in tension.* The elements of this triad are not separate or separable: exchanges occur only according to a set of cultural representations that renders them meaningful, and it is through exchanges that social formations are created, reproduced, and contested. … Cultural representations provide scripts and schemas for understanding the values of things exchanged as well as models for exchange. Yet cultural representations exist only insofar as they are themselves exchanged – if not shared, they are not social and collective (Peterson 2003: 15, my emphasis).

This passage captures an ideal synthesis rather than actual anthropological practice. In actual practice, anthropology still has great difficulties integrating the notion of cultural representation, on the one hand, with those of social formation and exchange on the other. For instance, a senior social anthropologist, Tim Ingold (2000b), has decried the growth of memetics, a field of study derived from the concept of 'meme' (Dawkins 1976). To memeticists, cultural representations (e.g., catchy tunes) are memes, i.e., mental 'viruses' that spread from one human brain to another through imitation. For instance, I can 'pick up' a catchy tune from my neighbour's radio and pass it on to my workmates, who in turn may spread it in their homes, and so on. Against what he rightly deems a crude model (see Sperber 2000, Aunger 2002), Ingold stresses that the key to understanding human life is its embedded sociality. It is for this reason that ethnographers study social context, not 'transferable content'. Similarly, Maurice Bloch (2000) takes issue with the memeticists' idea of discrete cultural units diffusing across social and cultural boundaries. Most of culture, he argues, cannot be divided into discrete elements; there is much more to culture than catchy tunes. Furthermore, those rare elements that retain some degree of cultural integrity usually blend with other elements, losing their original meanings across social contexts. The catchy refrain 'Don't worry, be happy' can mean one thing in Jamaica, quite another in Romania. To both Bloch and Ingold, cultural selectionism (the survival of the 'fittest' cultural elements through cultural selection) is a doomed Social Darwinist enterprise.

Whilst sharing some of these misgivings about memetics, having worked on the social uses of media I have to question the privileging of social context over transferable content. Surely, we need to consider the dynamic relationship between the two. How is a neighbourhood's 'production of locality' (Appadurai 1996) affected by the adoption of new media contents? What kind of cultural work do people carry out to assimilate or reject different contents (Morley et al. 1992)? Why are some cultural forms more widely distributed across the planet than others? What are the environmental, genetic and cultural factors influencing the uneven distribution of cultural forms? These are questions that the anthropology of media can and should address, questions that are of interest to all branches of the discipline.

Bloch and Ingold's views echo the rejection eighty years ago – during professional anthropology's formative years – of the very idea of diffusion. Diffusion can be defined in simple terms as 'the transmission of elements from one culture to another' (Barfield 1997: 118). An influential theory in nineteenth- and early twentieth-century anthropology, it gave rise to the interdisciplinary field of innovation diffusion, a field almost bereft these days of anthropologists (Rogers 1995, Barnard 2000: 54).[5] In the British anthropological tradition, the demise of diffusionism has been linked to the post-First World War emergence of functionalism under Malinowski and Radcliffe-Brown. These two founding fathers disregarded earlier debates about the relative weight of diffusion versus independent invention. Although accepting that cultural traits can diffuse, they stressed that their function was usually transformed beyond recognition within the adopting society (Kuklick 1996: 161, King and Wilder 2003: 56).

By contrast, neither the German-American Boas nor his students saw any incompatibility between identifying the selective principles behind the appropriation of diffused traits and studying the adopting society. On the contrary, those principles could tell us a great deal about social change and continuity in the importing society (Kuklick 1996: 162). By the Second World War, however,

> the question of independent invention *versus* diffusion had been rendered nonsensical in sociocultural anthropology: either it was irrelevant to explanation of the dynamics

of social life or it represented a false dichotomy. It persisted in certain anthropological quarters, however. In particular, archaeologists remained concerned to specify the nature of innovations, because, unlike sociocultural anthropologists, *they had not abandoned the effort to account for world historical change* (Kuklick 1996: 162, my emphasis).

The evidence I present in subsequent chapters lends support to Boas' position on this matter. It shows that we can indeed learn a great deal about change and continuity in Malaysia – and other modern states – from the study of diffused cultural traits, including near-global media forms such as writing, propaganda and television. By this I am not subscribing to the cultural relativism of Boas and his student Margaret Mead (see Eriksen and Nielsen 2001: 40). On the contrary, I concur with Derek Freeman's view that cultural practices are often deleterious to a people and its environment (e.g., Tuzin 2001), and that anthropologists should not refrain from pointing this out, whether they are conducting fieldwork 'at home' or abroad (see chapter 2).

An example from postcolonial Africa will illustrate the need to rehabilitate the notion of diffusion. Debra Spitulnik has carried out anthropological research into the circulation of radio sets (2000) and radio discourse (1996) in Zambia. She contends that meta-pragmatic discourse is particularly amenable to being decontextualised, recontextualised and creatively reworked beyond the immediate listening event. By 'meta-pragmatic discourse' she means 'speech that is about the communication context or about the functions of language in context' (1996: 183 f.), for instance 'Over to you!' or 'That was well put'. The long-lived radio programme *Over to You*, now broadcast in six languages, is run jointly from the Lusaka and Kitwe studios. Two disc jockeys take turns to present musical selections by uttering the words 'Over to you', a meta-pragmatic English phrase that has now been assimilated into several Zambian languages, e.g., *Ofata yu* (ChiBemba) and *Ovata yu* (ChiNyanja). Spitulnik recorded the recycling of this routine in the context of song turn-taking during a traditional wedding, at a 'modern' singing event, at an Adventist choral rehearsal, and along the bottom of an envelope she received from a 14-year-old girl. Following Bauman and Briggs (1990), she asks what we might call 'diffusionist' questions:

1. How are decontextualisation and recontextualisation possible?

2. What does the recontextualised text bring with it from its earlier context(s)?

3. What formal, functional, and semantic changes does it undergo as it is recentered? (Spitulnik 1996: 165)

She hazards three hypotheses as to why meta-pragmatic discourse is so 'readily seized upon' and reproduced by radio listeners. First, it is transparent in both form and function, for it helps to segment and coordinate communicative

13

practices. Second, since it is 'speech about speaking', it can be easily transferred to non-media speech events. Third, this kind of discourse is exceedingly common in Zambian radio broadcasting, often in connection to celebrities, or in humorous or dramatic instances (1996: 167). Meta-pragmatic discourse exhibits 'a peculiar built-in detachability and reproducibility' that allows it to spread and circulate through the population more successfully than other forms of discourse (1996: 181).

This point is critical. Where most media ethnographers would focus on how Zambians adapt mass media content to their own cultural goals (e.g., Kulick and Stroud 1993), Spitulnik also asks *why* certain discursive elements (or traits) spread and circulate more widely than others. Spitulnik's ultimate aim is to understand the role of radio in the emergence of a Zambian public culture across ethnic and linguistic divides. Her dual research strategy – one that considers *both* diffusion *and* appropriation – serves this aim admirably. She demonstrates that Zambian radio has formalised language hierarchies, influenced speech styles, and come to embody the state (Ginsburg et al. 2002: 11).

Social anthropology still has to overcome its eighty year-old resistance to the diffusionist idea that some cultural forms, including media forms, have a very high degree of integrity, autonomy and reproducibility. This is certainly the case with the phrase 'Over to you' across Zambia, as it is with radio and television worldwide. Recognising this fact does not commit us to the view that human beings are passive recipients of contagious memes or pernicious media effects. Humans often do select and use cultural forms in accordance with their own interests, but some forms (e.g., television) are intrinsically fitter for diffusion and survival across cultural boundaries than others (e.g., Chinese opera or Shakespearean theatre). This uneven fitness is fundamental to the ongoing making of a global state order.

Culture Areas, Not Imagined Communities

One of the key contributions to the study of nationalism and nation building has come from Benedict Anderson, the author of the acclaimed book *Imagined Communities* (1991 [1983]). Anderson locates the first wave of nationalism in the Americas. The pioneers were 'pilgrim' Creole (*criollo*) functionaries and provincial Creole printmen. 'Print-capitalism' stabilised and standardised dominant languages, so that today we can still understand seventeenth-century English or Spanish. According to Eley and Suny (1996), Anderson contributed, with Hobsbawm and other Marxists, to the 1980s shift from a material to a discursive focus. In fact, he never underestimated the material and ecological effects of new media technologies. In the second edition of his groundbreaking work, Anderson stresses the joint effect of temporal and spatial media upon the history of the world's political communities.[6] The effect of 'empty, homogenous time' wrought by clocks and calendars was reinforced by that of maps, censuses and museums. Thanks to John Harrison's invention of the chronometer in 1761, longitudes could be calculated precisely. Eventually, the colonial powers put the entire planet into 'boxes' (Anderson 1991: 173), delimiting quite precisely territorial boundaries in those areas they considered to be strategic.

Today a global grid of independent states supports the present world order. This territorial grid provides the rugged surface through which people, representations, and commodities migrate and circulate. In this section I wish to suggest, first, that modern independent states are the prime 'culture areas' of our age; and second, that a range of media are integral to their formation and maintenance. The notion of 'culture area' is closely linked to the school of diffusionism discussed earlier. Like diffusion, it is no longer a popular concept. In the present climate of social constructivism, anthropologists prefer to speak of 'ethnographic regions' or even 'regional traditions of ethnographic writing' (Fardon 1990). Originally the term culture area was applied to geographical regions with identifiable clusters of culture traits. For instance, East Africa was said to have a 'cattle complex' consisting of cattle, nomadic life, patrilineal descent, age sets, and bridewealth. Similarly, Dutch scholars identified a 'structural core' (*structurele kern*) beneath the bewildering cultural variations to be found across the Indonesian Archipelago (Barnard 2000: 55–58). Prior to the Dutch, P.W. Schmidt (1910), a Viennese diffusionist, discerned two complexes in the Archipelago: one associated with moon symbolism in the West, and another associated with sun symbolism in the East. This scheme was later discredited by Rassers and other Dutch ethnologists (King and Wilder 2003: 52).

In the 1970s, a set of concepts compatible with the notion of culture area was developed by Pierre Bourdieu (1984, 1998). In his comprehensive survey of French practices of 'taste' and social distinction, Bourdieu discovered clusters of cultural forms that correlated with people's relative amounts of economic and cultural capital. Thus, he found a cluster of whisky, golf, tennis, bridge and piano among the professions, and a cluster of pétanque, Pernod, and sparkling white wine among farm labourers (1998: 5). It may seem at first as if Bourdieu were positing a number of discrete, static class-based 'complexes' or clusters, but on closer inspection a more dynamic picture emerges. The whole of France is what Gellner (1983) would call a 'cultural space' with a continual readjusting of people's relative positions partly through visible practices of consumption. For example, when a low-capital group adopts a given hobby from a high-capital group, the latter will often abandon it in order to maintain its 'distinction'. In ethnological terms, France is a 'thick' culture area, that is an integrated system of cultural institutions and practices (albeit one with significant regional, class, age-group and ethnic variations). By contrast, both the European Union and France's former empire are 'thin', overlapping culture areas fractured by country-specific cultural systems. In France, a dense tangle of media-saturated social formations (families, schools, universities, radio and television stations, ministries, cinemas, post offices, banks, restaurants, etc.) sustains a distinctive culture area, some elements of which are exported to its former colonies in various media forms. France being a heavily centralised polity, the Paris region remains the main hub in this cultural network (Scott 2000). Analogous, yet less well integrated, cultural networks criss-cross newer independent states such as Malaysia, Papua New Guinea (Foster 2002) and Zambia (Spitulnik 1996).

Besides the strong scholarly evidence supporting this notion of modern states as today's prime culture areas, many of us have a wealth of personal experience to corroborate it. When moving to a foreign country, we soon discover fundamental contrasts with our country of origin in climate, language(s), administration, transport, cuisine, leisure, media, etc. Even when the total 'way of life' (or culture) of both countries is similar – particularly if they belong to the same geographical region – our overall 'cultural competence' (Bourdieu 1984) can never match that of a native. Such a competence relies as much upon visible forms of social interaction as it does upon subtle cues and tacit knowledge acquired over many years (Bloch 1998, Fox 2004). Yet current social theory tells us, against all the evidence, that the congruence between place, culture and people was a figment of a previous generation's imagination. The efforts by Ruth Benedict and her Second World War associates to identify Japanese and German 'patterns of culture' are seen today as having been misguided by their faith in such a congruence (e.g., Peterson 2003: 45–51). Few social scientists today share this faith, having turned away from notions of cohesion, stability or structure towards notions of porous cultural boundaries and multiple identities (Eriksen 2004). Instead, many make the opposite assumption, namely that there is no such congruence. For example, Ginsburg et al. (2002: 1) open their media anthropology reader by calling for 'a critical anthropological project that refuses reified boundaries of place and culture'.

This common stance explains the long-lasting popularity of Anderson's metaphor of modern nations as 'imagined communities'. The idea of an imagined national community harks back at least to Hegel, born in 1770, who described newspapers as modern man's substitute for morning prayers (Anderson 1991: 35). To illustrate his metaphor, Anderson portrays a newspaper reader imagining a national 'community' of millions simultaneously reading the same newspaper. It is ironical that Anderson's perceived contribution is so often reduced to this static metaphor, considering that he rightly emphasised, as did Gellner, the link between nationalism and mobility, e.g., the pivotal role of itinerant functionaries in Spanish America (1991: 205). It is a metaphor that recalls the atomised individual media consumer of both the Frankfurt School and American media effects research.

Anderson's metaphor has nevertheless spread as widely in academic circles as the 'Over to you' catchphrase has among Zambians. It is time, however, to abandon it, for it distracts us from cultural changes and continuities 'on the ground'. In its stead, this book sets out to demonstrate that modern independent states are culture areas with intricate webs of social formations, cultural forms and exchange systems. As John Thompson (1995) has argued, modern media do not sever the bond between cultural traditions and territories. Rather they 'reterritorialise' such traditions. Where Thompson has it that modern media yoke cultural traditions to *larger* political entities, I would qualify this position by recourse to Tarling's tribe-state-empire trinity. From the second half of the twentieth century onwards, modern media have helped to reterritorialise cultural diversity in our planet around states, undermining in the process the two main political alternatives to the state: 'tribes' and empires. In other words, the twentieth century global rescaling of human cultures has moved both upwards (from 'tribal' units to states) and downwards (from empires to states) – a massive process of political homogenisation (cf. Asad 1992). As both Foster (2002: 151–174) and A.D. Smith (2001: 137) have concluded, *national states constitute the global, they do not resist it.*

Book Outline

In this section I provide a sketch of the remaining chapters. Chapter 2, 'What Became of the Iban?' is a review of the Iban literature, with special reference to the work of its two most influential figures: the New Zealand anthropologist Derek Freeman, and the native Iban ethnohistorian Benedict Sandin. In 1981 Freeman, renowned for undermining Margaret Mead's once celebrated work on Samoan sexuality, published a scathing attack on Sandin's unscientific ways. The polemic reveals some of the dominant themes and preoccupations of both the anthropological and indigenous traditions, as well as their essential complementariness. Neither tradition has dealt with the question of media and nation building, even though both Freeman and Sandin made important print media contributions to this process.

Chapters 3 and 4, 'Propagating the State', form a two-part history of Iban and Malaysian state media production, including the work of Sandin and fellow state-sponsored producers who sought to salvage the Iban oral heritage through print media and radio. In the early years of independence, this aim was pursued whilst defending the new country from both a hostile Indonesia and home-grown 'communist terrorists' through Iban-language propaganda. With peace, the propagandists turned from psychological warfare to socioeconomic development. The arrival of television in 1977 (chapter 4) coincided with the demise of the Borneo Literature Bureau, until then the main outlet for indigenous literature. It is alleged that the federal authorities burnt and buried virtually all vernacular books published by the Bureau. This mass media grave signalled the accelerated 'Malaysianisation' of media in Sarawak in accordance with Gellner's (1983) theory of nationalism as the pursuit of the 'one state, one culture' principle. The history of Iban media production reveals a field of 'indigenous media' at the service of the state, in marked contrast with the indigenous media of white-settler countries such as Australia (Ginsburg 1993), Canada (Perrot 1992) or Brazil (Turner 1992).

Chapter 5, 'Sustainable Propaganda', shifts the analytical focus from media production to media consumption. It suggests that state propaganda in Iban lands has become a sustainable form of development, an integral part of people's lifeworlds. This chapter analyses a range of media practices and texts (school essays and homework, school textbooks, viewers' television commentary, longhouse speeches) across various social formations in rural Sarawak. It shows that in spite of this practical diversity, the ideological space is highly uniform and coherent. People make sense of media reports through what I call a local 'ideolect', that is a parochial 'dialect' of the state ideology. This is exemplified by a series of extraordinary crises that afflicted the region in 1997, including widespread headhunting and gigantic forest fires in Indonesian Borneo, a mysterious viral epidemic in Sarawak, and the collapse of Southeast Asia's financial markets. All through these crises, rural Iban media consumers lacked an independent ideological space from which to assess the official reports critically. This chapter addresses the old question of to what extent (state) media influence their audiences, an area where research results have so far been disappointing (Ginsburg et al. 2002: 12–14).

Chapter 6, 'Writing Media', opens with the protracted anthropological debate surrounding the cross-cultural significance of literacy. An earlier school of thought (Goody 1968, Ong 1982) associated literacy with the emergence of science, democracy, and complex states in Ancient Greece and modern Western Europe. A later school rejects this approach as being Eurocentric and ascribing 'autonomous' powers to writing. Instead this school celebrates human agency and the myriad 'literacies' found around the world (Street 1993, 2001, Olson and Torrance 2001). Like most media anthropologists and cultural studies theorists, scholars of this latter persuasion privilege creative appropriation at the expense of diffusion. This chapter examines the Iban evidence and suggests that both approaches are needed. On the one hand, Iban have indeed creatively adapted literacy to certain parochial goals. For instance, in some areas they employ Catholic prayer books containing pagan notions of efficacy. On the other hand, Iban parents (like parents in other developing countries) are well aware of the economic value of standard forms of literacy. As a consequence, the vast majority of Iban children are sent to state schools.

Chapter 7, 'Media Exchanges', documents the biographical profiles of television sets in rural Sarawak, an approach inspired by the work of Kopytoff

(1986) and Appadurai (1986). Two stages in the life cycles of television sets are analysed: their acquisition and their disposal. The aim is to explore the materiality of a much valued medium and its relationship to processes of nation building. Iban continually reckon one another's relative position within their modernising state. For the purposes of such a reckoning, a code including a television's price, brand, model, and size, has evolved. Not all, however, is 'nationalisation' or the search for Bourdieuesque distinction through differential consumption – some pockets of parochial practice do remain. Thus the semantic openness of material objects (Miller 1994) allows for flexible customary uses, for instance the burial of television sets as part of a deceased person's grave goods (*baya'*).

Chapter 8, 'Clock Time', opens with a critical review of the anthropological study of time. Where anthropologists theorising writing have debated the degree to which this medium has been transformed across societies (chapter 5), a similar debate has yet to take place amongst those theorising time. Inexplicably, Alfred Gell (1992), Nancy Munn (1992), and other major contributors have failed to recognise the effect of wristwatches, radio, television and other media on time-reckoning and social scheduling. This chapter analyses the uses of media in the daily cycles of activity that bind together local Iban children, women, men and the elderly. Whereas most men and children manage their time through the waged workplace and school, most women and the elderly rely on radio during the day. In the evening, all four segments of the longhouse community jointly 'domesticate' Malaysia's national time by watching television in the semi-privacy of the family rooms (*bilek*). Television has had a major impact by shifting the social locus from the communal gallery (*ruai*) to the family *bilek*. This finding challenges recurrent doubts among media anthropologists and other media scholars regarding the notion of 'media effects'.

Chapter 9, 'Calendar Time', follows logically from the previous chapter. The emphasis here is on the festive uses of chronometric media, with the annual Dayak Festival chosen as a case study. The data presented derive from ethnographic fieldwork among both elite and non-elite Iban. As Anderson (1991) and others have noted, clock-and-calendar time is essential to the formation of modern states. This technology creates a sense of collective destiny and coordinated action. The Dayak Festival was 'invented' by native intellectuals in the colonial period and resisted by the British, who feared it may lead to political demands. It was finally officially launched in 1965 by the first independent state government and met with instant popular success. Rather than fostering Dayak rebellion, the festival has become an integral part of Malaysia's nation building process. In this chapter I rethink Nick Couldry's (2003) concept of 'media ritual', stripping it of its mythic component. As I define them, media rituals are rituals designed to provide remote access to a modern country's seats of power.

Chapter 10 is a summary and a conclusion. It recapitulates the evidence and argument presented with reference to Smith's (1995) above mentioned definition of a nation.

Notes

1. Fausto Barlocco, a doctoral student at the University of Loughborough (UK), is currently undertaking a comparative study of media and nation building in the East Malaysian state of Sabah (formerly North Borneo) under my co-supervision.
2. An online review by Matthew Durington of the two principal media anthropology readers to date – Askew and Wilk (2002) and Ginsburg et al. (2002) – can be found in *American Ethnologist* 31 (1) August 2003 (www.aaanet.org/aes/bkreviews). Earlier discussions of media anthropology include Spitulnik (1993), Ginsburg (1994), Dickey (1997), and Drackle (1999). See also Peterson (2003) for an historical overview and Rothenbuhler and Coman (2005) for an interdisciplinary reader.
3. Among the exceptions listed by Lent (1994: 84–87) are Mohd. Hamdan Adnan's (1988, 1990) and Frith's (1987) studies of mass communications and consumerism, Grjebine's (1988) case studies of prostitutes and the media, Banks' (1985) content analysis of women in Malay films, as well as other women-related studies by Rodrigues (1983–1984) and Nasri Adbullah (1983). Lent himself has worked on the issue of freedom of expression (1979, 1984a, 1989), on the ownership of Malaysian media (1984b) and on telematics (1991). Other, more recent work includes Boulanger (1993) on government and press in Malaysia, Rahmah Hashim (1995) on television programming, McDaniel (1994), Anuar and Kim (1996) and Nain (1996) on media production, Uimonen (2003) on new media and nation building, Karim and Khalid (2003), Yong (2003) and Postill (2004) on e-governance, Tong (2004) on the online newspaper *Malaysiakini*, Gomez (2004b) on the press under Mahathir, and Anuar (2004) on media censorship.
4. As far as Sarawak is concerned, among the few exceptions are Reece's (1981) article on the first Malay newspaper in Sarawak, Lent's (1982) survey of mass media in East Malaysia and Brunei, Ngidang's (1993) article on the Bornean media's treatment of the land rights movement, and Amir and A.R. Awang Jaya's (1996) *Isu-Isu Media di Sarawak.*
5. One exception is Dan Sperber's (1996) 'cultural epidemiology', a cognitivist brand of diffusionism that remains marginal to the discipline but has greatly influenced my thinking on these matters. Sperber's programme is being followed by Pascal Boyer (2000, 2001) and others.
6. By his own admission, in the first edition he had not considered spatial media such as maps or censuses (Anderson 1991: xiii–xiv).

2

WHAT BECAME OF THE IBAN?

Most anthropologists of an earlier generation 'belong' with a given people. Thus, Malinowski will always belong with the Trobrianders, as will Margaret Mead with the Samoans and Evans-Pritchard with the Nuer (Geertz 1988). Likewise, the late Derek Freeman (1916–2001) is inextricably linked to the Iban of Sarawak – and vice versa. Such is the identification of the Iban with Freeman that specialists in other regions can be forgiven for wondering what became of this Borneo people since Freeman's classic studies in the 1940s and 1950s. Freeman's work remains the obligatory entry point to Borneo studies, and it is essential reading for those wishing to pursue studies among shifting cultivators anywhere in Southeast Asia.

In the previous chapter I discussed the ahistorical turn taken by Malinowski and Radcliffe-Brown, the key figures in the rise of (structural-)functionalism within British anthropology. The structural-functionalism of Radcliffe-Brown came to dominate British anthropology from the 1940s to the 1960s. The common practice was to analyse societies synchronically as bounded wholes. Each society was portrayed analogously to an organism; it consisted of a set of interrelated systems held together by homeostasis (Barnard and Spencer 1996: 624). To Radcliffe-Brown, who borrowed heavily from Durkheim, anthropology was a form of comparative sociology. At the heart of his comparative programme he placed 'social structure', made up of roles, norms and jural obligations (Fischer 1997: 211). These early professional anthropologists rejected the historical speculations of both evolutionists and diffusionists. Their aim was to produce detailed monographs derived from long-term field-work in order to understand how pre-state societies manage to create and maintain social order. The monographs were written in the 'ethnographic present' and made little allowance for historical change or colonial influences (Gledhill 2000: 41–44).

Southeast Asia posed a great challenge to this programme, for in this region there were reportedly no 'large-scale corporate descent groups' of the kind that had been found among the Nuer and other African peoples.[1] In the absence of descent groups, how was order achieved? (King and Wilder 2003: 56–59). Murdock stated the comparative problem succinctly. For those societies that

do not employ either patrilineal or matrilineal [i.e., unilineal, JP] descent as a major organizing principle in the grouping of kinsmen ... there still exists no solid consensus regarding organizational principles, typology, or terminology comparable to that achieved for unilineal social systems (Murdock 1960: 1–14, quoted in King and Wilder 2003: 59).

Derek Freeman was one of several anthropologists who tackled this problem in the British territories of Sarawak, Malaya and Singapore after the Second World War. These field researchers studied family units, marriage, bilateral descent groups, property, social stratification and related matters (King and Wilder 2003: 59). Freeman, born in Wellington (New Zealand), conducted his Sarawak research under the auspices of Britain's Colonial Social Science Research Council. In addition to Sarawak, he conducted fieldwork in Samoa and fought arduously to refute Margaret Mead's famous theory of Samoan adolescent sexuality (Freeman 1999, King 2001). For most of his career, he was based at the Australian National University (ANU), in Canberra.

Freeman's chief contributions to Iban and Borneo studies have been to two areas: cognatic social organisation and shifting cultivation (cf. King n.d. vii). In this chapter I discuss briefly each of these strands, relating Freeman's work to that of other scholars. I then focus on the other major figure in Iban studies, the indigenous folklorist and ethnohistorian, Benedict Sandin. In 1981, Freeman questioned Sandin's scholarly credentials, deeming him too close to the 'major tenets' of Iban culture to be sufficiently objective in his writings. As we shall see, this critique tells us more about Freeman's own anthropological priorities than it does about Sandin's *oeuvre*. It also reveals the limitations of Freeman's structural-functionalist approach. In the penultimate section of this chapter I describe the multi-sited field research upon which my study of Iban media and nation building is based, followed by some remarks on the ethnic make-up of Sarawak.

Social Organisation

One remarkable feature of Freeman's writing is its great clarity. The opening paragraph to his classic *Report on the Iban of Sarawak* (1955), reprinted as *The Iban of Borneo* (1992), deserves to be quoted in full. It introduces his influential – and contested – analysis of Iban social organisation.

The most salient characteristic of Iban social organization is the practice of long-house domicile. Anyone who has travelled in the interior of Borneo is familiar with the conspicuous shape of a long-house: an attenuated structure supported on innumerable hard-wood posts, it stretches for a hundred yards or more along the terraced bank of a river, its roof – of thatch, or wooden shingles – forming an unbroken expanse. Superficially viewed the Iban long-house has the appearance of being a single structural unit, and many casual observers have made the facile inference that the long-house is therefore the outcome of some sort of communal or group organization and ownership. For the Iban, at least, this inference is the reverse of true. Among the various families which make up a long-house community there does exist a network of kinship ties, but the Iban long-house is primarily an aggregation of independently owned family apartments. The fact that these apartments are joined one to the other so as to produce a long-house detracts little from their essential autonomy. Indeed the unbroken expanse of roof tends to conceal the fact that the Iban long-house is fundamentally a series of discrete entities – the independent family units of a competitive and egalitarian society (Freeman 1992: 1).

In Freeman's (1992: 1–60) analysis the family unit – which he calls *bilek*-family after the Iban term for room or apartment – is the 'basic unit' of Iban society. In the Baleh region where Freeman conducted his fieldwork in 1949–1951 and 1957–1958, these units consisted of an average of five or six individuals, of which two or three were children.[2] They were either elementary families (i.e., consisting only of parents and children) or, in approximately half the cases, extended to include the grandparents' generation. Recruitment to the *bilek*-family was usually through birth, adoption or marriage. In some rare instances (1992: 28) it could also be by incorporation, e.g., when a divorced woman brought to her second husband's *bilek* a child from her previous marriage. *Bilek*-families were economically independent households occupying a single longhouse apartment. They were 'allodial groups', that is, groups holding absolute ownership of both land and property.[3] The entire family estate was partible, except the sacred strains of ancestral rice (*padi pun*) and other objects of ritual value (1992: 60). All children, regardless of their gender and birth order, had 'equal rights of inheritance' (1992: 29). Partition took place when two married siblings became members of the same *bilek*. Eventually one couple would leave with a share (*ungkop*) of the *bilek* property. Two *bilek*-families could also create a new family through amalgamation (1992: 60). The resulting group was known as *bilek berakup*, from the joinery work (*berakup*) carried out by a longhouse carpenter. In the Baleh region, downriver families short of residents, but wealthy, would often amalgamate with poorer upriver families with access to virgin farmland (1992: 56–59). Freeman concluded that the *bilek* is a 'perpetual corporate group', thus providing a celebrated 'solution' to the elusive problem of group continuity in cognatic societies (Appell and Madan 1988: 8).

Freeman defined the Iban longhouse as 'a local confederation of *bilek*-families, based on cognatic kinship' (1992: 127). Cognatic kinship is a system of bilateral kinship whereby ties 'are traced both through father and mother, and relationships of the same order, whether through males or females are of equal value' (1992: 66–67, cf. Rhum 1997). He stressed the importance of kindred (*kaban*), 'that cognatic category which embraces all of an individual's father's kin, and all of his (or her) mother's kin' (Freeman 1970: 67, quoted in King 1976: 122). The entire Iban society was a dense web of kindreds that, when needed, allowed for the execution of tasks that were beyond the ability of any single *bilek*-family (Freeman 1961: 211, quoted in King 1976: 122). Given the influence of Freeman's kindred analyses on later studies of bilateral kinship, these analyses have attracted the attention of other Borneo scholars. Thus, King (1976) has identified inconsistencies in Freeman's usage of the term, and has called for the inclusion of affines ('in-laws') in the Iban category of kindred (but see Appell's 1976 reply). King suspects that Freeman was seeking to 'set up a category of consanguineal kin outside the *bilek* family which can perform some of the functions carried out by lineages in lineal societies' (1976: 133). Instead, King emphasises personal choice in the carrying out of collective tasks within cognatic systems. Drawing on his fieldwork among the 'Ibanic' Maloh of Indonesian Borneo, he points at the need to consider ties of residence, friendship and age as well as kinship.

Interestingly, Freeman had already recognised by the late 1960s his prior over-reliance on structuralist modes of analysis (1992 [1955]: v). Yet it was only from the 1970s that he began to highlight the significance of choice in cognatic and other social systems (Freeman 1981). Indeed in the last two decades of his life he gave choice pride of place in his dogged pursuit of a unified science of anthropology that could transcend its biological, psychological and sociocultural divides. The uniquely human ability to make choices had so far, in Freeman's view, eluded both biological determinists such as E.O. Wilson and cultural determinists like Franz Boas and Margaret Mead (Appell and Madan 1988, Fox 2002).

Freeman found that longhouses held 'virtually no property [or land] in communal ownership' and engaged in no economic activities of a corporate nature (1992: 128). In an oft-quoted passage, he states that the longhouse, despite its communistic appearance to the untrained European eye, is in fact 'a street of privately owned, semi-detached houses' (1992: 129). Every longhouse, he adds, has a 'core-group' of closely related cognatic kin which includes the community's founding *bilek*-families. These households often own the best land and are greatly influential. Dispelling any notion that these communities may be static, Freeman notes that in pioneering areas such as the Baleh there was a high level of family mobility. It was rare, he reports, to find a longhouse that had retained the same combination of family units from one year to the next (1992: 127). But this mobility came with ritual strings attached. New longhouse members had to abide by the ritual conventions and customary laws (*adat*) of their adoptive communities. They all had to undergo rituals of incorporation, and it was universally agreed that the welfare of the entire community depended on the strict observance of local custom by all residents (1992: 128). In Davison's (1987: 108) Freeman-inspired summary, the Iban longhouse is an

> acephalous meritocracy, bound together as a ritual community, but otherwise fragmented into autonomous *bilek* families which interact with one another in an egalitarian but highly competitive social milieu.

This model of the longhouse has been challenged by a number of scholars. In chapter 9 I discuss Sather's (1993) ritual alternative to Freeman's model. Here I wish to refer to another critique. During her fieldwork in Gerai Dayak longhouses in the Indonesian province of Kalimantan Barat, Christine Helliwell (1993: 51) found that the permeability of the partitions between neighbouring family rooms (*lawang*) allowed 'an almost unimpeded flow of both sound and light' between all longhouse apartments. Questioning Freeman's notion of the longhouse as a built structure of autonomous households, she describes the Gerai Dayak longhouse as a 'community of voices'. Gerai voices 'flow in a longhouse in a most extraordinary fashion; moving up and down its length in seeming monologue, they are in fact in continual dialogue with listeners who may be unseen, but are always present. As such they create, more than does any other facet of longhouse life, a sense of community' (1993: 51). Helliwell's phenomenological approach is in line with a growing interest among anthropologists in the role of the senses in human sociality, a shift from what are now seen as the 'objectivist' excesses of earlier scholars to 'the culturally organised lived-in world' (Rival 1997: 147, cf. Ingold 2000a). In my rethinking of the late twentieth century Iban longhouse (chapter 9) I seek to synthesise Freeman, Sather and Helliwell while updating our model of this resilient social formation.

Shifting Cultivation

Freeman's other notable contribution, both to anthropology and to the ethnography of Southeast Asia, is his painstaking research on Iban agriculture. This body of work is classic 'applied anthropology' at its best. 'To the Iban', he writes,

> virgin forest is the most highly valued of all resources: by felling it rights over land are acquired and, if weather conditions be favourable, virgin land yields crops of exceptional abundance for two years in succession. The 'rich, untouched vegetation' of the Baleh area was, to the Iban, the most inviting of prizes, and desire to exploit it was the overruling incentive of their advance and an important motive in prompting their fierce attacks on alien tribes that stood in the way. Headhunting and a craving for virgin land went hand in hand (Freeman 1992 [1955]: 276).

The Iban Freeman lived with were 'a virile and resourceful people with an insatiable appetite for virgin land' (1992: 282). In post-war Sarawak, the Iban economy was still dependent on the shifting cultivation of hill rice. This mode of subsistence economy is characterised by field (not crop) rotation, forest clearing by fire, the sole use of human labour and dibble sticks (no draught animals or manuring), and the alternation between short-term cultivation and long-term fallowing (Pelzer 1945, in Freeman 1992: 160). The Iban farming cycle observed by Freeman was highly variable, subject to the vagaries of weather, pests and *bilek*-family labour availability. To tame this uncertainty and ensure an abundant harvest, the Iban punctuate the farming process with a lengthy series of rituals. As Freeman stresses, traditional Iban agriculture hinges on 'an elaborate fertility cult' (1992: 153). Pagan Iban believe that their *padi* possesses a spirit or soul. The most revered spirits are those which dwell inside the *padi pun*, the strain of sacred rice mentioned earlier. These spirits are 'the lords of all' (*raja antu padi magang*). Every farming year, each family will plant some *padi pun* at a spot that will become the focal point of numerous rites. The *padi pun* is the medium used by Iban to communicate with all other *padi* spirits, for example to cure ailing young *padi*. Special prayers are said to win over the *padi* spirits which are always treated with great respect to avoid giving offence. These spirits are addressed as if they were real persons, for it is thought they live in a society similar to ours (Freeman 1992: 154–155, cf. Ingold 2000a). A set of ritual interdictions (*pemali*) surrounds the *padi pun*, which are an inalienable part of the *bilek* property. The set differs greatly from one family to the next. In many areas, however, a person who has eaten or touched pork is prohibited from entering a farm on the same day.

The extreme precautions attached to rice cultivation hampered Freeman's efforts at surveying the farms using modern equipment, for local Iban were concerned that the *padi* spirits may take offence and flee, as had been the case in the past with a survey team. Throughout the Iban farming year, Freeman found that 'ritual and labour are inextricably interwoven' (1992: 159). For example, the opening of the farming year is marked with a series of elaborate rites known as *manggol*. These rites, which again vary from one *bilek*-family to another, are aimed at (a) securing auspicious bird omens, (b) propitiating the spirits of the land and jungle, and (c) inaugurating the risky undertaking of felling. In spite of modernisation and the erosion of Iban belief-systems, *manggol* rites are still performed across Sarawak. In chapter 6, I discuss the influence of Catholic prayer books on the rites of *manggol* I witnessed at a Skrang longhouse, comparing them to pagan *manggol* prayers in the Saribas area (Sather 1992).

The farming cycle is described in detail by Freeman (1992: 171–218). The *manggol* stage is followed by clearing the undergrowth, felling the forest, firing the farms, dibbling and sowing, weeding, guarding the farms, harvesting, carrying in the *padi*, threshing, re-reaping, winnowing, and storing the *padi*.

There is a marked gendered division of labour, with men carrying out tasks requiring physical strength and women concentrating on more tedious, time-consuming activities. In contrast to colonial government officers, Freeman reported the widespread practice of farming land for two years in succession, a practice he considered wasteful and 'deleterious' (1992: 282). When Iban pioneers entered the Baleh in the nineteenth century, a 'land-rush' ensued, for the first settlers were aware that the future of their family lines depended on obtaining customary rights to the best land. The rush had further motivations, notably the added opportunities for headhunting, looting, and slave-taking (1992: 283–286). To Freeman, the Iban are not merely 'prodigal of the land', they are voracious '*mangers de bois*'. The strategy of pioneering groups was to extract as much wealth as possible from a primeval forest and swiftly move on to other virgin territory. In so doing they became 'semi-nomadic'; yet, in contrast to truly nomadic groups they had no incentive to return to 'inferior secondary jungle' (1992: 286).

In his recommendations to the colonial government, Freeman concluded that Iban shifting cultivation was sustainable only when virgin forest was farmed for a single year and then left to regenerate. Moreover, the land could be reused virtually in perpetuity should it be cultivated at infrequent intervals of 12 to 15 years. But in cases where the land was successively farmed for two or more years, the result was invariably 'serious degradation' or even 'devastation'. His final words read: 'If shifting cultivation in Iban pioneer areas is to be stabilized, it is of crucial importance that an attempt should be made to eradicate these prodigal methods' (Freeman 1992: 305).

Over the years, this portrayal of Iban agriculture has attracted praise and criticism in equal measure. Although hailing Freeman's studies as ground-breaking, later scholars believe he may have been influenced by a small number of colonial officers. It was during the inter-war years that the Sarawak administration first began to regard shifting cultivation as a liability. The Brooke government of the day began to favour settled cultivation, commercial plantations and controlled logging. Yet new research in various parts of Sarawak in the 1970s and 1980s suggested that in long-settled areas, Iban communities had achieved sustainable farming strategies. When the population pressure was too great, local people would cultivate more cash crops, swamp rice and/or dedicate more time to waged labour. Other flexible ways of adapting included borrowing land and introducing new cropping-fallow arrangements (King and Wilder 2003: 248–254). Sather (1990), who works in the Paku (Saribas) area, has also rejected Freeman's characterisation of Iban as '*mangers de bois*'. Paku Iban, says Sather, manage their secondary forests wisely in their long-settled areas. In addition to their economic and jural importance, forests provide the settings for relations of 'guardianship and benefaction' between humans and spirit-heroes (Sather 1990: 17). The Iban language of social relationships is suffused with botanic metaphors, and the forest landscape constitutes 'a visible chronology in the form of inherited trees, cemetery and former longhouse sites' that connects residents with past generations (1990: 37).

Be that as it may, there is little doubt that across Southeast Asia – and Sarawak is no exception – the pressures of modernisation and nation building have severely eroded shifting cultivation. The combined impact of plantations, settled cultivation, mass logging, schooling and migration has been incalculable (King and Wilder 2003: 254).

Freeman vs. Sandin

The earliest writings on the Iban, formerly Sea Dayaks (see below), date back to the times of James Brooke, the first White Rajah of Sarawak, whose reign began in 1841. They consist largely of private correspondence, government reports, personal memoirs, and at a later stage, of accounts by European travellers, scientists and missionaries. Before the establishment of European rule, the past was the exclusive domain of indigenous genealogists (*tukang tusut*), bards (*lemambang*) and storytellers (Jawan 1994: 21, King n.d. iii). Terry King (n.d. ii–iv), a specialist in the Maloh of Indonesian Borneo, marvels at 'the amount of material which is available on the Ibans in comparison with that for other indigenous groups of Borneo'. In his view, this abundance results from a number of historical circumstances. First, from the demographic importance achieved throughout northern Borneo by the Iban as they 'assimilated, subjugated or drove out other indigenous peoples' (see Sather 1994 and Sandin 1994). Second, from 'Iban resilience in the face of Western imperialism'. This led the Brooke Raj in Sarawak to commission a number of studies on them, a tradition continued by the British colonial government after the Japanese Occupation of 1941–1945. Third, from the work of a number of fine scholars, both foreign and native, including Freeman, Sandin, Pringle, Sutlive, Sather and Masing.

The highly competitive ethos of traditional Iban society forced each new generation to prove its worth, since social status was not inherited. Prior to the Brooke Raj, there was no formal Iban leadership. Leaders were chosen for a particular purpose, such as wandering in search of heirlooms (*bejalai*), or headhunting *(kayau)*. The elders *(tuai)* were chosen for their knowledge of the customary law *(adat)* and their rhetorical prowess – both skills much eroded today by literacy and other modern cultural forms (chapter 5). In this respect pre-state *adat* can be seen as a means of social regulation in the absence of political authority. The Brookes created the office of longhouse headman (*tuai rumah*), who was appointed by the governor or district officer, a departure from pre-contact Iban ways. Attempts to create a chieftainship by the Rajahs were, however, firmly resisted by the Iban. Eventually, the office of 'native

28

chief' (*penghulu*) was created in 1883. This male role entailed, amongst other things, running the administration, collecting taxes, and disseminating information. The *penghulu* was appointed by the administration and was responsible for a number of headmen. From 1949, Iban headmen have been democratically elected by longhouse residents, although district officers can still reject headmen and withhold their annual allowances. In practice, headmen have no power to command but through a 'subtle mixture of persuasion and admonition' (Freeman 1992: 113). Both offices have survived the post-independence era and are as important today as they were during the White Raj.

Freeman described pre-state Iban social ideology as being strongly egalitarian. Some differentiation existed in terms of wealth and influence, but there was no institutionalised subordination. With obvious admiration, he wrote: 'Iban society is classless and egalitarian – and its members, individualists, aggressive and proud in demeanour, lacking any taste of obeisance' (Freeman 1992: 129). This putative egalitarianism stood in stark opposition to other Bornean societies such as the Kayan – a fact the Iban themselves were always keen to point out. As one Iban elder once put it to Freeman (1981: 30): 'Among the Iban everyone paddles; Kayan chiefs just sit in their canoes'.

This portrayal, alas, has not gone unchallenged (see Sather 1996). In 1981, Freeman responded with characteristic vehemence to Rousseau's (1980) conjecture that the Iban are not an egalitarian society but rather a society with hereditary strata, comparable to the Kayan and other Bornean societies. Rousseau was calling for 'an historical approach' to Iban studies and supported his case with evidence from Benedict Sandin, the renowned indigenous scholar. To Freeman this was an unfortunate move, for Sandin was 'in no sense a trained social scientist' but rather an 'ahistorical collector of folklore' (Freeman 1981: 12–13). Moreover, Sandin had always placed 'full credence in the major tenets of Iban belief' (Freeman 1981: 54). Sandin's writings are, in Freeman's view, marred by 'conceptual paradoxes' such as his usage of the term 'hereditary' to describe individuals who had been appointed to office for the first time (1981: 12). They are also plagued by factual errors. In Sandin's *Sea Dayaks* (1967), says Freeman,

> we are treated to a genealogy (Mr Sandin's own) which begins in 'the Holy Land in the Middle East' (p. 97), to padi mortars that suddenly fly skywards (p. 51), to the slaying of stars in human form (p. 24), and to numerous other transempirical acts, such as ancestors cutting down invisible spirits (p. 32) and turning their adversaries into boulders (p. 11), in a continuous narrative that ends with the descendants of these miracle-working ancestors becoming clerks in the Government of Sarawak and the Borneo Company Limited (1981: 13).

To better appreciate Freeman's position, we require some background on the late Benedict Sandin, regarded by many as 'the foremost authority on the history and culture of his people' (Pringle 1970: xiii).

With the creation of the Borneo Literature Bureau in 1960 (chapter 3), Iban authors, most of them rural school teachers, began to make great efforts to record an oral tradition that was swiftly vanishing. Sandin was the most accomplished among them. He was born in 1918 in Kerangan Pinggai, a longhouse on the Paku river, in the Saribas basin of Sarawak. The Saribas area was at the time undergoing a rapid economic transformation following the successful adoption of rubber. After the Brooke 'pacification' of the area in the early 1860s, Saribas leaders had turned from headhunting to trade and cash crops. Literacy spread rapidly, as many learnt to read and write from kin who had acquired a basic mission education in more peaceful areas (Sather 1994: 75). The wealth generated by the rubber boom lead to the elaboration of ritual and ceremony, and public speech-making became a central institution (1994: 69). As in nineteenth-century Madagascar (Bloch 1998), new technologies and practices, including literacy, were being mobilised to pursue local aims. Like the Malagasy, the Iban distinguish between ordinary and formal language, or more precisely between 'shallow language' (*jako mabu*) and 'deep language' (*jako dalam*). Sandin learnt deep language from his father, a renowned orator and genealogist, and he himself became a famous practitioner of both crafts after his retirement from the government service.

> My father was one of the speakers who was always invited during Iban weddings ... Because he was so good at this. I started in the 1930s to learn from him all of the difficult words, that is, the words that have a very, very deep meaning which few people today understand. I wrote down many of his speeches in this deep language ... Having studied these things – it is for this reason that I can claim to be one of the few Iban who understands the deep meaning of the Iban language (in Sather 1981: 116).

The last sentence may strike European readers as boasting, but it certainly fits in with the Iban (and Malagasy) association of oratorical achievement with ancestral knowledge. To Sandin, literacy was both a way of increasing his own cultural competence and of fostering the cultural renewal of his people. It was not a radical departure from his origins, as Goody's (1968, 1987) model of literacy as an autonomous institution would have us expect. Sandin's father taught him that he descended from the god of war and headhunting, Singalang Burong, and from the culture hero Salamuda.

> By 1930, as soon as I knew how to spell Iban words, I started to collect genealogical trees [*tusut*] from my father, who gave me, for example, the straight line genealogy from Singalang Burong down to myself ... As I memorized these *tusuts*, I became interested in learning as much of the genealogies as I could (in Sather 1981: 115).

Sandin was formally educated in the Saribas and in Kuching, the capital of Sarawak, from 1928 to 1933. In 1941 he became a junior native officer and was transferred to the Information Office after the Japanese Occupation. There he became the editor of the first Iban news publication, *Surat Pembrita*. During this period he began to publish papers on Iban history and lore in the *Sarawak Museum Journal*. From 1952 to 1963 he worked at the Sarawak Museum as a research assistant. In 1954–1955 he studied museum methods and anthropology at the University of Auckland. Upon returning to the Sarawak Museum he embarked on an intense period of fieldwork, recording and publishing genealogies, ethnohistorical narratives, bardic chants (*pengap*) and a Saribas dirge (*sabak*) (Sather 1994: 72–73). He was appointed Curator of the Sarawak Museum and Government Ethnologist in 1966. Soon before this appointment, he began a fruitful collaboration with Robert Pringle, a Cornell historian. Their joint effort yielded two important works of Bornean scholarship: Pringle's (1970) *Rajahs and Rebels* and Sandin's (1967) *The Sea Dayaks of Borneo before White Rajah Rule* (Sather 1994: 74).

This is not the place for a Sandinist retort to Freeman's essay. For our present purposes, suffice to remark that Sandin's collective work is an outstanding example of ethnohistory, in both acceptations of the term: (1) 'the search for historical data on ethnic groups' and (2) 'the ethnic group's own representation of their history' (Seymour-Smith 1986: 99). As Sather (1994: 77) has cogently argued, Sandin's shortcomings must be set against his intimate knowledge of lore and history in the Paku-Saribas area. In fact, his evidence supplements, and often confirms, that of Pringle and other Western scholars.

Freeman's tirade reveals more about his own scholarly priorities and proclivities – partly shared by other regional scholars – than it does about Sandin. In particular, it betrays the ahistorical nature of structuralist-functionalism. Freeman is primarily interested in 'pristine Iban society' (1981: 7), not in social change. This is worthy of note, for other scholars have joined Freeman in his search for such an untouched society. A case in point is Jensen's *The Iban and their Religion* (1974: 1), an account which 'describes – in the ethnographic present tense – the situation, principally in the Second Division of Sarawak, as it was during the years 1959 to 1966'. It is only at the very end of his book that Jensen (1974: 213–214) mentions three factors that already in the 1960s were radically changing the Iban way of life: (1) the spread of rubber and a cash economy, (2) local authority schools and (3) mass conversion to Christianity. These factors are not, however, brought to bear on Jensen's foregoing discussion. Was this author not sufficiently acquainted with such changes? He was indeed, for like his predecessor, Freeman, he had carried out research for the government of Sarawak. It was in fact Jensen (1966) who reviewed the applied aspects of Freeman's early work on Iban agriculture. In the 1950s and 1960s, the vast majority of Iban, Jensen had then reported, turned to cash crops and individual (rather than *bilek*-family) property.

Queen Elizabeth in Sarawak

In February 1972, Her Majesty Queen Elizabeth II
of Great Britain and her husband Prince Philip visited
Malaysia.
Here she is seen chatting with chief minister of
Sarawak, Datuk Pattinggi Tan Sri Haji Abdul Rahman
Yacub inside one of the 'exhibition' rooms inside the
Sarawak Museum.

Published and Copyright By:
Anna Photo Company
16 Carpenter Street,
Kuching, Sarawak,
Malaysia.

Figure 2.1. A postcard showing Queen Elizabeth II during a visit to a mock Iban
longhouse inside the Sarawak Museum in 1972. She is with the then Chief Minister
Yakub (in Malay attire) and with Benedict Sandin (in a European suit) who was the
Museum's director at the time.

Source: courtesy Peter Wee, Anna Photo Company.

Jensen's 'Iban religion' refers to a primeval system of beliefs unaffected by Christianity or nation building. Seventeen years on, epistemological matters had changed little in this research area. In fact, the ethnographic present is still commonly used in Iban studies. Thus, in the early 1990s Davison and Sutlive (1991: 212) analysed Iban oral literature to conclude that Freeman was mistaken in thinking that headhunting is/was (the tense was irrelevant to their case) linked to a religious cult of phallic symbolism. To these writers, it is the idea of 'organic regeneration and vegetative growth' that provides the underlying model, or metaphor, for Iban headhunting. The authors, albeit admitting that headhunting was 'central to the Iban way of life as it existed up until the early decades of this century' (1991: 213) disagreed with Jensen's (1974: 6) view that headhunting had ceased to shape 'Iban behaviour' since its suppression in the 1920s. To argue their case, these authors drew on sources far removed in time and space, reaching as far back as 1846 in their quest to dig out the 'underlying model' for Iban headhunting (cf. Needham 1976). One is reminded of Heine-Geldern's (1956 [1942]) more ambitious hunt for an essential Southeast Asian cosmology. In Melanesian anthropology, Carrier (1992: 13) describes these debates over 'who got it right or wrong' regardless of historical change as 'synchronic essentialism'.

The Present Study

Today there are over half a million Iban in Sarawak, about one-third of that state's population. Brunei and West Kalimantan (Indonesian Borneo) each have 14,000 to 15,000 Iban, while in Sabah there are only around 1,000–2,000 (Wadley 1999b: 597). In the past they lived primarily along rivers in the interior hills, but over the past 150 years about half have migrated to flat delta areas. By the early 1990s, over 20 per cent of Iban in Sarawak had migrated to urban areas (Sutlive 1992: 2), a trend likely to continue. Iban society has been well documented in the areas of 'social organisation, agriculture, religion and oral tradition' (King n.d. vii). However,

> an enormous amount of research needs to be done in oral tradition and literature, in local historical detail, *in processes of modernisation* and the structure of political activity, analyses of ritual performances, and in aspects of material culture such as textiles; finally, the Iban-related peoples of West Kalimantan [in Indonesia], are still very much a *terra incognita* and basic ethnographies are still required of various of the groups there (King n.d. vii, emphasis added).

The present work centres precisely on those 'processes of modernisation'. It can be read alongside prior studies of Iban social change, namely studies of Iban urbanisation (Sutlive 1972), migration (Austin 1977, Padoch 1982a, 1984, Sutlive 1985, Kedit 1993), schooling (Seymour 1974, 1977, Eaton

1974) modernisation (Sutlive 1978, Kedit 1980a), tourism (Kedit 1980b, Zeppel 1994), agriculture (Padoch 1982b, Cramb 1985, 1988, Cramb and Wills 1990), rural development (Mertz and Christensen 1997, King and Parnwell 1999), and politics (Sutlive 1992, Jawan 1993, 1994). It is based on eighteen months of field research in Sarawak in 1996–2001, with the bulk of the research carried out in 1997. In June 1996 I carried out a pilot study which involved visiting prospective field sites to gain a first impression of contemporary life in Sarawak. Having established a good rapport with Iban in the Saribas basin, I decided to undertake most of the fieldwork in this area. A second field site would be Kuching, and the third site remained to be determined. The rationale behind working in three areas rather than one follows from the previous discussion: in a developing society with increased links – created through electronic media, migration, schooling, etc. – there is an urgent need for ethnographies that explore such links. These explorations can provide a sturdy analytical shield against crude notions of 'the global' having an impact upon 'the local'. Indeed, one of the strengths of multi-sited ethnographies is that they can generate intra-societal comparisons (Marcus

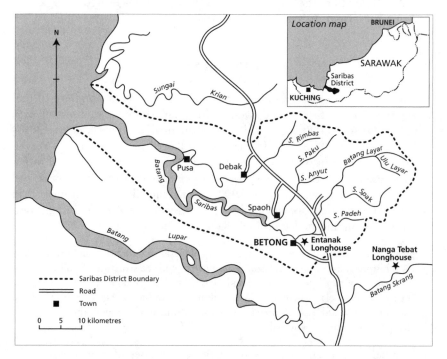

Figure 2.2. Location of main field site (Entanak Longhouse) and of ancillary field site (Nanga Tebat Longhouse).

Source: adapted from Sather (1992: 111).

1995: 107). For instance, my frequent visits to Kuching from 'the field' – that is, from the Saribas area, situated four hours away by coach – alerted me to the ideological similarities and differences among Iban from both areas (chapter 5).

First Field Site: the Saribas

The Saribas has long had a reputation as an area that experienced early social and economic progress (Pringle 1970: 208). Iban from Sandin's Paku branch of this river, in particular, took advantage of a high world demand for rubber in the 1910s and 1920s to amass considerable fortunes. At the height of their success, 'as many as one thousand Chinese, Iban and Malay labourers were employed by Paku Iban families' (Sather 1994: 71). Saribas Iban also demonstrated an 'early thirst for education', and many would travel considerable distances to acquire a mission education (Pringle 1970: 206). Today the Saribas Iban are no longer exceptional in their desire to 'develop' (*ngemansang*), but the cultural ideal of doing so while preserving their customs (*adat*) is arguably stronger than in other rivers. Central to my concerns is the early (1950s) involvement of Saribas Iban in the collective project of creating a 'modern' Iban culture through education, radio, print media and other state institutions. As Pringle (1970: 209) noted over thirty years ago, Iban from the Saribas and the closely-related Krian river

> probably make up no more than 15 per cent of the total Iban population. Yet the first man to serve as Chief Minister of Sarawak, Dato Stephen Kalong Ningkan, is a Saribas Iban. So are the first Sarawak-born State Secretary, Gerunsin Lembat, the first local Curator of the Sarawak Museum, Benedict Sandin, and the first Iban Resident of a Division, Peter Tinggom. The preponderance of Saribas-Krian staffing in certain departments of the State Government, such as Radio Sarawak, has from time to time generated mild resentment among Ibans from other areas. Nevertheless all would agree that had it not been for the Saribas community, the Ibans would have encountered far more difficulty ... in assuming their fair share of power and responsibility in the new era.

The effects of this 'brain drain' to Kuching and other urban areas are today apparent across the Saribas. Goody's (1987: 146) remark on the 1950s impact of literacy upon rural West African communities applies equally well to the Saribas Iban. Those who have not 'learnt book' and have stayed behind, says Goody, 'begin to see themselves as inferior to those who have learnt book and gone away'. In chapter 5, I develop this point in relation to literacy and print media in the Saribas.

I undertook field research in the Saribas (Betong) for a period of approximately thirteen months during 1996–1997. My then wife, Kyoko, accompanied me for some five months. We were based at a longhouse called Entanak, located some fifteen minutes on foot from the small market town

Figure 2.3.   Entanak Longhouse (Saribas) as viewed from the road.

(*pasar*) of Betong. At the end of 1997, Entanak had some 150 residents in 28 *bilek*-families led by a headman. Most men were earning regular wages working for a local construction firm, the Public Works Department (JKR), the local bus company or the police. Most women alternated between wet *padi* farming (*bumai tanjung*) and domestic chores. All local children attended school, while some teenagers had found local employment as labourers or shop assistants. Unlike some other longhouses in the area, all *bilek*-families in Entanak are now Christian. The last pagan families joined the Anglican Church in the late 1980s. Politically, the community has long been associated with PBB, the dominant party in the State coalition whose Saribas leader, Dr Alfred Jabu, is Sarawak's deputy chief minister (see chapter 9). The Entanak ideology or 'ideolect' (chapter 5) is a good example of the quintessentially Saribas search for a balance between development (*pemansang*) and tradition (*adat*) – a search epitomised by Sandin. Entanak was the first longhouse in the area to have a telephone line installed and one of the first to have electricity, in 1987. It is served by a good road with a frequent bus service (STC).

Figure 2.4. Entanak Longhouse. The author (second from right) with his adoptive mother, Indai Amoi, her nephew (far right), her son (third from left) and family, and a European friend of the author's (second from left).

Source: courtesy Samuel W.F. Onn.

On the other hand, its founding *bilek*-families are proud of the longhouse's ironwood (*belian*) posts and gallery floor and of its long history.

The main research methods I employed in the Saribas area were a household survey, semi-structured interviews, follow-up conversations, participant observation, genealogies (*tusut*), biographies of persons, biographies of radio and television sets, and children's school essays. The household survey covered 119 *bilek*-families in six Saribas longhouses. It was aimed at gathering (1) basic social and economic data, (2) information on the *bilek*-families' material culture (especially heirlooms [*pesaka*] and media artefacts) and values related to it, and (3) information on local media practices and preferences. Sir Edmund Leach, who carried out the first ethnographic survey of Sarawak which paved the way for Freeman, once argued that numerical social surveys count people as units, while the purpose of social anthropology is to 'understand people not as units but as integral parts of systems of relationships', and one can never count these (Ellen 1984: 258–259). The household survey was also good as an introduction to the local residents, and as a way of learning colloquial Iban and beginning to discern Leach's 'systems of relationships'. I arrived in Sarawak with a basic knowledge of Iban I had acquired through 1960s primers kept at the School of Oriental and African Studies (SOAS) library, in London. Having learnt Indonesian (Malay) in Jakarta some years earlier, the transition to the cognate Iban was relatively smooth, although I never achieved total fluency. In order to strengthen my Iban I did not use an interpreter, and gradually shifted from writing up field notes in English to Iban. For added security given the nature of my research topic, I wrote some notes on 'sensitive' subjects in a colloquial form of Spanish, my native language.

My occasional research assistant (a male university student from a local longhouse) and I separately carried out and audio-taped three series of semi-structured interviews in Entanak and, for comparative purposes, another two longhouses. Each series focused on one major topic: everyday routines, radio uses and television uses. Interviews were typically followed by 'off the record' conversations which often revealed more than the interview itself and helped to contextualise it.

Although based at Entanak, I often visited other longhouses in the wider Saribas basin – in particular those with close kinship ties to Entanak Longhouse. I also accompanied Entanak residents or the local Anglican priest (an Iban) to weddings, funerals and other gatherings at nearby longhouses. With the permission, and often encouragement, of the hosts, I videotaped many of these occasions, as well as other everyday activities (some 55 hours in total). Unexpectedly, screening these videos at an Entanak *bilek* became both a favourite local pastime and a research method in its own right. Ellen (1984: 217) considers the term 'participant observation' to be a both an oxymoron and an 'anthropological mystery'. Willis (1977) has nonetheless rightly defended it, in spite of its wooliness, as the social scientist's best chance of being surprised. Throughout the entire period of field research, open-ended participant observation made me rethink cherished assumptions (e.g., about local oratorical prowess; see chapter 5), and re-assess my research priorities in the light of certain unexpected events (e.g., a 'traditional knowledge' quiz night connected to the Dayak Festival; chapter 9). Besides the longhouse gallery and family rooms, other important social settings in which I participated included the coffee-shops in the market town, official functions, church gatherings, Iban pop and folk concerts, bus journeys, football matches, children's games, paddy farming, pepper gardening and fishing.

The genealogies I collected were both a disappointment and evidence of the decline of oral knowledge. Having read Sandin (1994) and Sather (1994), I expected my informants to be highly knowledgeable about their ancestors. Sandin argued that genealogical knowledge was most sophisticated among the Saribas Iban, whose experts (*tukang tusut*) could often trace descent up to fifteen generations. In my experience, by contrast, I found that most Saribas Iban knew little about their ancestors, to the extent that a good number of respondents could not even recall the names of one or two of their grand-parents. Very few *tukang tusut* are still alive, and those who remain have been made largely redundant.

I also collected 'biographies of things' (Kopytoff 1986: 67). George Marcus (1995: 106–107) has encouraged ethnographers to study artefacts in the 'speculative, open-ended spirit of tracing things in and through contexts'. In this spirit, I asked Saribas Iban about their radio and television sets: how they were acquired, for how much, by whom, and when. I analyse the results in chapter 7 by means of two phases or crises in the 'social life' (Appadurai 1986) of Saribas television sets – their acquisition and disposal. This analysis sheds light on otherwise concealed processes of social and material valuation as well as on the partly ritualised exchange system that binds the dead and the living. In addition, I collected a set of life histories of both men and women. Although initially I was hoping to achieve a balance between the accounts of (by local standards) high and low achievers, it soon became clear that successful men, particularly those with a proud military or civilian career behind them, had more detailed stories to tell than those women farmers who felt they had little to boast about (cf. Hoskins 1998). In chapter 5, however, I relate some episodes in the life of a generous informant; an articulate middle-aged woman. Finally, I asked two Saribas teachers to set a number of optional essay questions to 63 secondary school pupils (chapter 5). I take essays and exams to be media practices that help to spread and reproduce the state's nation building ideology across rural Sarawak.

Second Field Site: the Skrang

Tourists from as far afield as Iceland visit the Skrang in order to experience life in a remote Dayak longhouse. Ironically, the Skrang lacks that 'quality of community and continuity' that can be found in the economically more developed Saribas (Pringle 1970: 208). As I explain in chapter 6, the reasons have to be sought in the local history and geography. While the Saribas is sheltered by high hills from the formerly war-ridden Kanowit and Batang Lupar areas, the Skrang always had easy access to and from these rivers. For this reason, its communities were chronically disrupted well into the twentieth century (1970: 207). Until the recent (1970s) upsurge in tourism and pepper culti-vation, the Skrang had benefited little from the wider economic developments unfolding in Sarawak (Uchibori 1988). Literacy also arrived much later than in the Saribas, and many longhouses remain to this day resolutely 'pagan'.

I carried out an intensive four-week study in a longhouse named Nanga Tebat and visited nearby communities, mostly during February 1998. Tebat is located some forty minutes from the main road by longboat. At the time of fieldwork there were no roads connecting this area to the rest of Sarawak's

Figure 2.5. Longboat jetty at Pais Longhouse, where the Skrang river meets the main road.

Sri Aman (formerly Second) Division. Tebat had a population of 92 people spread over 22 *bilek*-families. The economic mainstay of these households was pepper and hill-rice farming, supplemented by income from rubber cultivation, tourism, and in some cases remittances from migrant kin. All *bilek*-families, except for one, had converted to Anglicanism in 1993. Owing to this ongoing process of conversion, I found the various uses of an unexpected print genre – the indigenised prayer book – to be of special interest.

In the Skrang I combined participant observation, questionnaire-based interviews and follow-up conversations. For purposes of comparison, the questionnaire was identical to the one I had used in the Saribas a year earlier. I usually took notes during post-interview conversations, which I often taped. Additionally I videotaped a number of events, most of them connected to the building of a new longhouse and other daily activities. In order to gain further insights into local life and repay in part my hosts' generosity, I also taught English at the primary school.

Figure 2.6. The gallery (*ruai*) of a Skrang longhouse. Galleries are often quiet in the daytime.

Third Field Site: Kuching

Kuching was an 'invisible' field site. For all foreign researchers working in Sarawak, Kuching is the unavoidable point of entry and departure. It is here that contacts are made and renewed with the local administration and intelligentsia before and after working in 'the field', generally a remote upriver longhouse. Few anthropologists, however, have chosen Kuching as their field site.[4] In all I worked in Kuching for some three months, often for short periods of time to attend seminars or conferences. Worthy of special mention are the workshops or conferences on Iban-language broadcasting (April 1998),

Figure 2.7. The external platform (*tanju'*) of a Skrang long-house, used for winnowing rice and drying rice, pepper and laundry. Notice the television aerials attached to bamboo poles.

Iban-language textbooks (April 1997), the Iban arts (July 1997) and the impact of globalisation on Sarawak cultures (December 1997), as well as the presentation of Dr Masing's (1997) book on Iban bardic lore (June 1997), the official opening of the Centre for Dayak Studies at the University of Malaysia in Sarawak (March 1998), and the Dayak Festival at the Crowne Plaza Hotel (May 2001). These occasions provided me with a good overview of contemporary official representations of Iban and Dayak culture (see chapters 4 and 9 and Winzeler 1997).

Additionally I interviewed radio producers on their professional life histories and current activities and sponsored an essay competition on the history of the RTM Iban Section from the listeners' perspective. I also interacted with urban Iban, mostly from the small professional class, outside an interview setting. Unfortunately, owing to sad family circumstances in Spain, I had to leave Sarawak before I could complete a comparative study on media practices among Siol Kandis (Kuching) residents. With hindsight, this impediment had a positive side to it, as it sharpened the contrast between 'ordinary' rural Iban and highly educated urban Iban (chapter 5). Before leaving Sarawak I was able to photocopy a considerable body of publications in Iban produced by the defunct Borneo Literature Bureau (chapter 3) which are now in the hands of private collectors.

A Note on Ethnic Terminology

For the sake of clarity, some brief remarks on the terms 'Dayak', 'Sea Dayak', and 'Iban' are now in order. The blanket term 'Dayak' is commonly used in many parts of Borneo – but not in Sabah or Brunei (Winzeler 1997: 28n) – to refer collectively to all non-Muslim indigenous groups. Traditionally, it has carried the negative connotation of 'yokel' or 'rustic' among coastal Malays, a perception that still lingers on today (King 1994: 1). Ethnologically, the term 'Dayak' has nonetheless the virtue of pointing at Borneo-wide cultural commonalities despite the island's bewildering linguistic and ethnic diversity. These commonalities include longhouse domicile, the belief in bird and animal omens, and the institution of headhunting (King 1994: 1–2). In Sarawak, the distinction between 'Land Dayaks' (today Bidayuh) and 'Sea Dayaks' (today Iban) is attributed to James Brooke, the first White Rajah, who noticed marked differences in language and custom between the two groups (Pringle 1970: 19). Brooke and his contemporaries regarded the Land Dayaks as timid, peaceful hill farmers who had been historically at the mercy of Sea Dayak headhunters.

The term 'Iban' only became popular with Western scholars when Charles Hose, the self-taught ethnologist and Resident, began to promote it in the early twentieth century. He did it to avoid the confusions surrounding the label 'Dayak', which nearly always stood for 'Sea Dayak' (Pringle 1970: xviii, 20). 'Iban' is thought to derive from the pejorative Kayan word *ivan*, which means wanderer (King and Wilder 2003: 209). Derek Freeman's *Report on the Iban* (1955) contributed to the consolidation of the term after the Second World War, when the British Crown took over Sarawak from the Brooke dynasty. Another important development was the creation of Iban political parties and Radio Sarawak's Iban Section (*Bagi Iban*) during that period. Benedict Sandin himself reluctantly accepted the term 'Iban' only around this time. Like many of his Saribas kith and kin, Sandin had always associated the word 'Iban' with people from the Rejang basin (Pringle 1970: 20).

Interestingly, although the labels Sea Dayak and Land Dayak have virtually disappeared, the 'supraethnic designation' (Boulanger 2000: 45) 'Dayak' has made deep inroads since the war. This can be linked to the 1950s emergence of Malay and Chinese political parties in preparation for independence from Britain (King and Wilder 2003: 209). As a reaction, the Sarawak Dayak National Union (SDNU) was established in 1956. The hope was to translate Dayak numerical superiority into political clout. But Dayak political unity has remained an elusive goal, as the various parties and associations came to represent the narrower interests of the constituent Dayak 'races' (Boulanger 2000: 55, cf. Jawan 1993). Concurrently, the great popularity of the annual Dayak Festival from the 1960s onwards, provided a more sustainable – albeit politically weak – avenue for the constitution of a Dayak identity (chapter 9). By the end of the twentieth century, urban Dayaks had settled for an instrumentalist view of the Dayak category, regarding it as a political tool lacking in cultural depth (Boulanger 2000: 54).

Conclusion

The Baleh Iban that Freeman knew in the 1940s and 1950s were shifting hill rice cultivators with access to vast reserves of primary forest. They practised a 'rice cult' that demanded constant ritual attention to the requirements of unseen beings. Their longhouse-based social organisation was cognatic, flexible and egalitarian. It was already, however, linked to a hierarchical system of administration that stretched all the way to Kuching and London. Freeman, and other anthropologists of a structural-functionalist persuasion, downplayed these links. Instead, they produced ethnographic accounts of largely self-contained, 'traditional' Borneo societies. There were good practical reasons for doing so, the same reasons that drove Sandin to zealously gather his data: unless it was urgently documented, oral knowledge of pre-state Iban culture would be forever lost. We owe these scholars, therefore, a great debt.

The present study seeks to add to the growing anthropological literature on social change in Southeast Asia. Unlike most studies of Borneo peoples, however, the culture area chosen as my frame of reference is not Borneo but rather Malaysia (cf. King 1993). This is not to deny the existence of Borneo as a culture area, but rather to suggest that, of the two 'thick' culture areas to which Sarawak belongs (Malaysia and Borneo), Malaysia is gradually becoming the more important one, as I try to prove in subsequent chapters. There is an entrenched division of labour in the scholarship of Borneo militating against my approach. Anthropologists and folklorists tend to concentrate on 'traditional' or marginal cultural practices (e.g., Freeman 1955, Jensen 1966,

Sandin 1967, Sather 1993), while political scientists, historians and economists specialise in elite practices within a given modern state (e.g., Leigh 1983, Jawan 1994, Reece 1998). Interestingly, this cleavage between culture and political economy is not confined to academia. It runs through the entire field of writings on the Iban and other Dayak peoples, not least through the Sarawak press. As I argue in chapter 4, newspapers in Sarawak represent the Dayaks in two contrasting ways. First, as colourful, camera-friendly indigenes with timeless cultural traditions. Second, as underdeveloped 'rural folk' awaiting modernisation. The two representations are kept separate through conventional rhetorical means. In this book I join those scholars who have sought to bridge the discursive chasm by integrating 'culture' and 'political economy' into their analyses of Iban social change. Perhaps the most notable of these contributions are R. Pringle's (1970) *Rajahs and Rebels*, mentioned above in connection with Sandin, and V.H. Sutlive's (1992) *Tun Jugah of Sarawak: Colonialism and Iban Response*, the fascinating biography of an Iban leader.

But in choosing a Malaysian frame of analysis, am I eschewing the functionalist idea of traditional societies as 'bounded wholes' only to posit modern states as the bounded wholes of our era? Am I not replacing Freeman's 'pristine Iban society' with an equally essentialist 'modern Malaysian society'? The answer is 'no' on three counts. First, unlike the functionalists I make history central to my analysis; more specifically, the main historical phases in the Iban media contribution to the building of Malaysia (chapters 3 and 4). Second, I take Malaysia to be an open rather than a closed cultural system (Bertalanffy 1969, Peterson 2003). This allows me to track the diffusion and appropriation of media forms originating in other countries. Third, the multi-sited ethnographic approach I adopt below, while practised by Freeman and other scholars as well, includes Kuching, i.e., it links rural and urban social formations.

Notes

1. Andrew Beatty (personal communication, 11 October 2004) point outs that '[a] number of Indonesian societies do in fact have corporate descent groups (e.g., in Sumatra and East Indonesia) – though the extent to which they are corporate has been debated'.
2. A longhouse survey of 119 *bilek*-families in the Betong (Saribas) area which I carried out in 1997 (see main text, below), yielded similar figures.
3. A useful definition of allodial is: '(of tenure) characterized by or relating to the system of holding land in absolute ownership' (www.wordreference.com).
4. Winzeler's (1997) article on Bidayuh ethnicity contains materials from the Kuching area, including an analysis of Bidayuh architecture in the Sarawak Cultural Village, a multiethnic theme park. Clare Boulanger (1999, 2000, 2002) has conducted interview-based research on Dayak identity in Kuching, whilst Kirsten Eddie Craig, a doctoral candidate from Duke University, in the United States, has undertaken fieldwork into cross-cultural healing practices in this town.

3

PROPAGATING THE STATE, PHASE I

In chapter 1, I discussed Gellner's (1983: 140–143) robust thesis that most states seek to monopolise legitimate culture through mass education and a national language. The driving principle of nationalism, contends Gellner, is 'one state, one culture'. A key neglected area of research is *exactly how, through which media*, states seek to transcend their cultural diversity and supposed backwardness and achieve a 'literate sophisticated high culture' (1983: 141). In this chapter I argue that one chief site of struggles between central and peripheral ethnic groups in Malaysia is language, and that the Iban and other Dayaks, who lack the 'political shell' of the state (1983: 140), are losing out to the politically stronger Peninsular Malays and their Sarawak allies.

We can distinguish two periods of media production impinging upon rural Iban society. First, an early period (1954–1976) dominated not by 'global' media but rather by Iban-language radio and books controlled by the Sarawak government and aimed at consolidating its hold across the territory. In this chapter I cover this phase. I dwell on some of the ambiguities involved in the task, for the early Iban producers were striving *both* to modernise their society *and* to protect it from the ravages of modernity. In the following chapter I analyse a second period (1977–1998) dominated by audiovisual and print media from three urban centres (Kuala Lumpur, Kuching and Sibu). This second period was characterised by powerful efforts to exclude the Iban language and culture from the mass media and promote a colourful, vague Dayak identity in its stead – a creative process familiar to students of other Asia-Pacific nations (e.g., Papua New Guinea; see Sullivan 1993).

The Rise of Iban Radio, 1954–1976

Radio Sarawak was officially inaugurated on 8 June 1954. Sarawak was then a British Crown Colony. The Sarawak Legislative Council (or *Council Negeri*) had finally decided to go ahead with hotly debated plans to create a broadcasting service (Morrison 1954: 391). Set up with the technical assistance of the BBC, the service had four sections: Malay, Iban, Chinese and English. The Iban section broadcast one hour daily from 7 to 8 p.m. In the early days the variety of programmes was limited to news, information on farming and animal husbandry (*betanam betupi*), and some Iban folklore, especially sung poems (*pantun, renong*) and epics (*ensera*). It was also used for medical and other emergencies in certain upriver areas (Dickson 1995: 137).[1]

The late Gerunsin Lembat (1924–1995) from Malong, Saratok, was the first Iban broadcaster. In January 1956 he was promoted to Head of the Iban Service (Langub 1995a: 56). He is still remembered by rural and urban audiences alike for his extraordinary voice, command of the Iban language and knowledge of the *adat* (customary law). In those days Radio Sarawak was jokingly known as 'Radio Saribas' owing to the prevalence of broadcasters born or educated in that region. Even today, a strong influence of the Saribas dialect can be detected in standard RTM Iban.

The Iban were the first Dayaks to have their own radio programmes. In 1957 the Iban example led influential members of another major group, the Land Dayaks (today Bidayuh), to express their 'great desire' to have their own radio section (*Sarawak Tribune*, 21 October 1957). Others, like the Kenyah and Kayan would follow suit in subsequent years. In the intervening years they were avid listeners of the Iban programmes.[2]

In 1958 the School Broadcasting Service (Ib. *Sekula Penabur*[3]) was set up in Kuching by a New Zealander, Ian Prentice, under the Colombo Plan. Most radio sets were donated by the Asia Foundation and the Government of Australia. A regular schedule of broadcast English lessons began in 1959, designed for native primary schools in rural areas, where most teachers had only a basic education. It was hoped radio would help overcome pupils' reliance on the English spoken by native teachers hampered by a 'limited range of knowledge, ideas, stories and vocabulary'.[4] By the end of 1960 there were 467 participating schools across Sarawak, and 850 teachers had attended 11 training courses.[5] Sarawak was a regional pioneer in radio-mediated teaching and learning. Indeed Malayan educationalists were to learn from their Sarawak colleagues at a later stage. The response from the target audience was very encouraging. In 1960 the Service received 700 letters from Primary 5 and 6 pupils around Sarawak in response to questions set to them.[6]

Meanwhile Radio Sarawak was preparing for independence. From 1961 to 1963 Peter Redcliffe, an alleged intelligence officer with Britain's MI5,[7] and John Cordoux were in charge of Radio Sarawak. They were replaced by Charles McKenna, the last expatriate Director, soon before the formation of Malaysia in 1963. With 'independence through Malaysia', Radio Sarawak became Radio Malaysia Sarawak. The inclusion of the term Malaysia signalled a shift in priorities for the Iban Section and all the other sections. The first task was to help the new country from the perceived threat posed by Indonesia whose leader,

Soekarno, claimed Malaysia was a new form of British imperialism designed to keep the Malay world divided[8]. In response to Soekarno, a Psychological Warfare (Psy-War) Unit was set up under British guidance. It deployed tactics already used successfully by Radio Malaya against the communist guerrillas in the 1948–1960 period. One of the weapons deployed was the *cherita kelulu* (radio drama) which adapted traditional Iban storytelling genres, themes and characters such as the Keling and Kumang epics *(ensera)*. Other dramas were set in contemporary rural Sarawak and promoted the need for development, religious and racial harmony and loyalty to the new country. The first producer of these dramas *(cherita kelulu)* was Andria Ejau, who also published a number of them through the Borneo Literature Bureau (see below). Vivid jungle and longhouse sound effects were fundamental to the task of producing compelling drama. Some were borrowed from the BBC, while others were home-made.

Other time-honoured tactics included interviews with war victims and patriotic songs. An Iban singer, Connie Francis, sang *Tanah ai menoa aku* (lit. my country's land and water, i.e., my Fatherland), the Iban/Malaysian answer to Indonesia's national anthem, while Hillary Tawan sang *Oh Malaysia!*. This was a time of growth for Iban pop. The 1950s influence of the Indonesian and Indian music industry gave way in the 1960s and 1970s to British and American influences. Pauline Linan was now joined by her sister, Señorita Linan, on frequent tours around Sarawak and recorded broadcasts. They were both brought up listening to Western songs. Señorita's personal favourites were, not unusually, Tom Jones and Engelbert Humperdinck. In her varied repertoire she sang in Iban but the rhythms and tunes were borrowed from the West. She knew her twist, rock'n'roll, country and sentimental. In those days Iban audiences lagged behind the more urbanised ethnic groups, says Señorita: 'for instance, the Chinese, were into The Beatles but back in the 1960s few Iban were exposed to world music'.[9]

There were other popular Iban singers, including Reynolds Gregory – also known as 'the Elvis Presley of Sarawak'. Ironically, the fruits of their pioneering efforts to create a 'modern' Iban pop scene are now collectively known as *lagu lama* (lit. 'old songs') as middle-aged Iban look back at those golden days and praise the depth *(dalam)* and subtlety of the lyrics, to them worlds apart from today's 'superficial' *(mabu)* Iban pop. Despite the foreign provenance of the tunes, the *lagu lama* are now regarded as legitimate heirs to the best Iban musical tradition. Why would this be so? According to the media theorist Debray (1996: 177) nostalgia is 'the first phase of mediological consciousness'. As a first generation of media producers and consumers reach their middle and late years, their discovery of 'a clear deviation from the old norm grasps the new order as a disordering'.

In the early stages of Iban pop, some songwriters and performers straddled both genres. For instance, Lawrence S. Ijau[10] (1966), a teacher and folklorist, wrote a number of pop songs that were broadcast by Radio Sarawak. Another case in point is Señorita Linan herself, who apart from being a pop singer was a traditional dance (*ngajat*) performer in the 1960s and 1970s. In the late 1990s, she was teaching this art form in Kuching. With the end of the Indonesian *konfrontasi* in 1965, priorities shifted from war propaganda to what a veteran Iban broadcaster has defined as the 'mental revolution of the people', that is to education, health and economic development. From mid-1971 a slump in the international timber market caused the economic situation in Sarawak to worsen, especially in the Sibu area. The combination of a rapid Malaysianisation, abject poverty and chronic unemployment led many Chinese to join the communist guerrillas (Leigh 1974: 156). Their Iban support was considerable. The communists used terror effectively by publicly executing informers. They also targeted virtually every school in Sibu with moralistic pamphlets and lectures. Students were urged to 'win the victory' and 'oppose and stop to wear Mini-skirt and funny dresses'. Teachers were often blamed for the pupils' decadent ways: 'some of them even teach the students how to twist, and thus really lead the students into darkness' (Leigh 1974: 158).

The Iban Section was again enlisted to deploy psy-war tactics against the insurgents. Two 15-minute programmes were broadcast daily: 'Topic of the day' (thinly veiled propaganda) and an appeal to the insurgents to surrender. In addition, special soap operas (*cherita kelulu*) were produced by Andria Ejau in order to, in the words of a colleague, alter the listeners' 'mental perspective' and 'get the people to report the terrorists' (*ngasoh rayat ripot tiroris*). In 1975 the gifted Iban storyteller and broadcaster Thomas T. Laka, still active in the late 1990s, was trained in drama techniques by a British psy-war instructor based in Kuala Lumpur. That same year television arrived in Sarawak – 12 years after it had done so in West Malaysia – and some of the radio staff were headhunted into the new medium.

At this point it is pertinent to ask to what extent we can consider the Iban Section part of the growing number of 'indigenous media' around the world that have attracted the attention of media researchers (Spitulnik 1993: 303). The anthropologist Faye Ginsburg (1993: 560–562) is one of the better known practitioners in this new subfield (see Abu-Lughod 1997). She argues that two resilient tropes dominate the study of indigenous media. First, there is the 'Faustian contract' approach derived from the Frankfurt School. This approach is pessimistic about the possibilities of indigenous cultures to withstand the onslaught of western media and their repressive ideologies. Second, there is McLuhan's (1964) 'global village' optimism with its utopian dream of a worldwide electronic democracy. Ginsburg (1993: 561–562) opts for a third trope: Appadurai's (1990) 'mediascape', a call for 'situated analyses that take account of the interdependence of media practices and the local, national, and transnational circumstances that surround them'. In settler nations such as

Canada and Australia which practise 'welfare colonialism', she notes, it is ironically the state that has to support these media given the lack of financial and technical resources available to the native populations. Another factor of growing importance is the globalisation of indigenous media, arts and activism. Thus, although Aboriginal culture has been exploited continually by the white majority for tourist and political gains, Aboriginal media producers have become more and more active at international film and video festivals and other forms of networking. In order to grasp the significance of these developments, says Ginsburg, we need to study how indigenous media producers 'enter transnational mediascapes in complex and multidirectional ways' (1993: 562).

While it may be useful in Australia, this approach would be of little use in Sarawak. Here it is not so much 'multidirectional ways' we should analyse but rather the unidirectional, collective endeavour of Iban radio producers to spread the dominant modernist ideology. Many Aboriginal producers have shown an active commitment to the romantic, post-industrial ideology of a global brotherhood of 'First Nations' or 'Fourth World Peoples' defined in opposition to white settler nations (Ginsburg 1993: 558). In contrast, Iban producers have remained committed to redefining, refining and modernising 'the Iban race' (*bansa Iban*) within the bounds of an avowedly indigenist, post-colonial state. This trend was reinforced with the advent of print media in the Iban language.

The Rise and Fall of the Borneo Literature Bureau, 1960–1976

In 1949, John Kennedy Wilson arrived in Sarawak from Scotland to become the Principal of Batu Lintang Teachers Training College. The chief aim of the college was to train young Sarawakian teachers and send them to far-flung corners of the new Crown Colony to set up and run primary schools, often under very harsh conditions. Its ethos followed in the Brooke tradition of symbolic respect towards the country's 'native cultures'.

> Batu Lintang, with its white washed walls decorated with splendid native designs, its encouragement of local handicrafts and interest in the tribal dances, had already set a pattern of pride in indigenous culture and artistic achievement (Dickson 1995: 27).

In November 1952 Wilson attended his last school-leaving ceremony. All students arrived in 'traditional dress, bright with hornbill feathers, silver woven sarongs and ivory earrings' (Dickson 1995: 27). Wilson was to go on to found a remarkably successful experiment in what today is known as 'sustainable development'. For four years he lived in the remote Budu area to set up a community development scheme from the bottom up, that is building on local Iban skills and cultural resources rather than importing them from the urban areas. Wilson saw this as the creation of new Budu 'elites' (Jawan 1994: 82). Alas, when Malaysia was born in 1963, his success was perceived as a threat by the new Kuala Lumpur rulers and he was eventually 'asked to leave Sarawak' (Jawan 1994: 121).[11]

The indigenist nature of Batu Lintang's ethos, or rather its blending of British education and native arts and ceremony, had a decisive influence on a core of motivated pioneering Iban teachers who would set out to modernise Iban culture while preserving what they considered to be the best of its heritage. On 15 September 1958 the colonial government inaugurated the Borneo Literature Bureau (Tawai 1997: 6). Like Batu Lintang and Radio Sarawak, the Bureau aimed at reconciling social and economic development with cultural preservation. The three official aims of the Bureau's publications in English, Chinese, Malay, Iban and other indigenous languages were:

(a) to support the various government departments in their production of technical, semi-technical and instructional printed materials for the peoples of Sabah and Sarawak.[12]

(b) to encourage local authorship and meet local needs

(c) to help in building up a local book trade

(*Borneo Literature Bureau Annual Report* 1960).

Production started in 1960. The following year, the book of Iban folk stories *Rita Tujoh Malam* by Anthony Richards (1961) sold the promising figure of 1,765 copies within six months. In the same year the Bureau also published the religious text *Jerita pasal Daniel* and took over the distribution of *Radio Times* from Radio Sarawak. The 1962 sales of English and Iban books were described by the Bureau as 'encouraging'.[13] Several booksellers reported selling books to illiterate Iban adults who would have their children read them aloud to them. Of the nine Iban books published, two were educational (geography and English), three were on Iban custom (*adat*), and four were oral narratives (*ensera* and *mimpi* [dreams]). The latter was Benedict Sandin's (1962) important *Duabelas Bengkah Mimpi Tuai Dayak-Iban*, a collection of dreams by Iban chiefs that had special historical significance.[14] Another prolific author who started publishing this year was Sandin's kinsman Henry Gerijih (1962) with *Raja Langit*, an *ensera*[15] on Keling and other heroes and heroines from the mythical world of Panggau Libau-Gelong.

In 1964 the Bureau celebrated its seventh annual literary competition. Seven Iban manuscripts were sent in, three of which were accepted. Sandin published *Raja Durong*, an *ensera* about the great Sumatran ancestor of Pulang Gana,[16] the Iban 'deity of the earth' (Richards 1981: 288). Another previous winner, Andria Ejau's *Dilah Tanah*, was published this year. Arguably the first ever Iban novel,[17] the author describes it as an *Ensera Kelulu*, that is a 'pedagogical story' (*tau pulai ka pelajar*), which he distinguishes from the traditional genre *Ensera Tuai* (or *Cherita Asal*). A more accurate translation might be 'morality novella', from the 'morality plays' staged in England between the fourteenth and sixteenth centuries in which personified virtues and vices were set into conflict.[18] Ejau's characters live in a longhouse situated in the imaginary land (*menoa kelulu*) of Dilah Tanah. They mean well, but keep running into trouble with the authorities for their reluctance to fully embrace the new *adat*, the so-called *adat perintah* (lit. government law), in particular the new laws aimed at curtailing slash-and-burn farming. It all ends well after the local councillor makes the locals see the need to follow the learned ways of the government regarding modern agriculture. There are obvious autobiographical elements in the story, for Ejau was a councillor from 1947 to 1956, frequently travelling to remote Iban areas, before he joined Radio Sarawak where he first started writing radio dramas. During his official trips to the backwoods he enjoyed talking to the elders, as he was 'seeking knowledge that could benefit my own people' (*ngiga penemu ke tau diguna bansa diri*). Previously he had been a security guard at an oil refinery in Seria (Ejau 1964). He was therefore well acquainted both with Iban customary law and with the state's own understanding of law and order. By means of his novellas and broadcasts he sought to bridge the two.

Ejau and Sandin represent two poles of the modernist-traditionalist continuum running through the entire field of Iban media production. Ejau specialised in transforming oral accounts, metaphors and imagery into contemporary, power-laden narratives that would 'benefit [his] people'. He was using old linguistic materials through new media technologies in order to promote 'modern' practices. Sandin took the opposite route as he sought to salvage as much of the Iban oral tradition as he could for the benefit of future generations. In other words, he was employing a new media technology to save (selected) 'old knowledge' (*penemu lama*). Their respective 1964 publications exemplify this marked contrast. While Ejau concentrated on modern agriculture, Sandin wrote about the Iban god of farming. Although both authors were undoubtedly the products and producers of a modern Sarawak, the generic divide they bolstered has indigenous, pre-state roots. Jensen (1974: 64) has divided Iban oral tradition into (1) stories about 'the origins of Iban custom, the rice cult, augury and social organisation' and (2) 'legends from the heroic past' whose purpose is to explain Iban behaviour and the potential consequences of wrongdoing. Ejau's contribution was to shift from this 'heroic past' to the contemporary Iban world he knew well, but his aim was equally to explain 'the potential consequences of wrongdoing'.

In 1966 an important change took place. The Bureau announced that whereas most previous entries had been first records of 'stories handed down orally for many generations', henceforth original writing would be encouraged (*BLB Annual Report* 1966). The scales were therefore tipped in favour of Ejau's line of work. George Jenang, aged 19, took up the challenge and published

Keling Nyumpit, an original[19] *ensera*, in 1967. Meanwhile A.A. Majang (1967) chose to publish in a new, para-journalistic genre: Iban reportage. His *Padi Ribai* deals with the rumours that spread across the Rejang in the 1950s that Pulang Gana, the god of farming, had passed away and his son, Ribai, was sending *padi* from overseas to grow in river shallows (Richards 1981: 289). Also in 1967, Andria Ejau himself published a sequel to *Dilah Tanah*, his morality novella mentioned earlier. In this new book, *Madu Midang*, Ejau resumes his preoccupation with social change and its effects on Iban culture. Two of his early themes re-emerge here: (a) the peasants' need to understand the new laws regulating migratory farming, and (b) their need to modify their customary law (*adat*) to allow for new developmental tools – in this case the wireless radio. He exemplifies the latter with an episode in which the longhouse elders ban the use of radio for a month in accordance with the *adat* regulating mourning (*ulit*).[20] Thus the community fail to learn about a dangerous fugitive presently roaming their land. One day the ne'er-do-well arrives and, posing as a government official, cheats the community out of their meagre savings.

The main Iban event of 1967 at the Bureau was the launching of *Nendak*, a magazine intended 'for Ibans who are unable to read with facility in any language other than their own'. The target readers were adolescents and young adults, both male and female. In order to attract them, a '[w]ide variety of material' was designed (*BLB Annual Report* 1967: 3–6). Appendix 3.1 captures some of that diversity. In its ten-year history, a total of 125 issues of *Nendak* were published. Besides being a rich repository of Iban lore, *Nendak* provides us with a privileged insight into the role of Iban intellectuals in state-sponsored efforts to modernise Iban culture and society on a wide front, from customary law through political organisation, agriculture and health to home economics.

In 1968 a second 'original work' was born, Janang Ensiring's *Ngelar Menoa Sarawak*, a passionate ode to Sarawak written in the *pantun* genre, i.e., 'a song sung in rhyming pattern' (Sather 1994: 60). Ensiring, who was 19 at the time, shows great love for both Sarawak and the five-year-old Malaysia. His *pantun* traces the history of Sarawak, from the cave-ridden, bloody chaos of prehistory through several stages of increased *adat* law and order to the glorious cry of Malaysian freedom from British colonialism in 1963: MERDEKA! (Ensiring 1968: 32). To the young poet, life before the Brooke Raj was hardly worth living:

Bekereja samoa nadai meruan	Their travails saw no profitable ends
Laban rindang bebunoh ba pangan	For they were busy murdering their friends
[...]	[...]
Sida nadai Raja megai	They had no Rajah to rule them
Adat nadai dipejalai	Had no *adat* to guide them

(Ensiring 1968: 2, my translation)

There is no trace in Ensiring of Rousseau's 'noble savage' who lives in harmony with nature, and a great deal of Hobbes' famous dictum on primitive man's life being 'solitary, poor, nasty, brutish and short'. For Hobbes (1651), the emergence of the state's monopoly of violence is a fundamental step towards peace, social evolution and prosperity – a view all Iban media producers would readily agree with. The teleological nature of modern Iban ethnohistory is a synthesis of foreign (British and Malayan) and indigenous elements. The foreign component supplies a view of nations as steadily marching along history towards greater unity and prosperity (Anderson 1991: 23), whereas the Iban tradition has *adat* regulating all spheres of life and severely punishing those who threaten the collective harmony.[21]

Another case in point is Sandin's 1970 ethnohistorical account, entitled *Peturun Iban* ('Iban Descent'). It recounts the history of the Iban people from their origins in the Kapuas, in present-day Indonesian Borneo, through their migrations into Sarawak, to the long pacification process under the White Rajahs culminating in the surrender of the last Upper Engkari 'troublemakers' in 1932:

> *Nya pengabis pengachau Iban dalam Sarawak. Udah bekau tu nadai agi orang deka ngaga pengachau ke nusah orang maioh. Ati berani agi dikembuan bansa Iban tang sida enda ngemeran ka nya agi. Sida berumah manah lalu besekula nunda pengawa enggau pemansang bansa bukai ke sama diau begulai enggau sida dalam menoa Sarawak tu.*

> This was the end of the Iban troubles in Sarawak. Henceforth nobody would cause suffering to the general population. The Iban are still endowed with brave hearts yet they pay little heed to them. They now build good solid houses and send their children to school following the example set by the other races of Sarawak (Sandin 1970: 123, my translation).

Iban readers are here again given a teleological framework, employed this time by Sarawak's foremost ethnohistorian who combines oral and written materials in order to prove that the state saved the Iban from themselves.

A new author, Joshua Jalie, put out a morality novella on rural development in 1972. Jalie's peasants have been blessed with a school, a road and a rubber scheme. Alas, they soon squander their profits gambling at the cockfights. To compound matters, most of them still believe in ghosts (*antu*). 'Since when have the rats run away from our spells?' says an unusually enlightened villager, 'The government has already given us poison to kill the rats but the others insist on following the old ways'.[22] In the preface, the author had made a clear distinction between rural Iban 'who know better' (*sida ti mereti agi*) and those who 'are still blind, who are not aware of the means and aims of development' (*sida ti agi buta, ti apin nemu julok enggau tuju ator pemansang*). Finally, also in 1972 W. Gieri had an *ensera* published on the adventures of a jungle ogre (*antu gerasi*). Here we have again a contrast of the

Ejau-Sandin kind identified earlier. While one author ridicules his rural brethren's belief in spirits and ogres (*antu*), another tries to salvage for posterity a most prominent member of that supernatural family, one whose name was traditionally used in the longhouse to quieten unruly children. Their contrast reveals the contradictory nature of the wider modernising project embarked upon by the early generation of media producers, caught up in preserving for the future what they, urbanised literate Christians, had discarded in their own lives.

The Bureau ceased to exist in 1977 when it was taken over by the federal body Dewan Bahasa dan Pustaka. That year Andria Ejau brought out another morality novella: *Tanah Belimpah*. It had episodes on the advantages of modern medicine over shamanic (*manang*) rites, on those of wet rice over hill rice cultivation, on the commendable efforts of the school authorities to create a Malaysian people (*bansa Malaysia*), and on the great potential of a newly arrived technology named 'television' to bridge the gap between rural and urban schools. We shall understand shortly just how tragically ironic Ejau's patriotic optimism would prove to be.

The Significance of the Borneo Literature Bureau

To the literary scholar, the Bureau's books are an 'excellent source' for the study of Bornean languages and literatures (Steinmayer 1990: 114), a study still in its infancy. As Sutlive (1988: 73), an authority on the Iban language, has remarked:

> Thirty-one years ago … Derek Freeman told me that Iban folklore 'probably exceeds in sheer volume the literature of the Greeks'. At the time, I thought Freeman excessive. Today, I suspect he may have been conservative in his estimate.

At a time when much of the oral tradition has disappeared, Iban books provide 'unparalleled insights into Iban social philosophy and epistemology'. They are 'instructive about Iban values, of achievement and self-reliance, of discretion, of restraint, of self-effacement and understatement' (Sutlive 1994: xxii). They also teach us about an under-researched area of study in Borneo: gender (see Appell and Sutlive 1991). Traditional Iban society was undoubtedly male-dominated. All the most venerated activities – pioneering, farming, headhunting – were the prerogative of men; they were designed to enable a man 'to become something else' (Sutlive 1977: 158). A close reading of the Bureau's stories on Keling and Kumang reveals how trouble often starts when a woman breaches a taboo, forcing Keling or another male hero to intervene and restore order. We said earlier that in modern Iban ethnohistory the White Rajahs 'saved the Iban from themselves' by restoring order. Similarly, Sutlive (1977: 164) concludes that in Iban narratives women 'must be saved from themselves', from their jealousy and naivety – by men.[23]

At any rate, thanks to the unrelenting work of Benedict Sandin, Henry Gerijih and other Bureau authors, Iban oral literature is today far better recorded than that of any other Bornean ethnic group (Maxwell 1989: 186, Sather 1994), even if some scholars have doubts about the usefulness of the Bureau's books, in which the oral accounts have been 'abridged and edited making them almost unreliable for serious studies' (Said 1994: 58). One neglected research area, however, has been the significance of the Bureau's books not for posterity but rather in terms of *the 1960s–1970s attempts to develop a modern, literate Iban culture.* This was precisely my aim in the preceding pages: to situate the books in relation not to a timeless past or a scholarly future, but in the contemporary flux of a rapidly modernising Sarawak. Three concluding remarks are called for:

First, the vision driving the Bureau's editors and authors was to modernise the native societies through social and economic development while preserving what they considered to be the best of their rich oral traditions through literacy. At the same time Sarawak had to be protected from the related threats of racial conflict, a belligerent Indonesia and communism. We have seen some of the ways in which the Bureau's authors, notably Andria Ejau, served their government. In all cases they were animated by the paradoxical project of having both to change and to preserve Iban culture. *What* Iban culture did they draw upon? Not a wholesale 'pristine Iban culture' (Freeman 1981: 7) untouched by modernity, but rather local oral fragments of an eroded 'tradition' (*adat Iban*) that Ejau and others reconstructed piecemeal as they went along. Yet salvaging a story in print is a radically different action from telling a story in the semi-darkness of an ill lit and illiterate longhouse gathering. It is part of the collective 'objectification' of Iban culture undertaken by these pioneering media agents. Writing about the Bidayuh, formerly known as Land Dayaks, Winzeler (1997: 224–225) applies Wagner's (1981) notion of 'objectification of culture', a process whereby implicit practices are rendered explicit as 'custom' or 'heritage'. To Wagner, such processes are part and parcel of the inventiveness of all human societies. Other anthropologists, however, have considered them to be unique to Western modernity. Winzeler seeks a middle ground. He argues that Southeast Asian societies adopted cultural objectifications of Indic and Islamic origin (notably *ugama* or religion, and *adat* or custom, respectively) well before the arrival of Europeans. Yet the tendency 'to turn native lifeways into matters of objective contemplation and selection of ethnic traditions' was greatly intensified under colonial and post-colonial governments.

Among the Bidayuh, for instance, the male ceremonial house (*baruk*), a strikingly designed building where enemy skulls were kept, has emerged in recent times as the 'ethnic emblem' *par excellence*. Winzeler (1997: 223) maintains that this choice of emblem results from its architectural beauty and from its being uniquely Bidayuh, for this multilingual group has little else other than architecture to distinguish it from neighbouring groups. Unlike the Bidayuh, the Iban have a common language with minor dialectal variations, a language with a long and rich history that is often invoked as the bedrock of the Iban culture. The Iban language was not only a *means* to the 'objective contemplation and selection of ethnic traditions'. The print media turned it into an *object* of study, contemplation and culturalist devotion in its own right. Indeed language has remained the most powerful emblem of Ibanness to this day (see Masing 1997), far more powerful than any item of material culture or architecture could ever be.

Second, as Appendix 3.2 shows, there was a predominance of authors from the Saribas-Kalaka belt, and in particular from Benedict Sandin's Paku river – an area noted both by its early economic and educational achievements and love of Iban tradition (Sather 1994: 71–72). The Saribas was a curiously modernist-traditionalist crossroads whose leading families were well aware of the economic advantages of a Christian name and education and yet had retained a deep respect for their own cultural heritage. Sandin and the other Bureau authors created a cultural feedback loop: they acquired oral items in the rural areas, processed them in Kuching and 'fed them back' to the rural areas in a new, literary form. In the process they were adding symbolic and market value to their stories, for the written word carried immense authority among illiterate and semi-literate longhouse residents. In so doing the Bureau was also standardising 'Iban culture' through the systematic use of orthographic, generic and rhetorical conventions. Moreover, after 1963, its authors 'updated' Iban ethnohistory with the incorporation of Malaysia into their developmentalist accounts.

Finally, King (1989: 243) understands ethnic categories as 'part of wider taxonomies and sets of social, economic, and political relations' and urges researchers in Borneo to relate ethnicity to other 'principles of social organisation'. Similarly, Eriksen (1993: 12) notes that 'ethnicity is essentially an aspect of a relationship, not a property of a group'. In the context of Iban ethnicity we have to stress a sub-ethnic domain: one's river of origin. Class, education and geography were inextricably conjoined in the making of the early Iban media producers. These pioneering authors were not only the products of a region. Their talents were fostered and channelled in a few educational institutions, which favoured the social and cultural development of the Iban. Appendix 3.2 demonstrates how nearly half the authors sampled obtained their secondary schooling at St Augustine, in the Saribas. Additionally, a sizeable number of authors trained as teachers at Wilson's Batu Lintang in Kuching. Virtually all were or had been rural schoolteachers. Four authors (Ejau, Jimbai, Kechendai and Jarraw) were also broadcasters with Radio Sarawak, another nativist institution. The exclusion of women from the new field of cultural production was a hidden, taken-for-granted principle of social organisation at work in this process. Very few women in those days had access to a secondary school education, let alone to further training in the capital. Besides, story-telling had always been yet another male Iban prerogative.[24] In sum, our authors were mission-educated men from economically progressive yet cultur-ally conservative areas, bent on developing their careers in a new field of cultural production while developing their people.

From the above discussion, it may appear as if there was no resistance to the modernising drive of these media producers. A closer reading of their texts, however, suggests a constant struggle to persuade reluctant rural Iban to modernise their ways, particularly in Ejau's educational work. In chapter 4 I argue that their efforts, at least in the Saribas and Skrang rivers, have paid off. This is born out by a history of ideas and media practices in these areas I have written from the perspective of local media consumers. Today there is little resistance to 'development' (*pemansang*) in its myriad institutional forms, from Christianity through agriculture to health and education.

Iban Print Media: from Boom to Bonfire

According to Leigh (1983: 160), the three key political issues in the decade that followed independence (1963–1973) were federal-state relations, the opening-up of native land to commercial exploitation, and the debate over whether English or Malay was to be the medium of instruction in Sarawak. The first Chief Minister of an independent Sarawak 'through Malaysia' was an Iban, Stephen Kalong Ningkan. He was seen in Kuala Lumpur as a con-frontational Dayak, especially because of his strong defence of English as the language of instruction and government and his reluctance to take on Malayan civil servants. In fact, like many other Sarawak leaders at the time, he consid-ered the union with Malaysia as a 'treaty relationship between sovereign nations' (Leigh 1983: 162).

In 1966, the Malaysian Prime Minister, Tunku Abdul Rahman, made use of emergency powers to remove Ningkan from power.[25] Instead he installed a more pliable Iban: Tawi Sli. The Tunku was a firm believer in the need for a strong national language, 'for language is the soul of the Nation' (in Leigh 1974: 88). He was convinced that under Tawi Sli 'there was a much better chance of the people developing a Malaysian consciousness' (Leigh 1974: 105, fn 79). The language issue was finally settled under the following Chief Minis-ter, Abdul Rahman Yakub, a Melanau Muslim, in favour of Malay[26] (Leigh 1983: 163). With Ningkan went the political support needed for the devel-opment of modern Iban-language media. Appendix 3.3 shows how the golden era of new Iban titles at the Borneo Literature Bureau came to a sharp end in 1968. Allowing for the backlog created by the deluge of new manuscripts reported in 1965, it is safe to assume that the drop was linked to the new, unfavourable political climate.

From the mid-1960s the Iban (and other Dayaks) increasingly lost political ground to the Malay-Melanau Muslim elites. The only outlet for Iban
discontent with the slow pace of rural development, the opposition party
SNAP, was financially weak and finally joined the government coalition in
1976. Throughout this period there were token Iban/Dayak representatives in
the state cabinet, but the real power always resided with the Melanaus and
their Malay allies (Jawan 1994: 124).

Radio Sarawak (later RMS and RTM) and Borneo Literature Bureau
producers and authors were struggling to preserve a language and a culture
that in the mid-1960s lost out to the new national language imported from
Malaya. Iban-language radio and literature were complementary media: the
former used oral/aural means, the latter visual means to achieve the same
goals. Their target audience was in the politically weak rural areas, away from
Kuching's corridors of power, increasingly linked to those of Kuala Lumpur.
The cultural system from which the authors of books and scripts drew oral
knowledge and to which they contributed literate knowledge was rapidly
becoming a subsystem within an expanding Malaysian polity.

Three decades ago, Leigh (1974: 94) predicted that 'the Iban school teachers may yet prove to be a politically pivotal group'. That appears to have been
the case, to some extent, in the 1987 elections (Leigh 1991). I now turn to
the abrupt end of the Iban medium with which those teachers were most
actively involved. This event arguably thwarted the development of Iban as a
language of high culture and social critique.[27] Oral tradition in Kuching has
it that soon after Dewan Bahasa dan Pustaka (DBP), Malaysia's language planning and development agency, took over the Borneo Literature Bureau in
1977, they had all the books in Iban and other Bornean languages buried.
Shortly afterwards, the mass media grave was discovered by a reader who
rescued some of the books. To prevent future finds, my informants allege that
the new cultural authorities resorted to a traditional agricultural practice
known as 'open burning'. If this is true, what in the 1960s had been a modest
literary boom had ended up feeding a bonfire.

DBP officials appear to be nervous on the subject of Bornean languages.
For instance, Z.A. Zulficly (1989) has stated that the role of his agency is to
publish works 'in the national language *or other vernaculars*' (my emphasis)
and that it 'does not disregard Sarawak's principal aspiration in relation to its
literature and local socio-culture, most importantly, its oral tradition in the
form of folklores in order that such folklores will not be obliterated thus'
(1989: 159). Soon after, however, he reveals the post-1977 function assigned
by Kuala Lumpur to the local languages: to supply the national language with
new words, a role he deems 'immensely significant for the purpose of fostering national integration'. Indeed, he says, '[h]itherto, 50 words in various
regional languages have been officially assimilated in the *bahasa* Malaysia word
vocabulary'[28] (1989: 159). He concludes that DBP cannot publish books in

regional languages 'because this would inadvertently contradict its policy and an apparently mediocre market' (1989: 161), thus inadvertently contradicting his own opening statement on the agency's role in publishing works in 'other vernaculars'.

The truth is that the protection and development of 'minority languages'[29] appears in Article 152 of the Federal Constitution which guarantees 'the right of all ethnic communities in Malaysia to use, sustain and develop their mother tongue' (Tawai 1997: 18). In practice, however, the sustained aim is to create a Malay-based national language and culture. This long-term goal was announced in 1971 at the National Culture Congress, in the aftermath of the 1969 racial riots in Peninsular Malaysia. The national culture would be 'founded on Malay core values, Malay cultural forms and the Malay language as the official national language' (Piyadasa 2002, quoted in Raslan 2004: 501). In 1988, to mark the 25th anniversary of the creation of Malaysia, the Sarawak government ran a number of workshops on each of the state's major ethnic groups in order to determine 'what to discard in the interest of 'development' and 'unity' and what to preserve and incorporate into a national (Malaysian) culture' (Winzeler 1997: 201). Well-placed Dayaks aid this process of linguistic and cultural assimilation. Another DPB official, Jonathan Singki, the editor of the Iban-language magazine *Nendak* from December 1975 until its reported cremation in November 1977, offers a different explanation for the insignificant output of Iban books under DPB. Singki, who now devotes his energies to Malay-language texts, blames the lack of professionalism of Iban authors and editors.

Other urban Iban I spoke to privately suspect that there are political reasons behind these 'technical delays'. A case in point is Andria Ejau's manuscript *Layang Bintang*, a morality novella on rural development he wrote in 1972 in which he warns rural readers of the perils of sheltering communist-terrorist (CT) guerrillas. This *ensera kelulu* won a 1973 BLB award, yet the Bureau never printed it. It was only in 1984, after a hiatus of 11 years, that Ejau learnt that his manuscript would not be published by DBP because it had originally been sent to the Borneo Literature Bureau,[30] an organisation no longer in existence (Ejau 1985: 5). DBP were willing, however, to return the original manuscript to Ejau. Fortunately for him, that same year (1984) the Sarawak Dayak Iban Association (SADIA) was founded. One of their very first tasks was to publish *Layang Bintang*, which finally came out in 1985 (by which time the anti-communist message was somewhat dated!). The rationale behind such an expenditure was enunciated in unequivocal terms by the Chairman of SADIA, Sidi Munan (1985: 3): 'For if we LOSE OUR LANGUAGE, we will LOSE OUR PEOPLE'[31] – a slogan tellingly reminiscent of Malaysia's first prime minister's aforesaid 'for language is the soul of the Nation'.

Conclusion

Ernest Gellner (1983: 140–143) has famously argued that the origins of nationalism in Europe lie in the rise of industrial society (see chapter 1). The requirements of a modern economy that aimed for sustained economic growth led to a new relationship between state and culture. Such an economy depended on a 'literate sophisticated high culture' in which members could communicate precisely both face-to-face and through abstract means. European states came to monopolise legitimate culture via mass education and a national language. The driving principle of nationalism, for Gellner, was *one state, one culture*. Across Southeast Asia, this principle is being relentlessly pursued today, in spite of the ubiquity of 'unity in diversity' symbols and slogans. For instance, the Thai government 'actively discourages attempts by foreign missionaries to provide its hill-tribe minorities with their own transcription-systems and to develop publications in their own languages: the same government is largely indifferent to what these minorities *speak*' (Anderson 1991: 45). Similarly, Iban radio posed less of a threat to the fledgling Malaysian nation-state than Iban print media, so it was allowed to live on. Provencher (1994: 55) overlooks this crucial distinction between orality and literacy when he states that the official policy is to teach the standard language (*bahasa baku*) to every Malaysian citizen 'and to officially criticize those who continue to speak and write in regional dialects'.

Eriksen (1993: 128) maintains that literate minorities have a better chance of surviving than illiterate ones. He adds: 'Groups which have 'discovered that they have a culture', who have invented and reified their culture, can draw on myths of origin and a wide array of potential boundary-markers that are unavailable to illiterate minorities'. That was precisely what was at stake when DBP took over the Borneo Literature Bureau.

Ethnicity studies within social anthropology since Barth (1969) have tended to focus on how cultural differences among ethnic groups acquire 'social significance'. Anthropologists who adopt this 'constructivist' approach are not overly interested in the actual cultural differences that may separate one ethnic group from another, but rather in how those differences are constructed. Yet there are anthropologists with an historical bent who maintain that cultural features matter a great deal. For instance, Peel (1989) has insisted hat cultural and linguistic distinctiveness was central to the strong consolidation of the Yoruba identity within the Nigerian state. Above I have adopted a 'culturalist' and historical approach centred on language, emphasising the importance of the Iban language during the first phase of modern media production (1954–1976) and the uniqueness of the re-invented cultural heritage preserved through it.

This early phase gave new opportunities to a generation of young Iban men who had acquired literacy skills at the mission schools and were eager to build, to quote Gellner again, a 'literate sophisticated high culture' combining cultural materials from their colonial masters and longhouse elders. Their project was remarkably similar to that embarked upon by late nineteenth-century Norwegian and other nationalists in Europe (cf. O'Connor 1999 on Ireland). The Norwegians, too, travelled to remote valleys in search of ancient words, stories and artefacts from an 'authentic culture' – a culture they believed distinct from that of their Swedish rulers. They too selected items from the peasant culture they studied to create a coherent ethnogenesis in the urban areas that was then re-routed to the countryside (Eriksen 1993: 102). The crucial difference was that the Iban teachers lacked an Iban state, for a literate culture 'cannot normally survive without its own political shell, the state' (Gellner 1983: 140–143). It is one thing to incorporate the state into a minority's ethnohistory and drama, like Sandin and Ejau did.[32] Quite another is to create a truly multilingual nation, as in the anomalous case of Switzerland (Deutsch 1966).

Notes

1. The development officer John K. Wilson (1969: 163) was a pioneer in the use of radio for development purposes. His first development centre was at Budu, near Saratok: 'That the people used the radios to listen in to organised programmes forwarded to Radio Sarawak either by tape or letter was of course encouraged to the limit. Budu news and educational features were a mainstay at Radio Sarawak in the early days. So if it happened that we were in Kuching and wanted a canoe to meet us anywhere, this was just very easy now. A telephone call to Radio Sarawak and that night the news had reached the longhouse'.

2. One well-travelled Iban informant told me that his language was much more of a *lingua franca* in Kayan-Kenyah areas in the late 1950s and 1960s than it is today owing to the popularity of the Iban-language service. Yet even today some Iban programmes are popular with other ethnic groups. An elderly Malay man from the Saribas assured me that he finds the Iban-language news programmes easier to follow than their Bahasa Malaysia equivalents, as he has no schooling. The Saribas Iban dialect is more familiar to him than the relatively new Standard Malay imported from Peninsular Malaysia.

3. The term *penabur* is a metaphorical neologism derived from the Iban farming term *nabur* (to sow or scatter).

4. *Sarawak Education Department (SED) Annual Reports* 1958–1960: 34.

5. *SED Annual Reports* 1958–1960: 35.

6. *SED Annual Reports* 1958–1960: 34.

7. I obtained this information from a reliable source.

8. There is a sizeable literature on the confrontation (*konfrontasi*). For Mackie (1974: 33) Soekarno was no great believer in 'Malay brotherhood'. He only used this notion for propaganda purposes. After having acquired by force West New Guinea from the Dutch and been subjected to official indoctrination for years, the Indonesian people, says Mackie (1974: 326–333), were predisposed towards Soekarno's slogans. His millennialism – a sophisticated version of a cargo cult – struck a chord with Indonesians and scared other governments in the region. According to Poulgrain (1998) it was not Soekarno who started *konfrontasi* but rather British and American intelligence agencies seeking to further the aims of their respective states. Jones (2002) who has studied recently declassified British documents, provides us with yet

another picture; one showing the Commonwealth powers and the U.S. confronting a hostile nationalist and anti-imperialist environment. According to this author, Britain was largely led by regional politicians throughout the process of the formation of Malaysia.

9. Interviewed on 1 July 1997 in Kuching.

10. The Borneo Literature Bureau (see below) published three folklore books by Lawrence Sanoun Ijau in the 1960s. Like many other folklorists, Ijau was from the Paku area and trained at Batu Lintang Teachers Training College.

11. One knowledgeable reader has suggested that it was not only Kuala Lumpur who had a hand in Wilson's expulsion but also Iban leaders such as the Tun Jugah. This reader believes the rivalry between influential Iban from the Rejang and other rivers may have played a part. I have not been able to pursue this matter. See also Wilson (1969).

12. Although based in Kuching, one interesting geopolitical anomaly of the now defunct Bureau is that it catered for the whole of Malaysian Borneo (Clifford Sather, personal communication). A much shorter-lived attempt at establishing an East Malaysian media organisation was television, as described in the next chapter.

13. Total sales in all languages rocketed from $38,739 in 1960 through $171,157 in 1961 to $348,528 in 1962. By contrast, Chinese books were selling poorly. The reason adduced was that neither Chinese adults nor children had much interest in books with Bornean themes (*BLB Annual Report* 1962).

14. Traditionally Iban have relied on dreams (*mimpi*) as much as on omens (*burong*) for guidance (Richards 1981: 220, cf. Catholic prayer books in chapter 5).

15. An *ensera* is an 'epic or saga sung in poetic language with explanations and conversations in prose' (Richards 1981: 87).

16. According to Richards (1981: 288), Pulang Gana '[r]epresents Indian Ganesh (Ganesa, Ganapati, lord of the troops accompanying (*sempulang*) or attendant on Siva) whose 'vehicle' is the rat (*cit*) from whom the Iban obtained PADI [rice]'.

17. Otto Steinmayer (personal communication, January 1999).

18. *Collins English Dictionary* (1994).

19. Jenang was born in Sungai Assam, Krian, Saratok. He learnt the art of storytelling from his father. A precocious author, Jenang wrote this *ensera* at the age of 16 'all by myself'; it did not follow from 'ancient stories' (*ensera tu ukai nampong batang ensera tuai tang iya empegal digaga aku kadiri*). Unfortunately this was to be, to the best of my knowledge, his first and last published work.

20. According to Paku custom, during the mourning period people are not allowed to 'make music, shout and put on flowery and red clothes' or cut their hair (Sandin 1980: 71). During fieldwork I found that rural Iban, at least in the Saribas, have bent their mourning *adat* to accommodate radio and television.

21. Larsen (1998) reports a very similar synthesis among Peninsular Malay peasants.

22. In the original: '*Dini chit tau rari ka puchau kitai? Perintah udah meri rachun dikena munoh chit tang sida agi majak ka penemu sida nya*' (Jalie 1972).

23. There is an important exception, however: the comic character Father-of-Aloi (Paloi), a mischievous old man eternally rescued from his self-inflicted misery by his wife and son. But then, comic fables 'satirize everyday life' while the heroic sagas of Keling 'celebrate Iban ideal and dwell in particular on wars, travel and romance' (Sather 1984: ix). Hence one could see the hen-pecked Paloi as the moral antithesis of Keling – a model of aborted manhood not to be tried in one's longhouse rooms. See Sather (2001) for a collection of comic tales in one of which Paloi challenges Keling and his followers to a cockfight. The agreement is that the loser becomes the slave of the winner. The heroes lose and their wives have to save the situation by trouncing Paloi and winning their husbands back. For once, it is not Paloi who has to be rescued (Clifford Sather, personal communication).

24. With the exception of the *sabak* (dirge) genre. Recall that Rajit (1969), the Anglican priest mentioned earlier, acquired his *sabak* knowledge from his mother.
25. A move applauded at the time by Malaysia's former Prime Minister, Mahathir, then a back-bencher. According to one biographer, Mahathir already held 'a dim view of democracy' in the early years of independence (Khoo 1995: 275).
26. Malay was accepted as the official language in Sarawak alongside English until 1985, when English was finally dropped (Zulficly 1989: 159).
27. It remains to be investigated whether the Internet and other new media are aiding the creation of such a critical space.
28. Including the Iban terms *berandau* (to converse, to chat) and *merarau* (to have lunch).
29. Ironically, in numerical terms Malay is more of a 'minority language' in Sarawak than Iban. The Malay population stood at 330,000 in 1988 (21% of the total), compared to 471,000 Iban (30%), the largest ethnic population in the state. Together, the Dayaks made up approximately 50% of the state population (Jawan 1994: 24).
30. John Lent (1994: 94), a media researcher, claims he was the victim of a different kind of restriction. His book manuscript on mass communications was banned from publication owing to 'a few timidly-critical points about Malaysian mass media'. The official line was that the manuscript had not been written in Bahasa Malaysia.
31. '*Laban enti kitai LENYAU JAKO, reti LENYAU BANGSA*'.
32. As Clifford Sather (personal communication, 23 May 2001) has rightly pointed out, the broad socio-economic and geopolitical factors that I stress in this chapter should not make us lose sight of 'the agency, the dogged determination, passion, at times even literary brilliance, of the Iban actors in this story'. Often we are dealing with 'creative and imaginative works, some of them quite moving, funny, etc'. Benedict Sandin, adds Sather, had to struggle throughout his life with both Sarawakians and foreigners hostile to his 'old fashioned' line of work (witness, for in stance, Freeman's 1981 dismissal of Sandin as unscholarly in his adherence to 'Iban tenets', chapter 2). Since the demise of the BLB, Sandin's memory 'is all but gone' in Sarawak, yet 'he loved what he did, thought it mattered enormously, and most of all he simply loved the language'.

APPENDIX 3.1

A breakdown of 7 issues[1] of *Nendak* magazine (1968–1975) by general (folk-lore vs. educational)[2] and specific subject-matter.

Penemu lama	Old knowledge
7 ensera	fictive narratives, usu. epic sagas
6 cherita lama/tuai	'factual' ethnohistorical accounts[3]
2 cherita mimpi	dream narratives
2 ensera anembiak	children's stories
2 entelah	riddles
2 adat Iban	Iban custom[4]
1 cherita kelulu	morality tale
1 pantun	sung poem
1 leka main	poem (official propaganda)
1 jako kelaung enggau jako sema	proverbs and parables
1 ngalu petara leboh Gawai Dayak	Dayak Day ceremony to welcome gods[5]
1 lumba enggau main	traditional Iban games

27 sub-total items

Penemu baru	New knowledge[6]
2 betanam betupi	agriculture and animal husbandry[7]
2 ungkop sida ka indu	home economics[8]
2 ajar pengerai	health advice[9]
2 jako melintang pukang	Iban crossword puzzle
2 belajar Bahasa Kebangsaan	national language lessons
1 pengawa kunsila	the office of councillor
1 tuai rumah enggau anembiak iya	the office of headman
1 rumah panjai	the longhouse [in a modern society]
1 ajar lumor	algebra
1 main sains dunya & gaya pengidup	geography quiz
1 sekula di menoa Malaysia	Malaysia's school system
1 Bujang Berani Anembiak Malaysia	Malaysian heroes
1 Taun Baru China	Chinese New Year
1 gambar tuai perintah	photographic gallery Sarawak leaders
1 gambar Taun Baru China	photographic gallery Chinese New Year

20 sub-total items
47 total items

Notes

1. Some parts were missing from two of the photocopies I was able to inspect, and I could not date another two of them.
2. The division of the items into two broad categories is my own. No such division is apparent in *Nendak*. Items from both categories are jumbled together in all issues examined. Furthermore, some of the 'Iban Folklore' items are also meant to 'modernise' the readers' supposedly traditional worldview.
3. See Sather (1994) for a learned discussion of Iban ethnohistory.
4. One contribution by Benedict Sandin on longhouse *basa* (etiquette, good manners), the other an interview with Tunggay anak Mulla, also from the Saribas, on *ngetas ulit* (rite to end a period of mourning) and *serara bunga* (rite to 'separate' the dead from the living) (Sutlive and Sutlive 1994).
5. A newly invented rite to receive and introduce to the longhouse the *Petara*, or heavenly guests (Richards 1981: 7), during the *Gawai Dayak* festival, adapted from Iban custom. *Gawai Dayak* was invented in 1965, three years before the publication of this issue of *Nendak* (see discussion of Ejau's novella *Batu Besundang* above).
6. I am following the Bureau's terminology here. In some items, e.g., '*Bujang Berani…*', read propaganda.
7. Prepared by the Agriculture Department.
8. Idem.
9. Prepared by the Health Department.

APPENDIX 3.2

Biographical profiles of 17 Borneo Literature Bureau Iban authors.

Name and year of first publication	River of origin	Secondary education	Training	Other experience
1962 Sandin	Paku, Saribas	St Augustine	Sarawak Museum	*tukang tusut*
1962 Gerijih	Paku, Saribas	St Augustine	St Augustine	*lemambang*
1962 Majang	Kalaka	St Augustine	Batu Lintang	
1963 Ejau	Kalaka	St Augustine	councillor	Radio Sarawak
1965 Duncan	Saribas	St Augustine	Batu Lintang	
1966 Pitok	Simanggang	Simanggang	Batu Lintang	
1966 Imang	Simanggang	Simanggang	Batu Lintang	craftsman
1966 Guang	Paku, Saribas	St Augustine	Agric Dept	
1966 Ijau	Paku, Saribas	Paku,Saribas	Batu Lintang	
1967 Inin	Kalaka	Saratok	Lubok Antu	
1967 Nyangoh	Kanowit	Julau	?	
1967 Gani	Balingian	Kapit	methodist pastor	
1968 Pelima	Rimbas	Debak	trader, Paku	
1968 Ensiring	Saratok	Saratok	Rajang TTC	
1968 Jarraw	Kanowit	Kanowit	Radio Sarawak	BBC
1969 Rajit	Saribas	St Augustine	Anglican priest	
1970 Kechendai	Paku, Saribas	Debak	St Augustine	Radio Sarawak

Note: I have included authors on whom information is available and arranged them by year of first publication, indicating river of origin, secondary school education, training and other relevant information where applicable. Sources: Borneo Literature Bureau publications and Steinmayer (1990). Key: St Augustine = St Augustine School, in Betong (Saribas); *tukang tusut* = genealogist; *lemambang* = bard; Batu Lintang = Batu Lintang Teacher Training College (Kuching); Rajang TTC = Rajang (Rejang) Teacher Training College.

APPENDIX 3.3

New Iban titles printed by the Borneo Literature Bureau from 1960 to 1976.

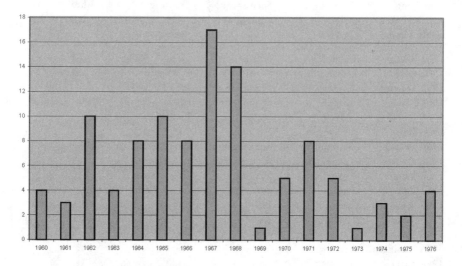

Source: Borneo Literature Bureau Annual Reports.

Other Literature Consulted

Newspapers and Magazines

Berita Harian, Peninsular Malaysia
Berita Rayat, Sarawak
The Borneo Post, Sarawak
The Daily Telegraph, U.K.
The Economist, U.K.
El País, Spain
Far Eastern Economic Review, Hong Kong/U.S.
Granta, U.K.
The Guardian, U.K.
The Independent, U.K.
London Review of Books, U.K.
Nendak, Sarawak
New Straits Times, Peninsular Malaysia
Newsweek, U.S.
Pedoman Rakyat, Sarawak
Pemberita, Sarawak
People's Mirror, Sarawak
Sarawak Gazette
Sarawak Tribune
Sunday Tribune, Sarawak
Time Magazine, U.S.
Utusan Sarawak

Official Publications

Bahagian Teknologi Pendidikan BTP. Annual Reports, Sarawak Government.

Borneo Literature Bureau BLB. Annual Reports, 1960–1976, Sarawak Government.

Dewan Bahasa dan Pustaka DBP. Annual Report, Federal Government.

Education Department Annual Reports, 1955–1957, Sarawak Government.

Information Malaysia Yearbooks, 1995–1998, Ministry of Information, Federal Government.

Radio Televisyen Malaysia RTM. Sarawak Yearbooks, Ministry of Information, Federal Government.

4

PROPAGATING THE STATE, PHASE II

This chapter covers a second stage of Iban and Malaysian media production, from 1977 to 1998. The latter year was a watershed, the year in which Anwar Ibrahim, at the time Malaysia's deputy prime minister, was imprisoned. Anwar's dubious trial and incarceration led to an explosion of alternative and oppositional media, especially news portals and websites (Anuar 2004). It is no exaggeration to say that Malaysia, and its media, underwent epochal changes in 1998 and 1999. Another reason for ending this chapter in 1998 is that this was the year in which I completed the main stage of fieldwork (in April 1998). I revisited Sarawak briefly in 2001 for a study of the Dayak Festival in Kuching (chapter 9). It would be impractical, therefore, to attempt to integrate post-1998 developments into the present account, although I do make passing reference to them, e.g., the 2003 ban on the Iban Bible.[1]

This second phase would witness a swift Malaysianisation of the media in Sarawak, with national television replacing Sarawak radio as the staple of evening entertainment in both urban and rural areas. At the same time, the thriving town of Sibu replaced the Saribas basin as the twin heartland, with Kuching, of an expanding Iban culture industry. Meanwhile, Kuching remained the capital of official, elite-driven Iban culture. The chapter is, for ease of presentation, arranged by medium: radio, print media, popular music media, television and interpersonal media. This somewhat artificial ordering should not distract us from the underlying commonalities across all media, notably the dominance of an extremely powerful state to which even private capital is subservient (Gomez 2004a). During this period, the nation-building ideals of the Malaysian state were relentlessly propagated across Sarawak, shaping the worldviews of both rural and urban Iban, as we shall see in chapter 5.

Radio

With the demise of the Borneo Literature Bureau (BLB) and the rapid spread of Malay-language rural schools and television, the Iban Section of RTM was the sole Iban-language medium of any import remaining in the 1980s. In 1980, after the communist threat had finally been quelled, the Psychological Warfare Unit at RTM Sarawak was dissolved. The main focus at the Iban Section was now the phasing out of shifting cultivation (see chapter 2) to give way to 'modern' agricultural practices. Interviews with successful cash crop farmers were a preferred method of persuasion. Other important areas were health, education, poverty and job vacancies. The purported aim was to change the rural population's conservative 'mind-set'. Meanwhile the Iban component of school broadcasting was undergoing fundamental changes. In the place of Michael Buma's spelling, dictation and traditional tales (*ensera*), more elaborate grammar-based Iban language lessons were now being broadcast to primary and lower secondary pupils.[2] This improvement must be set, however, against a far more transcendent 1980 shift: the establishment of Malay as the sole medium of instruction across the state school system in the place of English.

A further expansion of RTM airtime occurred in the early 1980s with the launching of Sunday programmes in Iban and two more hours in the evening from Monday to Saturday. The next increase was to arrive a decade later, with two more hours in the morning. Henceforth the total Iban-language airtime would be set at 66 hours a week, with 9 hours a day from Monday to Saturday and 12 hours on Sundays. In 1993 new studios were built and modern equipment acquired. Two years later some important changes in programming took place. First, the soap operas (*cherita kelulu*) were discontinued. According to the producer Laja Sanggin, this was due both to the low quality of the scripts submitted and to the Iban Section's lack of manpower. Second, 'loose slots' were introduced from 6 to 8.30 p.m. whose aim was both to inform and entertain the audience with varied capsules lasting 2 to 3 minutes instead of the accustomed 15 to 30 minutes. Some of these capsules were aimed at a young audience. Messages on the evils of truancy, loafing, drugs, etc., were 'injected' (see below) to this group in between the pop songs. Another novelty was to open up the lines to telephone callers with messages for their migrant kin on grave matters such as illness, death or financial hardship (*jaku pesan berat*). Callers could now also take part in a new programme called *Nama Runding?* (What do *you* think?) in which they could express their views on a given topical issue within the strict limits imposed by the Malaysian state, that is avoiding any direct reference to Malay privileges, land issues or Islam. These programming changes were both a response to perceived changes in the wider society (e.g., stiffer competition from private radio and TV, the rural-urban drift, a rise in educational standards, etc.) and a consequence of a lack of financial and human resources to produce new programmes. As a result the more 'traditional' programmes such as *Main Asal* (Folk Music) were relegated to what in rural Sarawak is a very late slot: from 10.15 p.m. to 11 p.m.[3]

In 1997 Sarawak's first commercial radio station, CATS[4] Radio, was launched. Its mission was to capture a wide audience across the state through 'light entertainment', especially music. It had an Iban Section run by an RTM veteran and former intelligence officer, Roland Duncan Klabu, transmitting two hours a day: from 1 to 2 p.m. Monday to Friday, from 3 to 4 p.m. on Sunday and from midnight to 1 a.m. seven days a week. To maximise his one-hour afternoon slot, Klabu opted for the 'hot-clock system', consisting of a five-minute news bulletin and a mixture of capsules, Iban pop songs, local reports, farming tips and suchlike. Klabu makes no bones about the true purpose of these broadcasts. The programme, he explains, was 'literally bought by a number of record companies seeking to promote Iban pop songs throughout Sarawak' (Klabu 1998: 2). The most prominent figure to emerge was undoubtedly Peter John anak Apai,[5] an Iban DJ who became hugely popular overnight with his personal brand of daft humour and ability to communicate on air with Iban callers from all walks of life. Peter John was an inveterate linker of two overlapping worlds: rural and urban Sarawak. CATS offered an amusing, hybrid alternative to a more sober RTM service. In addition, its crystal clear FM sound made listening a more pleasurable experience than RTM's crackling short-wave transmission.

In spite of Peter John's success, Iban-language broadcasting was in the late 1990s mired in a deep crisis. Educated Iban felt that the crisis of the Iban Section both reflected and accelerated the erosion and eventual demise of the Iban language and culture. With this bleak prognosis in mind and a sense of urgency, in April 1998 the Council for Customary Law (*Majlis Adat Istiadat*) in Kuching ran a one-day workshop on Iban-language broadcasting. The workshop, which I proposed and co-organised, was held almost entirely in the Iban language, a rare event in Kuching.[6] The problems identified included unclear objectives, inadequate audience research, insufficient manpower, lack of funds, no code of ethics, poor infrastructure and facilities, no print media support, no full-time women employees, a low command of Iban among urban broadcasters, etc. Further concerns about the Iban Section were voiced during the workshop or in private conversation elsewhere, including political pressures (both from Sarawakian and Peninsular quarters[7]); poor management; too many phone-in programmes replacing the forums, dramas, magazines and features of previous decades; growing competition from CATS as well as commercial radio stations and several television channels from the Peninsula; no programmes for women, children, or teenagers; and, as a result of all the above: a highly demoralised staff.

Although pushed to the margins of the workshop, the other two branches of Iban-language radio broadcasting were also discussed: School Broadcasting and CATS Radio. School Broadcasting (BTP) is also facing an uphill struggle.

The shared excitement of the early years about the educational possibilities of radio has gradually turned into bitter disappointment. A major stumbling block is that few schools in the urban areas teach Iban. In Kuching there remains but one school, St Mary's, still teaching this language. By the early 1990s, out of the 600 to 650 primary schools in Sarawak with a proportion of over 50 per cent Iban pupils, only 40 per cent listened to the Iban programmes.[8] A BTP survey blamed this low figure on the time pressures of an exam-orientated, textbook-based school syllabus, the poor reception in numerous 'shadow areas', a shortage of Iban teachers, and a large number of radio sets out of order (Untie 1998: 4).

The history of Iban-language broadcasting is therefore long and eventful. For decades it has not only served the government of the day with unflagging loyalty but has also contributed, in some measure, to the standardisation and preservation of the Iban language and culture across Sarawak. The Iban Section of Radio Sarawak (now RTM) has served the state well: it fought Indonesia in the 1960s, the communists in the 1970s and what the state defined as the (backward) 'rural mind-set' from the 1980s onwards. At present, however, the state has other priorities. Among the most pressing of these, to build a strong, unified national culture based on the Malay language and traditions (Raslan 2004). The host of problems affecting all three Iban-language radio organisations (RTM, CATS and BTP) can all be linked to a chronic weakness: the lack of adequate political representation of the Iban and other non-Muslim indigenous groups (Jawan 1994: 226–235).

There is, however, an unacknowledged problem facing producers: how to step out of their ideological certainties and recultivate the field of Iban media production. Melanesia provides us with a useful comparison. On the basis of her work in Papua New Guinea, Sullivan (1993: 551) has argued that the ideas and practices of media professionalism spread in parallel to the transfer of technology from the West to other regions. Quoting Keesing (1989: 23) she adds that, across the Pacific islands, the ideologues who idealise the past are usually 'hell-bent on technology, progress, materialism and "development"'. This observation applies equally well to Sarawak. The producers' faith in the potential of radio to transform their audiences given the right political, financial and professional resources has remained undiminished despite years of institutional stagnation. A case in point is the aforesaid belief that positive messages can be directly 'injected' into young listeners – what media scholars call the 'hypodermic needle model of communication' (chapter 1). This confidence can be explained by the fact that most radio staff were trained in the 1960s and 1970s – a period of rapid economic growth, multi-ethnic nationalism, anti-communism and deep faith in the infinite possibilities of modern technology. Their urban careers developed amidst the growing disparities in wealth and status between educated urban Iban and their illiterate or semi-literate rural brethren. Yet, in typically modernist fashion, this chasm was blamed on the latter's traditional 'mind-set'. Unlike indigenous media producers in Australia and other white-settler countries (see Ginsburg 1993, Turner 1992), Iban producers are too embedded in the state's material and ideological apparatus to provide alternative visions. As trained government servants, they reproduce the views of what Debray (1996: 176) calls the 'mediocracy', i.e., the 'elite holding the means of production of mass opinion'. A point made in the previous chapter has to be stressed once again: in countries such as Malaysia with tight media control and top-down communication, Appadurai's (1990) notion of 'multidirectional flows' of cultural influences holds little analytical promise. While it may apply to North America's intellectual diasporas, in the case of Iban radio the flow is largely unidirectional, from a few urban corridors of media power to countless longhouse galleries and rooms.

Print Media

Since the closure of the BLB a number of Iban books have been printed, most of them by a Kuching house named Klasik, including two traditional *ensera* (Donald 1989, Tawai 1989) and four *cherita kelulu* or morality novellas (Ensiring 1991, 1992, Garai 1993, Bangit 1995). We met Janang Ensiring (1968) in the previous chapter as a 19-year-old poet infatuated with Malaysia. His 1992 novella *Dr Ida* deserves our attention for its innovative use of urban settings and problems – a clean departure from the BLB's bucolic themes.

The second non-governmental print outlet for the Iban language today is provided by the first institutions ever to create texts in Borneo vernaculars: the Christian churches. The most successful religious texts appear to be those which have adopted a manner of 'BLB strategy', that is prayer books that seek to selectively adapt the Iban *adat* (in this case 'pagan' beliefs) to the modernising Christian project (in chapter 6, I explore the adoption of prayer books in the Skrang area). This dual strategy echoes those adopted in other Asia-Pacific societies. In Papua New Guinea, a European lay missionary directed in 1990 a television drama to teach villagers in a remote area new farming techniques. To Sullivan (1993: 537), this was part of a long missionary tradition of 'co-opting indigenous values (of community, mutual obligation, kinship and sharing) as the teachings of Christ and in so doing distinguishing church from private interests while easing a transition from barbarism to a market economy'. In Sarawak, the Catholic Church is ahead of rival denominations in its nativist-cum-modernist print media but has yet to use audiovisual media extensively, for reasons considered below. As Giddens (1984) has reminded us, social actions often have unintended effects. With the demise of the BLB, the Iban-language Christian texts have acquired greater significance as cultural repositories among the more literate Iban. This was undoubtedly not the intention of the authorities who allegedly ordered the destruction of the indigenous print media. For instance, in 2003 there was an outcry across Sarawak when the federal authorities banned the Iban Bible on the grounds that it used the Islamic name for God, *Allah (Taala)*. The authorities claimed that this may 'confuse' the populace.[9] Faced with mounting protests, the then deputy prime minister, Abdullah Badawi, ordered the immediate lifting of the ban.

Figure 4.1. The front cover of a *Berita Rayat* issue, probably dating from the late 1970s.

Two state-sponsored outlets for Iban authorship survived into the 1990s. One was *Berita Rayat*,[10] a monthly magazine founded in 1974 by the Rajang Security Command (RASCOM) in Sibu. This magazine was part of the government's efforts to defeat the Chinese-led communist insurgency in Sarawak's third division through military action and propaganda. The cover showed an Iban warrior in full ceremonial dress performing a sword dance (*pencha*). The contents were in the dual modernity-cum-tradition *Nendak* mould yet with an added emphasis on 'security'. As was the case in *Nendak*, a wide spectrum of Iban genres was represented. There were morality tales (*cherita kelulu*), sagas (*ensera*), riddles (*entelah*), ethnohistorical accounts (*jerita tuai*), hagiographies of Iban leaders and even a cartoon strip featuring Roky, a young law-enforcing hero. Unfortunately for Roky's author, the negotiated end of the armed struggle would also mean the eventual phasing-out of *Berita Rayat*. Production ceased in the early 1990s.

The one extant Iban print medium in 1997 was *Pembrita*, a state govern-ment mouthpiece published monthly by the Information Department.[11] *Pembrita* is yet another Iban medium with an original Paku-Saribas connec-tion, for it was the result of the pioneering Adult Literacy Scheme launched in 1950 in that river (Jawan 1994: 183). Aimed at rural Iban, it is a profusely illustrated newsletter containing two kinds of items: good developmental news (on exemplary longhouses, lucrative cash crops, animal husbandry, etc.) and exhortations to the rural populace to modernise their ways, with a typical headline reading (in Iban): 'FARMERS MUST CHANGE THEIR WORK HABITS'[12]. Unlike *Nendak* and *Berita Rayat*, though, *Pembrita* contains no traditional genres, despite repeated appeals to the readers for such materials, in an apparent attempt to broaden the readership base of what the editors call 'our Iban newspaper' (*Surat Kabar kitai Iban*).[13]

There is no such thing, however, as an Iban newspaper in the strict sense of the term. In 1996, eleven newspapers in other languages were published in Sarawak: seven in Chinese, three in English and one in Malay (see Table 4.1). A key constraint affecting all papers in Malaysia, and even more so in thinly populated states such as Sarawak, is the high cost of paper. In 1993 a ton of imported paper cost U.S. $1,000 in Malaysia but only U.S. $780 in the United States. A further problem for Malay-language papers both in East and West Malaysia is that advertisers regard most Malay readers as belonging to the low-income group, so advertising revenue is much lower than that for the English and Chinese dailies (Amir and Awang Jaya 1996: 13). Any fledgling Iban newspaper would have to overcome even more imposing barriers. One viable solution suggested to me by an urban Iban might be for one of the state's newspapers to carry a weekly Iban supplement, a practice already well established in Sabah with the Kadazan language.

The government controls virtually all newspapers in Sarawak, as it does in the Peninsula. This is achieved through a combination of 'restrictive laws' and

Table 4.1. Circulation of major Sarawak newspapers.

Newspaper	Circulation
Chinese	
1. *Chinese Daily News*	5,000
2. *See Hua Daily News*	n.a.
3. *Sin Hua Evening News*	n.a.
and 4 others	
English	
1. *Sarawak Tribune*	30,000
2. *People's Mirror**	10,000
3. *The Borneo Post**	n.a.
Malay	
1. *Utusan Sarawak*	20,000

Source: Amir and Awang Jaya (1996: 54).
Key: n.a. = not available; (*) = includes a Malay-language supplement.

personal connections (Anuar 2004: 489). The Chinese newspaper *See Hua Daily*, for example, is owned by Robert Lau, the mayor of Sibu and a Malaysian MP whose older brother is the timber tycoon, Lau Hui Kang (Gomez 2004b: 482). With the exception of one or two Chinese papers, writing favourably about any aspect of the much-diminished opposition is unheard of. On one noted occasion, a *Sarawak Tribune* editor was allegedly dismissed for publishing 'the wrong picture' of a powerful politician. According to press insiders, it is always safe to write pro-development articles. Another safe area is 'culture', that is the colourful side of Dayak cultures: music, dance, garments, etc. The Sarawak daily press represents Dayaks in two radically different ways: (a) as camera-friendly 'ethnics' with picturesque cultures in need of protection (and more tourism) or (b) as ignorant, backward peasants in need of enlightenment (and more development).[14] In both portrayals, which never appear together, scant allowance is made for the various ways in which actual Dayak agents may be making and remaking their social worlds.

The key to development, as seen by the Sarawak mediocracy, is for the rural Dayaks to change their collective 'mind-set' (a favoured term) so that development can proceed swiftly. There are similarities here with the ideology of Ejau and other Iban media producers from the earlier period (chapter 3). The key difference is that Ejau's generation drew largely from first-hand experience in upriver areas and an intimate knowledge of the Iban language and culture. Today's journalists, by contrast, write from urban areas for an urban readership.

Whilst Ejau and his contemporaries tried to blend culture and development in their texts (in pursuit of what today is known as 'sustainable development'), journalists constantly drive a harsh wedge between the two domains. A clear instance of the powerful interests behind this discursive wedge arose in 1987–1991, when a total of 30 Penan and other Dayak communities, including Iban longhouses, carried out anti-logging blockades in the Baram and Limbang districts. They were protesting against the destruction of the environment upon which their livelihood depended. The following extract sums up the role of the Sarawak press:

> The stories by the *Borneo Post* were orchestrated based on government press releases …; self-censorship by reporters was exercised to adjust to the media's organizational and official requirements. The only on-the-scene report the *Borneo Post* filed was on 21 July 1987, when the media escorted the State Minister for Tourism and Environment (who owns one of the largest timber concessions in Sarawak) to one of his timber camps in Limbang (Ngidang 1993: 94).

In its 11 July 1987 editorial, the *Borneo Post* lamented the fact that development had been hindered 'by two groups of people, namely the Penans and their allies and those who instigate people in rural areas to reject government efforts' (Ngidang 1993: 94). Sarawak newspapers are, in sum, at the service of the state government and their wealthy allies. Their modus operandi reveals the extent to which Sarawak is a rich 'resource frontier' (King 1988) in the hands of a small elite. The chances of an Iban newspaper ever being produced, therefore, are severely lowered by both the economies of scale required for it to be profitable, and by the same political imperatives that have led to the mass logging of Dayak forests and to the burning of Dayak books.

Popular Music

Sibu is the second largest town in Sarawak. From 1974, the timber industry grew rapidly in the state, with Sibu as its hub (Leigh 1983: 164). This attracted large numbers of Iban to an urban milieu where they were already well represented.[15] Many of the poorly educated Iban entered into patron-client relations with Chinese merchants (*towkay*) (Sutlive 1972: 119). The same pattern was to prevail in the budding music industry of the late 1970s.

Table 4.2. Subject matter of Iban pop songs produced in the 1990s, in percentages.

40%	broken heart	*ambis asa, tusah ati*
40%	longing heart	*lelengau, sunyi*
14%	happy heart	*ati senang*
2%	ode to Sarawak	*Menua Sarawak*
2%	*the meaning of life*[16]	*Dunya Sementara*

Sample: 49 songs from five well-known cassette tapes.[17]

By far the most successful Sibu record company during the 1977–1998 period has been Tiew Brothers Company, better known as TBC. Mathew Tiew Sii Hock, a former salesman, and two of his brothers founded TBC in 1977. Initially they sought to market Malay albums but found the competition from Peninsular record companies to be too stiff, so they chose instead to market Iban pop. Following the initial success of Iban cassette tapes, they began to release songs in Melanau, Kayan, Kenyah, Malay and recently Chinese. Iban has nevertheless remained TBC's mainstay. According to company sources, the uniqueness of Iban pop lies in its *rojak* ('mixed salad') melodies: a melange of Indonesian *dangdut*, global pop rock, heavy metal, Latin *baladas* and other styles, all performed to a peculiar Sibu-Chinese beat.[18] On another level, however, Iban pop is far from unique. If in the 1950s it followed Indonesian and Indian patterns, and in the 1960s–1970s Western ones, since the 1980s it has increasingly aligned itself with musical trends arriving from West Malaysia and absorbed concepts and words from the national language. Middle-aged Iban critics say today's lyrics are bland, sugary, lacking the subtlety and vigour of both 1960s Iban pop and the best contemporary Malay and Indonesian music. They are certainly politically safe: unlike some Indonesian popular culture,[19] Iban pop is about entertainment, not social critique. Most songs in my sample (94 per cent) deal with the vagaries of the human heart, as Table 4.2. clearly demonstrates. William Awing sings:[20]

Sepuloh taun dah lalu	It's been ten years
Tua nadai betemu	Since we last met
Tekenyit aku nerima surat nuan dara	Couldn't believe your letter, girl
Nuan mai aku nampong	When you told me that you wanted
Pengerindu tua	To start once again
Nama kebuah nuan	How can you say
Agi ka beguna aku	That you still need me?
Aku tu aku suba	I'm still the one I used to be
Ukai orang baru	I'm not a new person

Very occasionally singers will follow the lead of their Radio Sarawak forebears and step out of their love grooves to reproduce the views of the Establishment. In the following verse, the immensely popular Andrewson Ngalai praises Sarawak while promoting a commercial alternative to shifting cultivation:

Rakyat diau sama senang ati	The people all live merrily together
Mu[n]suh nadai agi dikenangi	Enemies are no longer remembered[21]
Tanah besai alai endur betupi	Plenty of land to rear livestock
Lantang senang dudi ari	So that one day we'll be happy

On other occasions, while still on the painful subject of love, they touch on current social problems, notably the inequalities wrought by education and migration (*bejalai*). Johnny Aman sings about the barriers of class and wealth now dividing the once egalitarian Iban society:

Malu amai asai ku dara	I feel really ashamed, girl
Ka jadi enggau nuan	I who wanted to marry you
Enda diterima	But was rejected
Laban aku orang merinsa	For being poor
Nadai pemandai bekuli ngapa	For being an ignorant coolie

And on the temptations of migration (*bejalai*):

Baka aku ti bejalai	I have to go away
Ngiga belanja sulu	To look for money, my darling
nuan ti diau rumah panjai	you're staying in the longhouse
Bejaga diri selalu	So look after yourself
Baka jako orang bukai	Don't listen to those
nusi berita enda tentu	who tell stories about me
Anang nuan arap ambai	Don't listen to them, my love
Nya mina berita pelesu	They're just lies
Nadai aku kala asai	Not once have I felt
Ngayah ka nuan sulu	Like betraying you, my darling

TBC has sponsored numerous song contests and 'discovered' rising starlets, many of them young Iban from the Rejang basin. They publish an Iban-language magazine named *Merindang* (Entertainment), purchase ample airtime on CATS Radio and have launched a website to promote both their starlets and established singers. In the late 1990s the company boasted two recording studios – one fitted with analogue equipment, the other with more advanced digital technology.[22] Their 1997 production was two albums a month. Besides cassette tapes, they produced karaoke videotapes and compact discs. Karaoke videos were significant as they provided the only regular audio-visual outlet for Iban artistes who seldom, if ever, appeared on television. Patterned on West Malaysian video clips, they were extremely popular at social gatherings in the longhouse and at public functions involving Iban leaders. The cassette and video cover illustrations project a dynamic urban persona devoid of any ethnic markers: the singers wear Western-style clothing and accessories (headband, sunglasses, mobile phone) reminiscent of those worn by Sarawak's visiting Filipino artistes and other Southeast Asian entertainers.

Irama, another Sibu company, often uses exactly the opposite imagery. Irama produces both Iban pop songs (*lagu Iban*) and folk music (*main asal*), including *taboh* (gong and drum ritual music) and *ramban* (love songs). The performers are clad in traditional Iban costume and surrounded by Iban motifs. Modernity is nowhere to be seen. These tapes appear, however, to be less popular than TBC's.[23]

Iban leaders and cultural organisations have decried the loss of the vast Iban musical heritage.[24] Suggestions have been made to introduce Bornean folk music in the Malaysian school curriculum[25] and the Dayak Cultural Foundation has announced the creation of a Dayak classical music orchestra.[26] At the same time, some leaders have called for tighter regulations in the pop music industry in order to protect Iban singers from exploitation by (ethnic Chinese) middlemen, and for official support to market their own tapes.[27] The Housing Minister, Datuk Celestine Ujang, believes some Iban artists would be millionaires if they were given a fair share of the industry's profits.[28]

The thriving Sino-Iban music industry in Sibu is the outcome of a number of favourable circumstances: the expansion of the music industry across the Archipelago, the economic growth and diversification of the Sibu area in particular and Sarawak in general, an urbanising Iban population with a growing demand for 'modern' forms of entertainment that RTM was failing to provide, the old symbiotic relations of patronage/exploitation binding Sibu Chinese and Iban, and the entrepreneurial acumen of one particular Sibu family.

Television

The invention of television in 1931 preceded by several decades the invention of Malaysia, a polity described by Benedict Anderson (1998), somewhat cruelly, as a 'hasty amalgam of Malaya, Singapore and the Bornean regions of Sarawak and Sabah' arranged by Whitehall.[29] Both Malaysia and Radio Televisyen Malaysia (RTM) were born in 1963. Unlike the BBC, RTM was never envisaged as a public service. Rather it was to be a *government* service with a crucial mission, as it was regarded as 'an important tool for facilitating or encouraging socio-economic development and for fostering national integration amongst the country's multi-ethnic peoples' (Anuar and Kim 1996: 262). Six years later, a second channel was launched. Its directives followed those for the first channel and remained unchanged into the 1990s:

1. to explain in-depth and with the widest possible coverage the policies and programmes of the government in order to ensure maximum understanding by the public;

2. to stimulate public interest and opinion in order to achieve changes in line with the requirement of the government;

81

3. to assist in promoting civic consciousness and fostering the development of Malaysian arts and culture; and

4. to provide suitable elements of popular education, general information and entertainment. (Nain 1996: 162)

Over the years, the realities of Malaysia's political life have tarnished these lofty ideals. Khoo (1995) provides three examples. In 1983, the populism of Dr Mahathir, then Malaysia's prime minister, was at its peak. As leader of the ruling coalition's (BN) dominant party, the United Malays National Organisation (UMNO), and undisputed national leader he was able to mobilise the UMNO-owned newspapers, especially the *New Straits Times* and *Berita Harian*, to carry 'reports, features, analyses and letters [...] slanted against the Malay royalty'. In addition, the state-owned TV stations ran a series of Malay films on the rampant tyranny suffered by the people 'under the Malay equivalents of the *ancien regime*' (1995: 206–207). Second, in 1986 RTM screened an edited police videotape to discredit the opposition party PAS (1995: 228). Third, in 1988–1989 the *Lagu Setia* (a song of loyalty to king and country, leaders and people, religion and race) was repeatedly broadcast over radio and television and sung at political, governmental and civic functions (1995: 321). A further example is given by Gomez (2004b: 477). During the 1990 electoral campaign, Mahathir used the mainstream media to discredit the opposition leader, Razaleigh, by accusing him of supporting Christianity owing to his links with the ruling coalition (BN) defectors Parti Bersatu Sabah. This campaign helped the BN to maintain a two-thirds majority in Parliament.

The late 1980s were marked by the increased authoritarianism of a vulnerable Mahathir. The BN used docile media organisations, notably television and the press, owned by politicians and businessmen 'to promote and legitimise itself' and to 'discredit political opposition and dissent more generally' (Gomez and Jomo 1997: 3). In recent years critics have argued that television's potential role as a tool of 'popular education' and national integration has lost out to the dictates of advertisers who favour entertaining foreign productions. In the 1980s, Mahathir's government began issuing licenses for the creation of private TV companies. His intention was to raise funds while retaining control over party political content by selling to carefully chosen bidders. All along, television has remained a key electoral tool for BN (Anuar and Kim 1996).

In 1984, the private channel TV3 was created. The official justification was that private television would foster competition, help reduce the size of the government debt and counter the VCR threat to national unity after growing numbers of ethnic Indians and Chinese had turned to imported videos in their own tongues, shunning the Malay-language domination of RTM's programming (Hashim 1995). TV3 was a huge commercial success. Despite a strong economic recession, it recorded a pre-tax profit of RM 2.16 million in

1985. Five years later, this figure had multiplied fifteenfold to reach RM 31.59 million. This led to rapid changes in the shareholding structure. By 1994 the majority shareholder was the group MRCB, controlled by close associates of Anwar Ibrahim (Gomez and Jomo 1997: 91–92). TV3's positive coverage of Anwar is said to have played a key role in his wresting the UMNO deputy presidency from Ghafar Baba, as part of his premiership bid (Gomez and Jomo 1997: 126–127). In 1997, Shamsuddin Abdul Kadir, close to Mahathir, became one of TV3's directors (1997: 73). The following year, Mahathir used TV3 and other mainstream media in an attempt to discredit his rival, Anwar Ibrahim, accusing him of being homosexual and corrupt. The blatantly one-sided reporting, however, backfired on Mahathir, and TV3's revenue suffered a sharp decline (Gomez 2004b: 479).

Some vocal sectors in Peninsular Malaysia have expressed dismay at what they see as a constant meddling of politicians in the programming, a wide-spread lack of professionalism and the unrelenting search for lucrative revenues from transnational advertising agencies. Both RTM and TV3 have been attacked for allowing un-Asian levels of sex and violence into their programming. RTM's hard-earned 1980s ratio of 60 domestic productions to every 40 imported ones had by 1993 been reversed. TV3 was even more western-ised: 80 per cent of its programmes came from the West, mostly from the U.S.A. (Hashim 1995). These figures, say the critics, indicate that the post-1969 policies to foster a national culture are under severe threat (Nain 1996). Pressure from non-Malay quarters led to a compromise: RTM would devote its first channel to the promotion of the Malay(sian) language and culture, while TV2 would target the needs of the non-Malay groups by broadcasting in Chinese, Tamil and English (Hashim 1995). Despite this adjustment, a number of pressure groups still feel that their constituents are under-represented, including women's groups, small ethnic minorities and non-Muslim religious groups (Anuar and Kim 1996). Another area of concern is the decline in the quality of investigative journalism, affecting not only television but other media as well. Gomez (2004b: 483–484) has suggested a combination of four possible causes: the consolidation of 'an extremely strong state' with power increasingly concentrated in the prime minister; an 'extreme subservience of capital to the state'; the influence of the political elite on editorial decisions; and self-censorship among journalists and editors.

A persistent bone of contention is religion. Islam is a main ingredient in the synthetic Malaysian culture dreamed up by the UMNO leaders after the serious 1969 racial riots in Peninsular Malaysia. It is the only religion with TV coverage, a perennial source of resentment from other religious quarters. So far moderate Muslim values have dominated local production. Most RTM dramas revolve around the concerns of the Malay community, notably how to reconcile the demands of modernisation with the Islamic faith and family responsibilities.[30] In chapter 5, I explore the negative reactions of rural Iban to these dramas. Two Malaysian researchers describe how 'Islamic values are injected [in many dramas], partly as an indirect response to the government's desire to instil Islamic values into the administration and wider society' (Anuar and Kim 1996: 270).

In their television history, the Bornean states are again a special case. Transmission commenced in Sabah in 1974, eleven years after it had done so in West Malaysia. From 1975 Sarawak was allowed to use the Sabahan facilities. Various cultural, musical and religious programmes were produced and broadcast by the two states over a joint channel known as Channel 3. However in 1985 Channel 3 was closed down following directives from Kuala Lumpur – predictably, it was seen as a threat to national unity. Programming was taken over by the centre, with which airtime was now 'shared'. Non-Muslim religious programmes were never again broadcast.[31] Today, in spite of Sarawak's impressive economic growth of the past two decades, local production is lower than it was in the 1970s. Three kinds of programmes are produced in Sarawak:

1. *Rampai Kenyalang*[32], the state's oldest television programme, launched in 1976. This 30-minute newsreel is broadcast every Wednesday from 12.15 to 12.45. It covers political events, sports and cultural celebrations such as Gawai Dayak (see chapter 9);

2. Documentaries on development and culture. Irregularly broadcast, on average twice a month;

3. Music, the arts, entertainment; also irregular broadcasts.

Television in Sarawak is a West Malaysian import that arrived more than a decade late. Together with the Malay-medium school system, this medium is an integral part of the wide-ranging process of 'double westernisation' affecting Sarawak and Sabah since the Federation was created in 1963 and accelerated since the mid-1970s. By 'double westernisation' I mean the two-step flow of ideas, images and practices from the Western world (especially the U.S.A.) selected and recycled in West Malaysia and then re-exported to East Malaysia. Television is also a reliable propaganda tool for the ruling coalition (BN), and it was so in particular for the country's authoritarian prime minister, Mahathir, who retired in 2003. It is a strong conveyor of nation building and modernity visions. Finally, it is the site of many a struggle for political and economic clout. Attempts by the Bornean states to develop an autonomous channel in the 1970s were soon thwarted by Kuala Lumpur in the interest of 'national unity', the same interest that led to the burning of Iban books. The result is that Iban and other Dayak groups are systematically excluded from television. The sole recurrent Iban contribution is that of a female singer on a prime-time nationalist video-clip. This is an example of the nation-state's indefatigable efforts to tame cultural diversity by overcommunicating the aesthetic appeal of the various cultures to a nationwide audience while *undercommunicating* (Eriksen 1993: 84 following Goffman) their chief perceived threat to national unity: unique languages and cultures. The Dayaks can be seen occasionally on television, but their tongues cannot be heard.

Interpersonal Media

Interpersonal media are technologies that allow two-way communication, including letters, telephone, fax, email, and public-address systems (cf. Thompson 1995). In a country such as Malaysia where the mass media are under strict government control, the interpersonal media have a special significance. Thus, Internet reports of all kinds reach Iban longhouse through indirect (and imperfect) channels. In 1997, a deluge of 'flying letters' accusing the Chief Minister, Taib Mahmud, of fleeing Sarawak at the height of the forest fires in neighbouring Kalimantan (chapter 5), reached all areas of the state (see *Sarawak Tribune*, 13 October 1997, for one of many pro-Taib retorts). Rumours that Taib had deposited 8 billion ringgit from his logging ventures in a Swiss bank reached the rural areas and were quietly relayed in coffee shops and longhouse galleries. In this instance, a number of interpersonal media (especially e-mail, telephone and letters) and face-to-face exchanges were mobilised to discuss allegations over which the mass media had imposed a blackout. With the gradual diffusion of digital technologies it is likely that web-based independent media organisations such as malaysiakini (Anuar 2004, Tong 2004) will increasingly shape interpersonal communication in Sarawak and elsewhere in Malaysia.

Conclusion

In this and the foregoing chapter I have discussed two generations of media production tied to profound changes in Sarawak. The first period (1954–1976) saw the rapid development of language-based Iban media – radio, books and magazines – driven by a generation of Saribas teachers drawing on oral Iban culture. Their aim was to reconcile economic development and cultural preservation. At the same time they were furthering the state's aim of 'saving the Iban from themselves', from their presumed backwardness. The second period (1977–1998), covered in this chapter, began with the alleged mass destruction of books in Dayak languages by the postcolonial, Malay-dominated state. This act of state violence contributed to the aborted ethnogenesis of a modern Iban culture. It ushered in a period of accelerated Malaysianisation and increased circulation of visual media contents, relegating Iban radio to marginal niches. At the subfederal level, the Sarawak state and its Dayak allies consolidated a safe, colourful Dayak identity supported by a wealth of musical and visual media used most intensively during the Dayak Festival (chapter 9). This identity displays all the signs of what Rival (1997: 138) calls 'tolerable difference'. A parallel discourse in the government-controlled press flourished and was pressed into intensive service at critical junctures of intolerable resistance from the Penan and other indigenous groups: the representation of the Dayaks as an underdeveloped people in need of a modern 'mind-set'. Partly as a reaction to the state's monopoly over legitimate media, this period also witnessed the growth of interpersonal media (telephone, fax, email, etc.) that sometimes challenged the ruling elite's accounts of rural development.

With King (1989), King and Wilder (2003) and other anthropologists, I understand ethnicity not as an isolated category of analysis but as part of a broader context of social, economic, and political relations – as part of what Comaroff (1996) calls the 'politics of difference'. *Contra* Barth (in Hann 1994), I am suggesting that the study of ethnicity in the post-colonial world cannot be divorced from the study of media, public culture and nation building. Indeed in Borneo as in other Asia-Pacific islands, ethnicity and nationality are two aspects of common development projects that seek to spread primordial notions (of 'custom', 'heritage' and the like) through various media. It is precisely those 'various media' that I have sought to explore in historical detail, for this is a sorely neglected area in the literature. This approach reveals behind-the-scenes struggles not so much over vague symbols, but over the development and consolidation of a modern national language and culture in Malaysia (see Musa 2004) – a question that is far from resolved given the continued strength of English, Mandarin and several Chinese 'dialects'. The attempts by Saribas Iban media producers to create a literate Iban high culture were thwarted by the new Malaysian state's will to monopolise legitimate language and culture. A literate culture 'cannot normally survive without its own political shell, the state' (Gellner 1983: 140). In this regard, Iban radio posed less of a threat to the new Malaysian polity than Iban books, so it was allowed to live on. Drawing on Appadurai's (1990) 'mediascape' trope and the ubiquitous notion of 'globalisation', Ginsburg (1993), Sullivan (1993) and others working on non-Western media production have highlighted the multidirectional nature of media influences. While we need to capture some of the complexity of contemporary media flows, I have insisted on the largely *unidirectional*, top-down flow of state propaganda from West to East Malaysia – a 'Westernisation' of sorts – and from urban elites to the rural population.

Notes

1. I shall be assessing these new developments in a forthcoming book on new media and local governance in Peninsular Malaysia.

2. This innovation was known as *Pelajar Jaku Iban ke Sekula Primari & Sekondari* (Untie 1998: 2).
3. In my Saribas and Skrang experience, most rural viewers retire for the night between 8.30 and 9.30 p.m. (See chapter 8).
4. CATS is an acronym. It stands for 'Communicating Aspiration Throughout Sarawak'. It is also a pun, as *kucing* (pronounced like Kuching, the state capital of Sarawak) is the Standard Malay word for 'cat'.
5. His artistic name is a wordplay on the Iban teknonym 'Father-of' (*Apai*). It literally translates as 'Peter John Son-of-Father'. I once attended a longhouse sermon in which the priest jokingly told his flock that 'We humans are all like Peter John; we're all children of the Father" (*Semua kitai mensia baka Peter John meh, semua anak Apai magang*).
6. However, some of the participants, all of whom were native Iban speakers, had at times to revert to English. Like many middle-aged, educated Sarawakians of other ethnic groups, they found it difficult to sustain a work-related discussion exclusively in one language, especially in a language different from English. Moreover, most of the terminology associated with broadcasting has no Iban equivalents. Other participants chose to use English to stress particular points, a common practice among English-educated Sarawakians.
7. Some Iban politicians are said to treat the Iban Section as if it were 'just another government department'. Pressures can also come from Malay politicians from Kuala Lumpur and their Sarawak associates. Religion is a particularly thorny issue. RTM Sarawak, unlike its Peninsular counterparts, has regular Christian broadcasts in Iban and other languages. These have been discontinued at least twice during the past few years owing to pressures 'from high places'.
8. Kaji Selidik Tahunan Tentang Penggunaan Radio (*Bahagian Teknologi Pendidikan* 1993).
9 See http://www.cnsnews.com/ForeignBureaus/archive/200304/FOR20030417b.html and http://www.malaysiakini.com/letters/200304220034275.php
10. Literally, '*The People's News*'.
11. Its Malay version is called *Pedoman Rakyat*.
12. *ORANG BUMAI DI MENUA PESISIR ENDA TAU ENDA NGUBAH CHARA PENGAWA SIDA* (*Pembrita*, May 1996).
13. In my experience, *Pembrita* is more popular in the Skrang than in the Saribas area.
14. For the second kind of portrayal, see Minos's 'Dayak attitude and NCR Land Development', *Sarawak Tribune*, 19 October 1997. Minos is a Bidayuh Dayak.
15. In 1947 there were less than 300 Iban in Sibu. In 1972, there were at least ten times this figure (Sutlive 1972: 466).
16. A most unusual philosophical investigation into life's transience conveyed in a moralistic tone by Andrewson Ngalai and entitled '*Dunya Sementara*', from his album *Ambai Numbur Satu*.
17. The five tapes are: *Ambai Numbur Satu* and *Andrewson Ngalai* by Andrewson Ngalai, *Taju Remaong* by Johnny Aman, *Iban Karaoke* by several artists (Johnny Aman, Andrewson Ngalai, Josephine, Wilson, and William Awing), and *Joget Iban* by several artists (Andrew Bonny James, Angela L. Jua, Johnny Awie, Jus Allen, Gibson Janggum, Jackson Dana and Alice Awis). Only the latter album is an *Irama* production; the other four are all TBC.
18. 'Iban music industry fast catching up with the rest of the world' (*Sarawak Tribune*, 22 March 1998). This catchy headline from *Bernama*, the Malaysian national newsagency, conceals the fact that it is a Chinese family who controls the lion's share of the 'Iban music industry'.
19. See, for example, Peacock's (1968) classic study on 'proletarian theatre' (*ludruk*) in the East Javanese town of Surabaya or Van Groenendael (1985) on the *wayang* in rural Java as, among other things, powerful sites of social critique.
20. '*Nuan enda ngasoh nganti*', in *Iban Karaoke Vol. 7* (TBC audiocassette).
21. Probably a reference to Sibu's recent past. More generally, the notion that there are no longer any 'enemies' (*munsoh*) thanks to the pacifying efforts of the government is widespread among the Iban.
22. TBC website (http://www.tbc.inet.com.my).

23. Even though the folklore tapes were considerably cheaper. In 1997 they were selling at RM 7.25 compared to the pop tapes' RM 12.50 to RM 13.50. I do not have at present, however, any sales figures from either company.

24. A case in point is the Iban politician and former headmaster, Jimmy Donald, who has worked on the musical heritage of the Iban. In a recent paper (Donald 1997), he singles out a number of traditional genres, including *didi* (lullabies) and other songs for children, *ramban* (used to correct someone's behaviour), *pelandai* (to entertain and egg on a warrior), *dungai* (an entertaining form of 'conversation'), *kana* (a sung epic), *pengap* or *timang* (invocation of the deities at major festivals), *renong* (to recall a love story, to heal a shaman's patients, to open a *pengap*), and others.

25. *Sarawak Tribune*, 8 April 1997.

26. *Sarawak Tribune*, 2 April 1998.

27. These views were put forward by an Iban councillor (name not recorded) at a workshop on Iban arts held in Kuching in April 1997.

28. *Sarawak Tribune*, 2 April 1998. Ujang himself is a millionaire. He is said to be a member of the 'Linggi Jugah' group formed by the three most influential Iban tycoons-cum-politicians in Sarawak (Jawan 1994: 122).

29. See Jones (2002) for a more complex interpretation.

30. An interesting parallel with the Radio Sarawak dramas and BLB novellas discussed earlier.

31. When the Christian Kadazan-dominated *Parti Bersatu Sabah* (PBS) swept into power in Sabah in 1990, the rebirth of a state television station was at the top of their electoral manifesto (Jawan 1994: 220–221). The federal government, however, successfully blocked such attempts.

32. Previously known as *Majalah Sarawak* and *Mingguan Sarawak*.

5

SUSTAINABLE PROPAGANDA

In May 2003 I interviewed a Malay town planner on the subject of information and communication technologies (ICTs) in Malaysia. When I asked him about the viability of the countless ICT pilot projects launched across Malaysia, he replied along the lines of: 'No, we're not worried about sustainability. Rural people will catch up. You see, when you bombard them with IT propaganda you're already doing sustainable development!' I found this idea of propaganda as a form of sustainable development deeply intriguing, and soon after that interview I coined the term 'sustainable propaganda'. Unfortunately a Google search revealed that the term had already been minted by an Austrian artist,[1] proving once again that science often trails behind art.

Another source of inspiration for this chapter has been K. Ramakrishna's (2002) *Emergency Propaganda*, a book devoted to British counterinsurgency efforts in Malaya in 1948–1958. This period is known as the Malayan Emergency. Ramakrishna rethinks previous studies of the Emergency. According to these, the British won the hearts and minds of Malayan Chinese guerrillas through a combination of effective propaganda, the massive resettlement of rural Chinese in 'New Villages', and small-unit military action. To Ramakrishna, there are a number of problems with these assumptions. First, they conceal two very distinct groups under the blanket term 'Chinese'. Whereas for educated urban Chinese the question of achieving citizenship rights was of paramount importance, what the Chinese peasantry desperately needed were tangible improvements to their economic lot. To persuade the ethnic Chinese as a whole to accept the proposed Malayan Union, the British would need to send very different messages to the urban educated from those intended for the rural masses. Eventually the British succeeded on both fronts, but not before a lengthy – and costly – struggle, as is painstakingly documented in the book.

A second flaw in previous work on the Emergency, says Ramakrishna (2002: 12–17), is the idea that propaganda refers merely to radio broadcasts, printed materials and the like. For Ramakrishna, we need to broaden the concept of propaganda to encompass non-discursive forms such as the behaviour of leaders, the creation of new settlements, and even events that have unintended effects on the target audience. In other words, in order to be effective, words and images must be backed up with deeds. In this respect, the communist leadership in Malaya failed miserably. From the outset they departed from Mao's teachings, which were curiously similar to those held by the British. While the British generally avoided broadcasting outright lies, the guerrilla leaders sought to control their rank and file through manipulation, deception and intimidation.

For Ramakrishna, the key criterion to distinguish propaganda from non-propaganda is neither intentionality nor means of communication nor truthfulness, but rather *relevance*. He gives the example of someone who wants to buy a car. This person will ignore the classifieds on vacuum cleaners and go directly to the car section. The section on vacuum cleaners, however colourful, is irrelevant to her present concerns. Likewise, during the Malayan Emergency, propaganda items on the promised granting of citizenship to the Chinese would have been largely irrelevant to a peasant audience but highly relevant to the urban intelligentsia. Emergency propaganda, then, succeeded because it was truthful, relevant and supported by deeds.

The problem with Ramakrishna's definition is that it appears to downplay intentionality. As Jowett and O'Donnell (1999: 6) define it, propaganda is

> the *deliberate*, systematic attempt to shape perceptions, manipulate cognitions, and direct behavior to achieve a response that furthers the desired intent of the propagandist (my emphasis).

By 'deliberate' they understand 'wilful, intentional, and premeditated'. That is, propagandists think ahead to consider various alternative possibilities in promoting an ideology and gaining an advantage over their rivals. They do so systematically, in an organised manner. Both private companies and governments set up agencies or departments devoted to the creation and dissemination of propaganda or advertising campaigns (Jowett and O'Donnell 1999: 6). As we have seen in previous chapters, the Malaysian state inherited from the British a range of agencies and techniques for psychological warfare and socio-economic propaganda. In this chapter I wish to apply Ramakrishna's Malayan insights and Jowett and O'Donnell's definition of propaganda to Sarawak. How applicable are these ideas about propaganda to the development of post-independence Sarawak? What happens when state propaganda becomes 'part of the culture', as I believe is the case among Iban in Sarawak? How does propaganda spread and become appropriated? More importantly for our present purposes, how does it contribute to nation building?

Ideologies and Ideolects

Towards the end of my fieldwork in Sarawak, I discovered a marked contrast in local media praxis. On the one hand, I had recorded a great diversity of media practices, including listening to the radio, watching television, using clocks and wristwatches, reading school textbooks, giving longhouse speeches through PA systems, celebrating the Dayak Festival, and speaking over the telephone. On the other hand, each of the two rural areas I studied – Saribas and Skrang – appeared to have its own highly consistent, uniform local ideology – a derivative of the Malaysian state's nation-building ideology. In other words, at the local level I found both media diversity and ideological unity. Below I discuss only the Saribas ideology, on which I have a great deal more data, but some aspects of the Skrang ideology – and its relationship to print media – are presented in chapter 6. Let us first turn to the highest levels of ideological production in Malaysia and make our way 'downhill' towards the Saribas.

In 1991, Malaysia's then prime minister, Mahathir, launched a new agenda for the nation officially promoted as Vision 2020 (*Wawasan 2020*). The aim was to transform Malaysia into a 'fully developed country' by that year. The five core components of this project (see Khoo 1995: 327, Gomez and Jomo 1997: 169) were:

- united, harmonious nation
- freer capitalism
- society driven by science and technology
- moderate Islam
- family-based welfare system

Implied in the vision, but never explicitly stated, were the following:

- scripted populism
- authoritarian government (Khoo 1995: 327)
- clock and calendar time (e.g., 2020)
- residual anti-Communism

Mahathir's nationalism changed over time from being primarily concerned with strengthening the economic standing of the Malays vis-à-vis the Chinese to promoting the idea of a united Malaysian nation, 'psychologically subservient to none, and respected by the peoples of other nations' (quoted in Khoo 1995: 329). This was to be achieved through industrialisation and a more profound 'economic liberalization' (1995: 328). Science and technology were regarded as central to this drive. Malaysian society would become a 'scientific, progressive, innovative and forward-looking society' (Gomez and Jomo 1997: 169). The moral underpinning of a future national culture would be provided by a moderate, progressive form of Islam resulting in a 'fully moral and ethical society whose citizens are strong in religious and spiritual values' (Khoo 1995: 328). Mahathir's political style was always 'people-centred'. A former rural doctor, he was confident that he understood the masses' (*rakyat*) ills thoroughly. He knew 'what [was] good for them' (1995: 200). His populism was not, however, spontaneous; it was based on carefully worded scripts disseminated by a compliant media apparatus (1995: 201–203). Finally, Vision 2020 was designed to foster a 'mature democratic society', yet for the foreseeable future the masses were not deemed sufficiently mature to live in a democratic society (1995: 329). This stance was confirmed in 1998, during the arrest and imprisonment of Mahathir's deputy, Anwar Ibrahim, under dubious charges of corruption and sodomy.

The Sarawak state government has been led since 1981 by Taib Mahmud, a Melanau Muslim whose slogans closely resemble those of his federal mentor, Mahathir. The official Sarawakian sub-ideology can be gleaned from reading the state government-controlled press, from street hoardings, public events and from the ruling coalition's Sarawak Manifesto of 1991 (for the latter, see Ritchie 1994: 127–130). When compared to the Mahatharist creed, two of the areas listed above show some discrepancy. First, in the Sarawak sub-ideology there is one item that does not appear in its parental system of ideals: the need to achieve 'sustainable land development'. Unlike Peninsular Malaysia, Sarawak is still a predominantly rural state in which much of the land is in the hands of indigenous communities. Changes to the native customary law under Taib's leadership have gradually undermined the position of the Dayaks. His official aim is to transform Sarawak from a backward state dependent on small-holding farming to an industrialised one with large-scale estate development, timber processing (Ritchie 1993: 106–107) and an efficient tourist sector that can profit from the state's 'rich cultural heritage'. Although ostensibly committed to a balanced pattern of urban-rural development, his 'Integrated Regional Development' (IRD) concept is clearly tilted towards the urban domain. It is intended to urbanise what are seen as inefficient rural areas (Kassim 1996).

Second, there is no mention of Islam in the Sarawak manifesto. Sarawak is again different from the Peninsula, where Muslims make up the majority of the electorate (60 per cent), and exert a decisive influence upon electoral strategies and policy. In Sarawak, Muslims are in the minority, with only 27 per cent of the population (Jawan 1994: 24). Taib, the Chief Minister, may count on the support of pivotal Malay Muslim leaders in Kuala Lumpur, but he is careful not to alienate non-Muslim voters in Sarawak. For this reason he has relentlessly expounded his 'politics of development' through the press, hoardings, speeches and other means as a healthy alternative to the 'communal politics' allegedly pursued by his Dayakist opponents (Ritchie 1993: 106).

Having sketched the official, and therefore contested, Malaysian ideology and its Sarawakian derivation or sub-ideology, I would now like to outline the Saribas Iban local ideology, which I shall call an 'ideolect'.[2] This proposed concept is a combination of the terms 'ideology' and 'dialect'. It is intended to convey the parochial, politically marginal nature of the Saribas Iban system of ideals; a system which integrates political ideals from the literate, mass-mediated power centres – Kuala Lumpur and Kuching – with local ideals inherited from an oral tradition based in the longhouse. The linguist Max Weinreich once described a language as 'a dialect with an army and a navy' (Pinker 1997: 28). In the context of Malaysia's nation-building project, the Saribas ideolect can be seen as 'an ideology without an army and a navy', that is a parochial system of ideals derived from a range of state ideals which in turn does not contribute much to Malaysia's nationalist ideology. The following set of ideals lies at the heart of the Saribas ideolect:

- united, harmonious nation
- peace through military deterrence
- local tradition (*adat*) compatible with modernity
- oral knowledge compatible with book knowledge (*penemu surat*)
- successful individuals who respect elders
- family-based welfare system

Although there are some variations in how the ideolect is reproduced depending on the social occasion, medium, person's status, occupation, age, gender, etc., the core ideals cut across all these distinctions.

Boys Will Be Policemen

In a collection of essays on the 'ethnography of moralities', Howell (1997: 4) stresses the dynamic relationship between moral values and social practices: 'Values are continuously changing and adapting through actual choices and practices, while, at the same time, they continue to inform and shape choices and practices'. Contra Howell, I wish to suggest that in the case of Saribas Iban society, values are not 'continuously changing'. Despite the dramatic pace of technological and economic change experienced by all middle-aged residents, there has been a remarkable continuity in the local ideology. As Raymond Williams remarked long ago: 'A main characteristic of our society is a willed coexistence of very new technology and very old social forms' (quoted in Silverstone et al. 1994: 1).

Howell (1997: 5) goes on to ask: 'Which social domains most profoundly articulate moral values and which are most (or least) affected by such?'. In what follows, I will argue that the moral order of Saribas Iban children is most explicitly and repeatedly articulated through classroom media practices in which they are asked to faithfully reproduce, often verbatim, the dominant modernist ideolect shared by their teachers, parents and adult kin. Saribas children learn about their world in a variety of ways – through social inter-action with adults and other children, through radio, television, comics and textbooks, through direct contact with a man-made environment, etc. Yet it is only in the context of the teacher-pupil relationship, and mostly through written tasks such as essays and exams, that they are asked to spell out a preformed moral order. In other contexts, for instance while they are watch-ing television, moral ideals remain implicit or at best poorly articulated. Therefore, in terms of moral and ideological reproduction during childhood, the school essay is a far more salient, and researchable, media practice than watching television.

I asked two Iban language teachers in the Saribas to set the following optional essay questions to 63 lower secondary (*Tingkatan 1* and *2*) pupils:

1. *Hobi (pengerindu) maia lapa*
   Your favourite hobby (or hobbies)

2. *Julok ati nuan jemah ila*
   What do you want to be when you grow up?

3. *Cherita television ti pemadu dikerindu ka nuan*
   Your favourite television programmes

4. *Nama tuju 'Wawasan 2020'?*
   What are the aims of Vision 2020?

Most Form 1 pupils chose to answer either the first or the second question, while most Form 2 pupils wrote about the first one. Both groups, however, wrote along very similar lines. Most of the boys would like to become police-men, soldiers or football players. I will concentrate on the first category (policemen) in order to trace this career choice to conditioning from the wider interpersonal and mediated milieux in which boys grow up. Ganggong, aged 13, is well aware of the importance of written exams:

> When I grow up I want to be a policeman. I like the idea because one day I want to be a policeman who people like and are fond of. If I want to become a policeman I have to pass the PMR, SPM, and SPTEM exams and go to the highest school of all, that is university. The reason why I want to become a policeman is so I can arrest [wrongdo-ers] and protect our land. So that our land is in peace and harmony and free from trou-bles. If I become a policeman I will not become just any ordinary policeman [*polis ngapa*], I want to be an ASP, that is a police chief or officer. If I become a policeman I must behave well so that there are no complaints about us. If I become a policeman I must respect the local customs [*adat*]. People who become policemen must be strong and honest [*lurus ati*] and feel compassion towards others [*sinu ka orang*] and must always help others.[3] I have to become a policeman because I really like this job. If there is a thief I can arrest him and put him in jail. This is why we have to obey the law so that we're not arrested by me.

Ganggong's intention of studying hard in order to secure a high social status is tempered with his desire to help others by protecting them from wrongdoers. This same balanced outlook is expressed by others, including Williamson:

> When I grow up I would like to be a police officer. The reason I have chosen this job is because I can help people like if somebody's house has been burgled I can help catch the person who did it.

Chris, who accidentally collapsed all four essay questions into one, finds in the protagonists of an American serial his policing role-models for the highly developed Malaysia of the year 2020. His view of the future is undoubtedly influenced by the electronic media:

> When I grow up I would like to be a policeman. I want to arrest people who have committed crimes and protect the country so that there is not one single person left among all the people of Sarawak committing crimes. [M]y favourite TV programme is The X-Files. It is about two Fbi agents who have not lost hope [M. *putus asa*] and are still looking for evidence, they are looking for people who have committed crimes. We all know what the aims of Vision 2020 are. I reckon there will be no cars in the future only aircraft because in the year 2020 Malaysia will already be developed [M. *maju*] [...] Perhaps we will have telephones at home and we will be able to see the picture on television. Who knows, there may be more and stranger diseases. Perhaps the police will carry laser guns.

The X-Files is a finely crafted and acted U.S. serial on the efforts of two glamorous FBI agents, Mulder and Scully, to solve classified cases involving supernatural beings or humans with so-called paranormal powers. It is highly popular with young Saribas Iban viewers, partly perhaps because it resonates with Iban and Austronesian ideas about *antu* and other supernatural agents, now avidly published as pulp fiction in Malay and Indonesian. It is unlikely, however, that Chris can follow the fast-moving plots with any accuracy by reading the fleeting Malay subtitles. This essay passage reveals the kind of interpretive work he has carried out on the serial. In short, he has integrated a rather subtle (by television standards) foreign serial into a simple, schematic, ideolectal representation of the work of policemen everywhere: 'they are looking for people who have committed crimes'. In fact, Mulder and Scully, two self-assured Ivy League graduates, are far more interested in probing into the paranormal than they are in mundane policing tasks.[4] Arresting simple mortals was the speciality of Starsky and Hutch and other unsophisticated *orang polis* familiar to Saribas Iban viewers of an earlier generation.

Another aspiring policeman, Nyawai, weaves together three recurrent concerns of young Saribas Iban: (1) farming as the unenviable fate of those who fail to excel at school, (2) the duty to repay one's parents for all their efforts, and (3) the need to secure the national borders from the threat of 'foreigners':

> When I grow up I would like to be a policeman if I can. The reason I want to be a policeman is to protect the behaviour [*ulah*] and the well-being of our country. [...] If

I cannot become a policeman I will work in the longhouse with my parents. I always think of what I want to be when I grow up.

Another reason why I want to be a policeman is because policemen do not have to do a lot of heavy work. [...] Another reason why I want to be a policeman is because I want to protect the masses [*rayat*] from the troublemakers who come in from other countries. I want to become a policeman so that I can repay the generosity of my parents who pay for my school.

Similarly, Simon writes:

When I grow up I want to be a policeman. The reason why I would like to be a policeman is because I want to protect the country.

Where did these 'stable representations' (Sperber 1996: 57–59) about a future career come from? How did they spread and consolidate? I believe they are prevalent because they are supported by a number of entwined social formations, agents and media, notably: (a) the long-standing Iban preference for employment in the security forces, a culturally-sanctioned legacy from the Brookes' 'pacification' of Sarawak, based on the principle of *divide et impera*; (b) positive textbook and radio representations of the police as 'our friends' (*pangan kitai*) since the Communist troubles in the 1960s (chapter 3), which influenced an earlier Iban generation; (c) newer versions of these early propaganda items repeatedly influencing the present generation; (d) the daily television spots showing proud uniformed men and women parading across Kuala Lumpur to mark special days on the national calendar; (e) glamorous television shows such as *The X-Files*; and (f) the compatibility of this profession with core components of the Saribas Iban ideolect, such as courage (*pemerani*), endurance (*tan, nakal*), personal achievement (*niki pangkat*), a modernist desire to escape from rural backwardness, a conservative love of law and order, and the customary obligation to help kindred in need (*nulung kaban*).

A comparison of three items from school textbooks demonstrates the unbroken continuity of these representations since the advent of mass print media. In Buma's pioneering Iban textbook, *Pelajar Iban 2*, published in 1970, we find (my translation):

A POLICEMAN

Laja is a policeman. He joined the police when he was still young. Many people besides Laja join the police.

Every morning Laja practises how to parade. He parades with a rifle. Many other policemen parade with Laja. They parade in a field. Often they march to a piece of music. The music is played by a band. After he has finished parading, Laja works in an office. He often guards the office, too. He carries a rifle.

There are times when Laja guards the main road. He looks out for people who drive in the middle of the road. When people ask for help, Laja helps them. Laja is extremely kind. He always helps people. He never gets angry. He feels compassion towards people.

Laja always visits Beji and family. Laja often spends the night there. Beji likes Laja. Laja tells Beji about his job. Beji understands the job. He wants to be a policeman. Beji knows how to feel compassion towards people. He is kind to people.

Many people know Laja. They praise him. They say he is a kind policeman. They are not afraid of talking to him. Even their children are not scared. They are Laja's friends.

The police are our friends. The police help us. We should not be scared of the police. We ought to be friends with the police. They protect us.

These flattering accounts were bolstered through radio broadcasts, political rallies and interpersonal relations to entice a new generation of Iban males to join the police and armed forces in the 1960s and 1970s, at the height of the Indonesian conflict and communist insurgency. Twenty-seven years on, an Iban-language book written by and for Primary 6 teachers, *Malin Pengajar Jaku Iban Taun 6*, published in 1997, furthers the same cause among a new generation (my translation):

BECOMING A POLICEMAN

In my view, not many people really understand the work of the police. The truth is that the police are our friends.

The work of the police is to protect people and country, and arrest those who steal, murder, swindle and commit many other crimes. The police do not arrest people who have not broken the laws passed by our government.

This is why the task of those who become policemen is not an easy one. It is a very stressful job. They always have to beware of any incident or misfortune that may befall them should they not be alert, for they themselves would be the first to be struck by such a misfortune.

We children or citizens of Malaysia should always help the police who protect the lives and country of the masses so that our troubles will lessen as time goes by. Therefore we should all stand behind our police force to guarantee the safety of our citizens and country.

In addition to ideological continuity over time these print media products display a high degree of consistency across the various school subjects, forming an intricate web of mutually reinforcing ideals, *a stable framework of intertextual consistency* (cf. Peterson 2003). Take this poetic example from the Form 1 English textbook (Chua 1996 [1987]: 234):

AUNT SUNITA

Have you ever seen Aunt Sunita?
So very smart she looks,
She drives her blue and white police car,
And catches all the crooks.

She writes many reports,
She directs traffic well,
Everyone gives her support,
So that she can do her duty well.

She helps everyone, young and old,
She's friendly and always fair,
People who do what they are told,
Won't be afraid when she is there.

Besides historical continuity and intertextual consistency, this ode exemplifies one significant change in Malaysian society over the past two decades: the increasingly active role of women in fields previously monopolised by men. In chapter 3 we saw that the first generation of Saribas Iban teachers to publish with the Borneo Literature Bureau was exclusively male. Similarly, in chapter 6, I quote two sisters from Entanak Longhouse whose *bilek*-family priorities prevented them from either attending school or furthering their education beyond primary school. Matters for girls are far better today. The Saribas Iban ideolect, especially as it is routinely articulated by influential adults, does not single out boys as their *bilek*-families' sole hope for educational achievement. Today boys and girls stand, as far as schooling is concerned, on an equal footing. In fact, teachers and parents alike often remark that girls are better pupils, with a keener interest in reading for pleasure and enlightenment outside school hours, a view corroborated by a survey I carried out in the Betong public library and participant observation in longhouses.

Girls Will Be Teachers

A majority of girls expressed a preference for a career in teaching. Notice the moral grounds on which Lucy justifies her choice:

> When I grow up I would like to be a teacher. The reason why I would like to be a teacher is because I want to make worthy persons [*urang ka beguna*] out of children and teach them the difference between right and wrong [*nama utai ti patu[t] dikereja enggau utai ti enda patut dikereja*].

The Saribas ideolect clearly separates out intelligent and well behaved children from stupid and badly behaved ones. Patricia, aged 13, writes:

> Compare those children who have not learnt anything with the clever ones. Look how the stupid children wander aimlessly around the market town [*pasar*].

With adequate guidance, some children can become intelligent. Magda explains:

> The reason why I want to be a teacher is to teach children so that one day they will be well-behaved[5] and intelligent [*awak ka mereti serta pandai jemah ila*].

A fourth girl, Lisa, draws upon the ideolectal emphasis on policing to imagine her future teaching practice:

> When they are too noisy I will have to report them [...] When they run away from the classroom, the teachers must look for them until they find them so that they do not get lost.

In the Saribas ideolect, high moral standards are often associated with filial piety. Molly conjoins piety with individual achievement in her career projection:

> When I grow up I would like to be a teacher. The reason I have chosen this job is because I want to teach young children, so that they grow up to be clever and to respect their parents [*awak ka sida pandai enggau hormat apai indai sida*].

Saribas Iban concur that one fundamental prerequisite for professional success is a fluency in reading and writing. If one cannot read, says Tanya, from Form 1, 'people will call one letter-blind (*buta urup*)'. Many girls showed a keen interest in the print media. Notice again the explicit moralistic tone of their essays:

> 1. Madeline (Form 1): Every human being must have a hobby. My hobbies are reading story books and studying. The reason why I chose these hobbies is because we benefit from them [*meri penguntung ngagai kitai*].

> 2. Molly (Form 1): I like playing with my friends [...]. I also enjoy reading story books, magazines, and newspapers in my *bilek* [...]. They not only fill in my spare time but also make me more intelligent [*meri pemandai ngagai aku*].

> 3. Sylvia (Form 1): I always read story books in my spare time. Reading story books makes us more intelligent. They also provide us with moral teachings [*jako ngajar*] for example people who are obsessed with money will end up with nothing. I always read stories about ghosts and spirits [*antu*] and stories that move me to pity [*ngasoh ati aku berasai sinu*].

> 4. Alison (Form 2): Every human being has a hobby. My favourite hobbies are playing volleyball and reading story books. I always read story books in my spare time. Reading story books makes me and everybody else more intelligent. Intelligence comes

not only from textbooks. But also from story books. Reading books helps me to fill in my spare time [and keeps me away] from wrongdoing. When we go to the public library we must have seen a sentence that reads 'Reading is the Bridge to Knowledge'. Thus reads the moral teaching for those of you who are not too fond of reading [*Nya munyi jako peransang ngagai kita ti enda berapa ka macha bup*].

The final two sentences are exemplary. They capture perfectly the style, moral tone and ideological certainties that result from years of joint school, long-house and mass media propaganda. Alison's memorisation of the state's graphophiliac slogan and her slippage into the second person in order to brandish the slogan against her sluggish classmates prove to what extent the hegemonic ideolect has been internalised by Saribas children – especially by those who do well at school. In turn, it is the latter who will in future reproduce these ideals from positions of influence. The main features of the ideolect, as expressed on paper, can be summarised in one imaginary essay paragraph based on a close reading of 63 real essays:

IDEOLEKT KITAI

Semua orang patut bisi julok hati jemah ila. Semua kitai mensia mesti belajar bebendar ba sekula awak ka ulih nyadi orang ti beguna, orang ti nemu nama utai ti patut dikereja enggau utai ti enda patut di kereja. Buku meri pemandai. Anang muai jam, laban 'masa itu emas'. Kitai Iban bedau tentu mansang enti banding enggau bansa bukai, baka sida Melayu enggau China. Patut kitai anembiak Iban sama seati nuju pemansang menoa kitai maia taun 2020. Menua kitai enda tau enda dijaga ari dikachau orang ti datai ari menoa bukai. Kitai Iban rebak baru tu ti udah ngambi pangkat jemah ila enggau sumbong enggau urang tuai. Patut kitai meri basa enggau sukong ngagai apai indai enggau semua urang tuai ti bukai ke bisi nulong kitai maia agi besekula.

OUR IDEOLECT

Everyone should have a goal in life. All human beings must go to school and study very hard so that they can one day become worthy persons, persons who know the difference between right and wrong. Books make us intelligent. Do not waste time, for 'Time is Gold'. We Iban are not as developed as other races such as the Malays or the Chinese. We Iban children should unite to develop our country by the year 2020. Our nation must be protected from troublemakers arriving from foreign countries. Those of us Iban from the new generation who manage to achieve a higher status should not be arrogant towards our elders. We should respect and support our parents and all the other adults who helped us while we were still at school.

A Shared Paradigm of Inference

To understand the huge significance of this standardised cluster of ideals we need a working theory of human belief acquisition. Richard Rorty (1991), the pragmatist philosopher, has developed one. Rorty (1991: 94–95) distinguishes between 'paradigms of inference' and 'paradigms of imagination'. The former occur when the logical space does not change, that is 'when no new candidates for belief are introduced', for instance when we add up a column of figures or run down a flow-chart. Paradigms of imagination include 'the new, metaphorical use of old words (e.g., *gravitas*), the invention of neologisms (e.g., 'gene'), and the colligation of hitherto unrelated texts'.

It should be apparent from the essay extracts given above that Saribas Iban children operate largely within a paradigm of inference. Their teachers, parents, peers, textbooks, story books, and television all provide them with highly consistent chunks of knowledge about the world. Over the years they learn how to practise what Rorty calls 'minimal reweaving' in order to incorporate new items into their web of beliefs and desires. Some examples from Tracy's (aged 10) Iban language exercise book will clarify this point. On 17 February 1997 she was set the following tasks:

Tulis sekeda ari orang ti patut dibebasa ka kitai ke anembiak
[List some of the people we children should respect]

Nama pengawa ti patut dikereja kitai dikena nulung apai-indai?
[What kinds of things should we do to help our parents?]

Kati ko kitai tau malas budi apai-indai kitai ti udah ngaga leboh agi mit sampai ka besai?
[Can we ever repay the kindness our parents have shown us all through our lives?]

The expected 'correct' answers are, of course, entirely consistent with the form and content of the essays studied earlier. A week later, Tracy had to rearrange jumbled sentences, a classic language learning activity which in her school often comes with moral strings attached:

1. *betundi leboh anang kelas dalam pengajar ngajar enti*
   [joke while do not classroom in the teacher is teaching while]

   [Answer: Do not joke in the classroom while the teacher is teaching]

2. *sebedau jari kitai dulu makai basu utai*
   [before hands we before eat wash (any)thing]

   [Answer: We must wash our hands before we eat anything]

101

These exercises add very little to the child's web of beliefs and desires. They are hackneyed, predictable and demand no inquiry beyond their tight parameters. There is no 'colligation of hitherto unrelated texts' at work, but rather the tedious reproduction of well-established moral certainties. Instead of metaphorical leaps of imagination, pupils are expected to work metonymically to fill in gaps or reorder pre-set bits of information. This kind of low-order inferential learning is not confined to rural Sarawak (Seymour 1974) – it is reportedly prevalent across the entire Malaysian educational system.[6]

'Recharge Your Batteries!'

Having discussed state schools, I will now turn briefly to a second site of ideolectal (re)production: the longhouse. In chapter 9 I study the spatial and temporal ordering accomplished during the Gawai Dayak festival by the few men who were allowed access to the PA system. Here I wish to use those festival examples and add another three to explore some of the ways in which the Saribas ideolect is reinforced through the PA system:

1. At around 9.30 pm the official speeches began. The first person to take the microphone was the headman who thanked the native chief, the organising committee, the *gendang* ensemble and the entire community for the smooth running of this year's much expanded programme. He also thanked those who helped financially with the prizes, especially a local politician, and Aki James for repairing the wooden Hornbill. He concluded his speech praying to the Iban Supreme Deity (*Petara*) that those in the government service would be promoted (*niki pangkat*), that farmers would reap abundant harvests and that labourers would earn high wages (*bulih duit, bulih ringgit*).

2. Then the native chief took the microphone. His speech centred on the presence among them of a student of Iban culture from London University who had followed in the footsteps of Robert Pringle, the eminent scholar, to study Entanak and other leading longhouses in the Saribas.

At another electrified, economically developed longhouse in the Saribas, a funeral ceremony (*anjong antu*) was held in honour of a distinguished elder:

3. The deceased's nephew, Apai Minggat, reputed to be a successful lawyer, stressed his late uncle's deep respect (*basa*) and consideration towards all fellow humans, whether rich or poor, young or old. Despite his humble origins, he achieved much in life, and yet he was never arrogant (*sumbung*).

4. Datuk Telichai, a former member of Sarawak's State Council, highlighted in his speech the deceased's dedication to the preservation of the Iban heritage. He provided young people with a role-model (*teladan ke manah*), for if the Iban do not preserve their traditions (*adat*), their 'culture' [English word used] will be severed (*culture kitai putus*). 'We must remember the things we are told; keep the good things, discard the

Figure 5.1. Addressing guests over the PA system at a Saribas longhouse Christian wedding.

bad ones' *(iya ke manah simpan, iya ke jai letak).* 'Don't forget to write. Write everything down' *(Anang enda nulis. Nulis semua utai).* And he encouraged his audience to follow the examples of the late Benedict Sandin and Michael Buma, the accomplished Saribas Iban authors.

There is a fundamental difference between school textbooks and television on the one hand, and PA system speeches on the other. The former are mass media addressing an anonymous, faceless audience made up of both rural and urban, Malay and non-Malay, Peninsular and Borneo citizens. Producers have no feedback from the immense majority of users, so production proceeds largely independently from its reception (cf. Ang 1991) – certainly to its reception in the Saribas, an area whose existence may be unknown to most Peninsular producers. The PA system, in contrast, is an interpersonal medium in which the immediate, face-to-face reactions of the audience are an integral part of the unedited 'production process' (see Thompson 1995). Competent public speakers in all societies must be sensitive to the likes, dislikes and mood of their audiences. Barrett and Lucas (1993: 574–575) have described public speaking in Iban society in the following terms:

> In oratory, depth of meaning is a key to engaging the audience. At weddings the groom's community and the bride's community are each represented by orators and the

Figure 5.2. Cutting the wedding cake in front of the cameras.

long duel between them is likened to defending or attacking a fort (Barrett and Lucas 1993: 574–575).

Knowledgeable Iban, both urban and rural, say that the art of oratory has declined dramatically since the post-war spread of Christianity, school education and migration. I did not witness any 'long duels' at Saribas weddings, nor was 'depth of meaning' (*jaku dalam*) a key defining feature of speeches on these and other occasions. What I did witness and record was the oratory bind in which many a speaker found himself, caught between two complex, 'deep' (*dalam*) systems of knowledge – literate, cosmopolitan Malaysian knowledge and oral, parochial Iban knowledge – neither of which they mastered. It is customary these days to offer each speaker a glass of distilled rice-wine (*chap langkau*) or liquor as he prepares to address a gathering and to egg him on with the jocose neologism '*Chas dulu!*' (lit. Charge [your batteries] first!). Alas, the energising beverage can be no substitute for the speakers' ancestors' long hours of daily oratory practice in the poorly-lit *ruai*. In those days, storytelling was mediated by neither literacy nor television.

Another recurrent feature of PA system speeches is the other side of the epistemological coin: speakers constantly seek to rhetorically bridge the widening gaps that are opening up within Iban society. In brief, they pursue a 1990s version of the cultural project I identified in chapter 3 with the early producers and writers at Radio Sarawak and the Borneo Literature Bureau: the dream of a developed Iban society, yet one steeped in a rich tradition (*adat*). Thus the headman (Extract 1), an Anglican Christian, asked the Iban God (*Petara*) not the Christian God (*Allah Taala*), for his blessings in the ongoing development of the longhouse. Similarly, both the native chief (E2) and the first politician (E4), emphasised the compatibility between 'knowing book' and the preservation of custom. Apai Minggat (E3) made the same point whilst stressing the importance of respect and good manners (*basa*) as a pillar of a modernised *adat* that can help the Iban to achieve parity with other peoples without losing their moral bearings. A second politician (E5) will provide us with a significant contrast. At a fund-raising dinner organised by the Anglican Church in the Saribas:

> 5. ... the politician, a Saribas Iban, delivered a flawless speech in Iban. He told his audience that being a Christian does not consist simply of attending the Easter and Christmas services and banquets. That would be like washing oneself but twice a year. Anglicans must practise their faith continuously. They must also unite now that other churches have come to the Saribas 'to cause trouble' (*ngachau*). It is no use being baptised an Anglican only to run off to embrace other churches until the time comes to be buried, as others have no proper cemeteries. 'We should all unite' (*Patut kitai serakup magang*), he insisted, and told a local parable (*sempama*) to drive his point home. He reminded the audience of the prime minister's recent words to the effect that we can all see on television how people in other countries are always killing one another over ethnicity and religion. In Malaysia there is peace, ethnic harmony and religious freedom.

Speaking on church premises rather than in a longhouse, this speaker had to pitch his speech at a higher geopolitical level. He offered his provincial audience a nationalistic, Mahathirist message that reinforced the well-established belief that other countries are chronically at war, as discussed below. He also called for the unity of all Iban Christians. In his skilful blending of domains he encouraged his audience to reconcile the variegated *Christian* Iban heritage with the national culture project. He did nevertheless *implicitly* support the preservation of the oral heritage through his use of the parable and other relatively 'deep' (*dalam*) rhetorical devices. In chapter 2, I mentioned the work of a European missionary in Papua New Guinea. The Anglican Church speech summarised above is equally part of a long Sarawak tradition of 'co-opting' strikingly similar values to those promoted in PNG (see also Gewertz and Errington [1991] below).

All five speeches, in contrasting ways, lent support to core areas of the Saribas ideolect. In the final section I analyse the key tensions and contradictions in some of the media practices that shape the maintenance of the ideolect. Prior to that analysis, I wish to highlight the resilience of the Saribas ideolect during a 'black year'.

A Black Year

In 1997 a series of crises affected directly the lives of people across central and northern Borneo. These included a mysterious Coxsackie-B epidemic, a more familiar outbreak of dengue fever, gigantic forest fires billowing thick clouds of 'haze', the collapse of regional financial markets, and the return of head-hunting to Indonesian Borneo. Rural Iban reactions to these major crises are telling. A general sense of bewilderment enveloped the longhouses. For decades, longhouse dwellers had learnt to view major events through the frame of official radio and television. They had learnt about a rapidly developing Malaysia at peace with herself and her neighbours – a prosperous Malaysia that sent UN blue helmets (some of them Iban) to restore the peace in less fortunate countries. Meanwhile, the world beyond Malaysia was mired in chaos: pictures of starving African children, chronic warfare in the Middle East, assassinated Western leaders, said it all. One Iban woman complained to me: 'Those foreign countries, there are so many wars!'. Another said: 'You white people, when you disagree with someone you just shoot them, like you shot Kennedy'. Malaysian politicians, she added, do not even need bodyguards.

The televised crises of 1997, alas, revealed that all was not well with Malaysia. Yet, with minds nurtured since childhood by official and unofficial propaganda, local viewers lacked autonomous spaces from which to query the government's reports. It was not merely a problem of lack of access to non-governmental media. To be sure, unlike urban intellectuals, rural Iban had no direct access to the Internet, or to foreign television channels. More significantly, they were not in the habit of envisaging, let alone discussing, alternative interpretations of events to those presented by the governmental media. Gradually, as the crises eased, rural Iban returned from their initial bewilderment to a sense of normality. Doubts may have arisen, but they did not find a discursive outlet. All along state radio and television news broadcasts presented the prime minister and his cabinet making steady progress in overcoming the crises. For example, pictures of Malaysian helicopters flying over the border to assist the Indonesian fire fighters were repeatedly broadcast; as were soundbites by Mahathir reassuring the populace that all would end well.

Ramakrishna's expanded definition of propaganda as consisting of both discursive and non-discursive elements is helpful here. Decades of sustained official propaganda – both of words and deeds – have moulded rural Iban worldviews to such an extent that the political ideals of the urban establishment have become perfectly naturalised. For instance, rural Iban have tangible evidence that studying hard can lead to a clerical job that will generate a steady income, which is exactly what they have been told for decades. The propagandists – the priests, headmen, headmasters, radio broadcasters, politicians, schoolchildren, etc. – were right all along: school knowledge can be hugely important to individuals and their dependants. As a result, very few Iban parents doubt today the power of the printed word, so the vast majority of children are sent to school. This finding is at odds with the recent anthropological celebration of diverse 'literacies' in marginal areas of the globe (Street 1993, 2001, Bloch 1998, Kulick and Stroud 1993, etc.). When it comes to literacy, Iban parents feel they have little to celebrate and much work to do – as indeed do parents in Papua New Guinea (Sillitoe 2000: 210–211), Ghana (Goody 1987: 140–146) and across the developing world (chapter 6).

We should not disregard, however, the role of intentionality – as I suggested at the outset. The strong congruence between the aspirations and ideals of government and governed in Sarawak would have been unattainable without the 'wilful, intentional, and premeditated' efforts of state propagandists down the decades (Jowett and O'Donnell 1999: 6).

Sustainable Contradictions

No system of ideals is free from tensions and contradictions, as both Marxian and Jungian thinkers have often observed. New beliefs and desires, says Rorty (1991: 93), put strains on the old. Human agents use different techniques to tackle these tensions and inconsistencies. Throughout fieldwork in the Saribas, viewers complained about the declining standards of television. Malay soaps, very popular with RTM programmers in Kuala Lumpur at prime-time, were conspicuous for their absence from a popularity survey[7] I carried out early in 1997 in Saribas longhouses (see Table 5.1). The following three responses are characteristic of the general attitude towards Malay soaps.

1. Indai Saur is in her early 30s. When I asked her about television in the old days (*suba*) she told me there were no 'company stories' (*cherita syarikat-syarikat*) then, stories full of rich urban Malays always eating in expensive restaurants. She doesn't enjoy watching them. After the interview we watched a video they had rented, *George of the Jungle*, a new American comedy on the old theme of Tarzan and his troubles with

Table 5.1. Most popular television genres among Saribas Iban adult viewers.

Favourite Genre	*Responses*
News (*berita*)	54
Music/dancing (*lagu/joget*)	14
Football (*bul*)	11
War (*perang*)	10
Cartoons (*katun*)	4

Sample: 119 households in six longhouses.

Civilisation. Indai Saur, her husband and their young daughter enjoyed the action, especially the 'lies' achieved through 'computer animation' (*nya bula, dikena computer animation*). These lies allowed monkeys to speak and elephants to leap about like dogs. They also enjoyed George's uncouth antics in New York and admired the luxury shops. 'City people don't mind spending in shops, do they?', she asked me.

2. Indai Kamba is 30. She told me television programmes used to be better (*suba manah agi*) for there were no rich people, and the stories were true (*suba nadai urang kaya, betul-betul suba*). There were no companies run by arrogant urban Malays in those days. 'We in the longhouse don't like these stories. They've got cars, they eat well, they live in brick houses…' (*Kami rumah panjai enda rindu cherita nya. Sida bisi motor, makai manah enggau rumah batu…*).

3. Indai Rita, aged 33, upset my interviewing schedule, for she was reluctant to talk about radio. 'I don't know a thing! I'm not interested in radio' (*Enda aku nemu! Enda minat ka radio*), she said. 'What I *do* like is television. I'm a *modern* Iban!', she added with characteristic irony (*Tibi baru rindu meda. Aku Iban moden!*). She told me only old people know about *renong*, a type of sung poem sometimes broadcast on the radio, not young people such as herself. Besides, there was no one willing to teach them – 'and it's boring!' [English. term used], and we both laughed again. So we decided to talk about television. The trouble with television, according to Indai Rita, is that the standards have declined. 'Malay dramas are not very good, they're always about money' (*Wayang melayu enda manah, selalu pasal duit*). Broadcasters are no longer keen to air white-man films, she explained. Last night, however, there was a nice 'action movie' [English term used. The film was about four U.S. policemen who team up to destroy a foreign pimp]. She watched it with her siblings until midnight: 'When they have a sponsor, the films are better, like Dunhill for example'. She also enjoys watching quality soaps, such as *Santa Barbara*, which she intends to follow week after week until the end (*M. sambong-sambong sampai abis*). She has enjoyed similar white-people serials in the past, especially *Dallas* and *Dynasty*.

This collective rejection of an entire television genre (contemporary Malay soaps) on the basis of their being 'full of rich people eating in expensive restaurants' demands an explanation. A useful starting point is Freeman's thesis that Iban social ideology is profoundly egalitarian, as discussed in chapter 2. Freeman found that there were inequalities in terms of wealth and influence, but no institutionalised subordination. With his usual eloquence, he writes:

> Iban society is classless and egalitarian – and its members, individualists, aggressive and proud in demeanour, lacking any taste of obeisance (Freeman 1970: 129).

If Saribas viewers reject the Malay soaps because they clash with this egalitarian ethos, why then do they enjoy watching *Dallas, Dynasty,* or *Santa Barbara,* all three equally about the rich and powerful? In my view, their comments reveal an inherent contradiction in the Saribas ideolect – they tell us where the hinges creak, to paraphrase Debray (1996). The problem is best broached in terms developed in Gewertz and Errington's (1991) ethnography of the Chambri of Papua New Guinea. The Chambri are part of an

inter-ethnic regional exchange system premised on the equality of autonomous trade partners and knowledgeable elders – what these authors have
termed a 'system of commensurate differences'. By contrast, the exchanges
with overseas tourists and the wider world system are both incommensurate
and hierarchical (1991: 56, 164). During their extended fieldwork in the area,
they came to know a young man who had set out to write the first-ever
Chambri Bible, an attempt at reconciling Catholic and Chambri truths. In
an ethnographic twist that echoes a well-known Borges tale,[8] this man found
the resemblance between the two traditions to be so close that some passages
from his Bible read exactly like the Catholic original. He soon ran into difficulties, however. The elders, who were otherwise proud and relieved to see
their traditions preserved in print, would not relinquish the deeper levels of
their knowledge to the aspiring Evangelist. Having done that would have
allowed the literate young man to 'transcend and thus subvert the system of
commensurate differences' (1991: 166).

The sight of urban Malays flaunting their wealth on television is at logger-
heads with the Saribas Iban rejection of those fellow Iban who have 'climbed
the ladder' (*niki pangkat*) and become arrogant (*nyadi sumbung*) towards their
rural brethren. This rejection was apparent in the school essays analysed
earlier. Moreover, the RTM serials belie the daily propaganda videos on television and more irregular speeches on the radio and *ruai* in which all Malaysian
peoples (*bansa*) are walking abreast 'along the path to prosperity' (see chapter
9). The Saribas Iban system of commensurate differences is geopolitically
broader than the Chambri's – it is no longer riverine, as it encompasses the
whole of Malaysia. Ever since the consolidation of the state ideology in the
1960s and 1970s, Saribas Iban make use of an *inter-ethnic frame of reference*
in which the low standard of living of 'we Iban' (*kami Iban*) is constantly
contrasted with the higher standards of 'the Chinese' (*sida China*) and 'the
Malays' (*sida Melayu*). Alternatively 'we in the longhouse' (*kami ba rumah
panjai*) is counterposed to 'them in the cities' (*sida ba nengeri*) and similar
expressions. Television dramas are an important source of materials in this
ongoing comparative exercise: they provide viewers with what is seen as updated information on the brick houses, sports cars, exclusive restaurants, and
so on, of the rich. The remote, semi-mythical land of the white man is beyond
the pale of this system of commensurate differences. In other words, it is
incommensurate. As Indai Awas put it, 'The way they act in *Dallas* is different. They are truly developed (*maju endar*)'. White-man programmes, like all
white-man products, are considered to be of superior quality, as befits the
most advanced race (*bansa*) on Earth. The stories, as one viewer put it 'have
a logic' (*bisi logic*): they are beautifully shot and acted, whilst Malay dramas
are seen as pale reflections or shoddy imitations of the genuine articles (*sida
'ka nunda ka urang putih*, 'they want to follow the white people'). In the Iban
worldview, aesthetic accomplishment and race are inseparable.

The crucial difference between the Chambri and the Saribas Iban is that the Chambri elders successfully managed to prevent a literate man from subverting their egalitarian, parochial, fragmented, oral ideology. The Saribas elders have been less fortunate. They have long been relegated to a mostly ceremonial role with little real power or prestige knowledge within a nation-wide system premised on the mastery of cosmopolitan, literate knowledge. The Saribas Iban ideolect evolved in the 1960s and 1970s from a false premise: that 'knowing book' (*penemu surat*) would allow the Iban to march hand-in-hand with the two hegemonic peoples of Sarawak while helping to preserve (in print form) the egalitarian longhouse *adat*. In reality, states are built not on customary equality writ large but rather on modern inequalities.

Can Saribas viewers' rejection of Malay dramas be interpreted as a way of opting out of an ideological 'game' already rigged by the urban elites? Is it a short-term 'tactic' pitted against the longer-term strategies of the powerful (de Certeau 1984)? This interpretation would be in line with current metropolitan social theory. Yet a better way of looking at the problem is in terms of Douglas' (1984) textbook concept of dirt as 'matter out of place'. To Saribas Iban, the soaps are an irritating anomaly: they fall within the ideolectally-correct genre of television drama (*cherita tibi*), a genre classified as 'entertainment' (*hiburan*) and yet they subvert the old, prescriptive egalitarian ethos of their ideolect. For Clare Boulanger (pers. comm. 1998) a central question social scientists must address is 'how human beings collude, despite their better efforts, in fabricating and replicating conditions of oppression'. The rejection of these soaps is *both* an indirect form of 'peasant resistance' (cf. Scott 1985) to a hegemonic state system *and* a form of collusion in that it is tantamount to recognising: 'We know that our leaders' inter-ethnic egalitarianism is a sham (*bula*), but we don't want to be reminded of it'. What is crucial is not so much the existence of this opposition-collusion interpretive duality (analogous to Hall's [1973] 'negotiated reading'), much favoured in the recent media research literature (e.g., Mankekar 1999, Rofel 1994, Abu-Lughod 1997), but rather the fact that refusing to watch Malay soaps is a thoroughly ineffectual form of resistance, for it perpetuates the illusion of a nationwide equality despite mounting evidence to the contrary.

Migrant Propaganda

This account of Saribas Iban sustainable propaganda, focused on media practices and institutions, would be incomplete without a consideration of a non-media practice: migration. Like other peoples in the Archipelago, the Iban have an old tradition of young male migration (*bejalai* or *pegi*) in search of riches and adventure (Kedit 1993). As the Sarawakian economy developed, this indigenous institution came to resemble the rural-urban migrations found in developing countries around the globe. From the 1960s, large numbers of rural Iban – both men and women – have abandoned rice farming and migrated to urban areas, timber camps, offshore oil rigs, etc., in search of wages to support their families. More than any school lesson, this first-hand experience working for members of far wealthier and more powerful 'races' has taught rural Iban that status (*pangkat*) and reputation come to those with book knowledge, family riches and the right connections. Here Ramakrishna's Giddensian point about the unintended propagandistic effects of certain actions is apposite: migration has had the unintended consequence of reinforcing official nation-building propaganda.

Conclusion

We can now outline the main features of nation-building sustainable propaganda among the Saribas Iban. First, it is the result of *deliberate* campaigns by dedicated state propagandists and agencies over a period of decades. Some of the more influential of these agencies have been Radio Televisyen Malaysia (RTM), the Information Department, the Ministry of Education, the Borneo Literature Bureau, and its successor Dewan Bahasa dan Pustaka (chapters 3 and 4). These recurrent campaigns were supported by grassroots state agents, including local politicians, native chiefs, longhouse headmen, priests, teachers, parents and pupils. Second, nation-building propaganda has remained *relevant* to local people's concerns and aspirations. Here we can distinguish between long-term aspirations (e.g., a fully developed Malaysia by 2020) and short-term concerns (e.g., overcoming the 1997 crises). Third, this kind of propaganda is highly *consistent* across media and social formations, as we saw when we reviewed propaganda forms in the school, longhouse and church. Fourth, *non-media institutions*, such as migration, can have the unintended effect of aiding nation-building propaganda, in this case, by offering migrants and non-migrants alike yardsticks with which to measure their relative 'progress' or stagnation in the race to national modernity. Finally, negative reactions to Malay soap operas are but one example of *ineffectual resistance* to the dominant ideology. In terms of Hall's (1973) influential model of audience reception, most Saribas Iban television viewers adopt a 'dominant' (i.e., dominated) position with regard to official discourses. Having been socialised into a parochial dialect of the ruling coalition's ideology, they have no critical haven to repair to when bombarded with state propaganda.

Notes

1. See the project 'Sustainable Propaganda' (*Nachhaltige Propaganda*) by Oliver Ressler, at www.kunstundbuecher.at/propaganda.
2. My usage of the term 'ideolect' refers to *ideology*, not language. It is not to be confused with the linguistic notion of 'idiolect' (occasionally misspelled 'ideolect'), that is an individual's idiosyncratic way of speaking her mother tongue. Further, it should be confused neither with the German term *Ideolect*, that is the language of privileged groups such as intellectuals (www.sociologicus.de/lexikon/lex_soz/f_j/ideolect.htm), nor with Paul Dowling's 'high discursive saturation practices' (www.ioe.ac.uk/ccs/dowling/c2000/level.html), nor further with Bakhtin's suggestion that speakers of 'different generations, classes, places, professions, have their own dialects, or ideolects' (www.brocku.ca/english/courses/4F70/bakhtin.html).
3. This sequence of pitying followed by assisting the needy has deep cultural roots. It closely resembles one of Richards' (1981: 350) dictionary examples of the uses of the term *sinu'*: '*laban penyinu' hati ia, ia ngusong aku*, because he was moved to pity, he came to help me'.
4. *The X-Files* has generated a strong international following, including a large number of websites and chat groups on the Internet. For a range of textual analyses of this series see Lavery et al. (1996).
5. Jawan (1994: 268) glosses *enda mereti* as 'bad mannered; mischievous'.
6. According to Shaw (*Newsweek*, 1 September 1997), when the currency crisis of 1997 struck Southeast Asia, governments in the region spent $15 billion in foreign exchange markets, 'all for naught'. This sum, he argues, would have sufficed to endow a number of world-class universities in the region. In his view, without 'intellectual capital' Southeast Asia will remain a centre for cheap labour and low margin products, and will still have to rely on higher-cost, knowledge-intensive imports from the developed countries. See also Musa (2004) on the Malaysian education system, Jawan (1994: 208–213) on the politics of rural education in Sarawak and Sweeney (1987) on orality and literacy among Peninsular Malay university students.
7. The question 'What is/are your favourite programme/s on television?' (*Nama cerita ba TV dikerindu ka nuan?*) was open-ended, that is no set menu of genres was suggested to the respondent. In this manner, a standard ideolectal classification of television programmes into 'genres' or kinds emerged, a sample of which is captured in Table 5.1.
8. J.L.Borges, 'Pierre Menard, Autor del Quijote', in his *Ficciones* (1995).

6

WRITING MEDIA

From Wet Womb to Dry Tomb

In 1984, the French anthropologist Maurice Bloch attended a conference in Eastern Madagascar on regional history. The attendants were mostly Malagasy academics and students, although there were a few foreign scholars as well. As is the usual practice in Madagascar, the papers were delivered in French, the language of the former colonial power. There was one exception. Arthur Besy, a renowned regional politician and intellectual, delivered a speech in Malagasy that lasted some two hours – well beyond the allocated fifteen minutes. The speech dealt with the origin of a local place name. It was traditional in its formal structure, 'stuffed full of proverbs and scriptural illustrations, redolent with repetitions, certain passages recurring again and again rather like the chorus in a popular song'. Besy's academic compatriots, accustomed to more Cartesian renditions, were not overly convinced (Bloch 1998: 155). At certain passages in his speech, Besy boasted about his great accomplishments in life as a diplomat and as a man of traditional learning. He found that the work of the young Francophone scholars had its own rationale but lacked the deep historical significance of his own contribution.

According to Bloch, Malagasy culture places great significance on the distinction between everyday language and oratory (*kabary*), which parallels that between the young and the elderly. Young people are 'wet', their bones are not yet hardened, their words and deeds lack wisdom. Knowledgeable elders are different: they have developed a dry, ancestral element over the years. Their oratory prowess is proof that they have the blessing of the ancestors. The process of drying up will be completed after their deaths, when they will have 'lost all wet individuality and will be entirely dry ancestor' (1998: 156). Bloch sees this process as a form of lifelong possession or colonisation: individual persons are colonised by the 'dry coral' of the ancestors, which is all that will remain in their tombs in the form of dry bones. Besy saw his speech as the passing down of ancestral knowledge to a wet audience. He was blessing the hearers with the dry wisdom of his words.

The purpose of Bloch's story is to undermine Jack Goody's (1968, 1977, 1986) 'autonomous' theory of literacy (Street 1993). Goody is usually seen as the chief proponent of the 'great divide' model, based on the notion that orality and literacy have radically different social, institutional and cognitive effects. Although Goody has modified his stance slightly in response to his critics (Goody 1986) he is still associated with the idea of literacy as an 'autonomous' institution. Authors of this persuasion are said to 'conceptualise literacy in technical terms, treating it as independent of social context, an autonomous variable whose consequences for society and cognition can be derived from its intrinsic character' (Street 1993: 5). In essence, Goody argues that literacy is a fundamental institution in the history of mankind. It allowed the ancient Greeks to build a democratic state and the rudiments of a modern science. Pre-literate societies, in contrast, bury knowledge in a web of social relations; what really matters in a statement is not its truth but who says it. For instance, genealogical knowledge is ceaselessly reshaped to fit present interests. With the advent of literacy, people were able to challenge the elders using historical documents. The seed of critical thought, says Goody, had been sown. Over time, literacy allowed the passage from small-scale groupings to complex state societies.

Against this thesis, which he deems Eurocentric and deterministic, Bloch (1998: 153–154) contends that we have to locate literacy within the wider cultural and historical processes of a given society. In Madagascar, literacy did not alter in any fundamental way the indigenous systems of knowledge. When nineteenth-century missionaries translated the Bible into Imerina, local leaders reacted by producing their own 'Bibles' in which they sought to legitimise their own genealogies and myths of origin. They saw the Bible as a threat not because it brought to the country a new kind of knowledge, but because a new technology was being harnessed to promote the same kind of knowledge. For the Imerina Queen, the missionaries wanted 'to make the Malagasy worship the ancestors of the Europeans: Moses and Jesus Christ in order that they stopped worshipping my ancestors: Andriananpoinimerina and Radama'. The Malagasy, a highly pragmatic people, took this and other European technologies and turned them to their own uses (1998: 159–160). As a result, they regard the written or printed word as an extension of oratory. To Bloch, Besy is not a naïve indigene stumbling upon a new medium. He is a knowledgeable elder working within a century-old tradition of Malagasy literature that continues to flourish alongside oral forms.

The Merina are certainly more literate than the English middle classes yet most of their work is like that produced by Besy, though usually shorter. Literacy has not transformed the nature of Merina knowledge – it has confirmed it (Bloch 1998: 161).

One is tempted to export Bloch's suggestive model of Malagasy literacy to Borneo. After all, the island of Madagascar is considered an integral part of the Austronesian world, albeit a remote one (Fox 1993). Like the Merina, rural societies in Insular Southeast Asia

> tend to have deep stockpiles of oral knowledge about the past. They typically present such knowledge in public ritual speech performances at such events as the dedication of new villages, funerals, stone monument dedications, and bone-reburial ceremonies. Such occasions call for poetic evocations of a transcendent past, recalled via such spoken genres as rhymed couplet speeches. During these special ritual times, which often go on for several hours, orators sometimes are said to speak "with the voice of the ancestors", and the living world of contemporary humans momentarily touches the shadow world of dead forebears (Rodgers 1995: 30).

As I read about Arthur Besy, I was reminded of Benedict Sandin, the Iban folklorist and ethnohistorian mentioned in previous chapters. Like Besy's people, the Iban speak of ordinary versus formal language, or 'shallow language' (*jako mabu*) as opposed to 'deep language' (*jako dalam*). Sandin, like Besy, turned literacy to his advantage by drawing on his vast oral knowledge and oratorical skills. For both distinguished men, literacy became an avenue to improving their cultural competence while helping to renew their indigenous cultures. Literacy was not, therefore, a break with their cultural traditions, as a strong version of Goody's autonomous theory would predict. On the contrary, it reinforced those traditions. Bloch's understanding of literacy would seem, then, more suited to the Iban case. There are, however, difficulties with this approach, as I explain below (on Bloch's anti-diffusionism, see chapter 1).

Ibangelism

A more recent example of Iban uses of literacy comes from my own 1998 fieldwork along the Skrang river. Our historical knowledge of this river is scant by comparison to that of the neighbouring Saribas. Few genealogies have survived, probably as a result of the migration of leading Skrang families and ritual experts to the Rejang basin and beyond during the nineteenth and twentieth centuries (Sandin 1967: 29). The rubber boom that transformed many parts of the East Indies, including the Saribas, from the turn of the century to the 1930s, bypassed the war-ridden Skrang (Uchibori 1988: 256). The time-honoured solution to overpopulation and political instability, migration, was still practised in the 1930s, when numerous families (*bilek*) migrated to other areas of Sarawak in search of virgin forests. Often the 'migration leaders' (*pun pindah*) took along with them the local ritual specialists, i.e., the chief augur (*tuai burung*), the bard (*lemambang*) and the healer or shaman (*manang*). Thus numerous longhouses were left behind without a single ritual specialist. With hindsight, we can say that the way was paved for future missionary activities. In my own chosen field site, a longhouse at Nanga Tebat, my best historical informant could not trace the origin of the community further than five generations. Today, as I said in chapter 2, the Skrang lacks 'that quality of community and continuity' that one finds in the Saribas basin, and especially along Sandin's Paku river (Pringle 1970: 208). This is ironical considering that tourists from around the world come to the Skrang to experience what is packaged as a 'traditional Iban longhouse'.

In 1998 Nanga Tebat had 22 *bilek*-families living in temporary houses (*dampa*) while they completed construction of a new longhouse (perhaps too 'modern', some feared, to attract future tourists). Five years previously, and having been bereft of ritual experts for sixty years, the residents became Anglican Christians, with the exception of one remaining pagan family. According to D. Bingham (1983: 121), a veteran Catholic missionary from England who works in the Rejang, for most longhouse dwellers who have converted 'the all important functions of the Christian religion are the family blessings of the [long]house, home and farm'. New converts, he adds, 'really do feel a great sense of deliverance from the burdens, fears and taboos of paganism … the simple saying of a Hail Mary can be sufficient to give them courage and

Figure 6.1.   A Skrang healer (*manang*) treating a patient.

remind them that God is with them' (1983: 121–22). This is precisely how Nanga Tebat converts feel about their new religion. As two men put it to me:

1. *[Jalai pendigup kami diatu] manah agi laban nadai penanggul, terus kerja, nadai jaku mali-mali, nadai burung-burung.*

2. *Nyamai nyadi keristen: nadai mayuh pengawa.*

1. [Nowadays our way of life] is better because there are no longer any hindrances, we can get on with our work, there's no talk about taboos or omens.

2. It's nice to be a Christian: there's not much [ritual] work to do.

We should be aware, however, of the strong continuities that characterise many Christian practices in Austronesian societies. Bloch (1998: 87) has this to say about Catholicism among the Zafimaniry of Madagascar:

> [E]ven for those most involved in the church, Catholic belief and practice is, and has always been, only an *added* element on top of traditional religious beliefs and practices … Foremost among these traditional beliefs and practices are those concerning ancestors. These seem to remain almost totally unaffected by equally strongly held Christian beliefs.

Similarly, despite the best post-pagan intentions of the priest and his Nanga Tebat deputy, the local lay reader, a close examination of the longhouse's service register revealed that both performed a significant number of rites based on pre-Christian beliefs and practices. Indeed far more pagan-derived services were officiated (18) than strictly Christian ones (5), and the list could have grown to be even longer, to judge by the contents of the prayer books.[1] This demonstrates the strong continuity of religious practices despite the priest's repeated anti-syncretistic tirades. I shall mention briefly but one of the services based on pagan notions and practices: *sambiang manggol. Manggol* is a term traditionally reserved for 'the rites and technical actions that mark the commencement of the annual rice-farming cycle' (Sather 1992: 109, cf. Freeman 1992 [1955]: 173). The first rites are known as *mantap*, literally to slash or cut, and they centre on slashing the undergrowth that occupies the site of the *bilek*-family's 'seed pillow' (1992: 117). In pagan families they are followed by a *mantap* invocation (*sampi kena mantap*). The one recorded by Sather in 1984 took place in the Paku area and was recited by the farmer's brother-in-law:

O, ni kita	O, where are you
petara aki	Spirits of our grandfathers
petara ini?	Spirits of our grandmothers?
Ti dulu kalia ke dulu nubah	You who long ago opened the
tanah mungkal menoa tu.	bountiful land of this domain.
Kita ka dulu berumpang,	You who first felled the jungle,

besawang,	Cleared the land,
berimba,	Cut down the virgin forest,
ngaga temuda dulu kalia?	Who first created an estate of farmland?
Kami tu anak,	We are your children,
telesak,	Your offspring,
uchu ambu kita,	Your favourite descendants,
Deka bumai dalam menoa tu.	Who wish to farm this land.
Nganti tulong urat	We take your place,
kita ka dulu menya	You who have long ago gone before us,
Nya alai kita enda tau enda	We attend with care to the work
ngemata,	Which you have entrusted to us,
lalu ngintu pengawa kami tu	
Laban kami tu meh uchu	Because we are your beloved
ambu kita,	grandchildren,
Darah getah kita,	Your flesh and blood,
nampong nerujong,	your true descendants,
Ngintu bilik penaik kita	We carefully look after your legacy.
Nya alai kita enda tau enda	Therefore help us so that I do
nulong nukong aku dalam	not suffer unhappiness while I
umai tu.	work this farm.
Beri penglantang ngagai aku	Bring me spiritual contentment
baka kita ka dulu kalia	such as you enjoyed in former times.

(Sather 1992: 118–119)

This invocation, as interpreted by Sather (1992: 119–120), serves two purposes. First, it establishes the family's legal right, in accordance to the local custom (*adat*), to the cultivation of land secured by their ancestors. The family members are, after all, the ancestors' 'favourite descendants'. Second, the invocation asks the spirits of the ancestors (*petara aki, petara ini*) for protection from misfortune and the assurance of farming success.

In June 1997, I attended a *sampi manggol* officiated by a native Iban Anglican priest on behalf of the headman at Nanga Tebat. Instead of reciting from memory, as a pagan officiator would have done, the father read out of a Catholic book of prayer based on both Iban and Christian notions and appropriately entitled *Adat Kristian* (Marcus n.d.). The following is an extract from that prayer:

O Allah Taala aki, Allah Taala ini	O, God grandfather, God grandmother
Allah Taala apai, Allah Taala indai	God father, God mother
Apai Jesus Kristus ti di-regang ka kitai	Father of Jesus Christ who was crucified for us
Kami bepanggai betuai	We have faith in you and follow
Ka Nuan siko aja Allah Taala	No other than you, the one and only God
Kami arap kami ngadap	We have trust in you and appear before
Ka Nuan, Tuhan Jesus, ti Penebus dunya.	You, Lord Jesus, Redeemer of the world.

Figure 6.2. Skrang men working on a burnt hillside. They are using long staffs (*tugal*) to dibble holes for rice seed.

Nuan udah ngalah ka Sitan leboh di-regang	You defeated Satan while on the cross.
Lalu Nuan udah besemaya	You promised
Deka ngubah samoa dunya nyadi baru,	To make the world anew,
Nudok ka perintah ti manah,	To build a just Kingdom,
Endor samoa orang deka nitih ka ator	A place where all men will abide by the laws
	of our Father who is in Heaven
Apai ti di serega	
Endor nadai laya, nadai apa nama;	A place free from strife and sorrow;
Endor senang, endor lantang,	A place of peace and joy,
Endor tanah lemak, tanah luchak	A place where the land is soft and fecund,
Endor padi, endor puli.	A place richly fertile.[2]

(*Adat Kristian* n.d.: 14, my translation)

This prayer does not simply invoke a new Christian God in place of the old pagan gods or spirits. It actually calls on a manner of 'Holy Sextinity' consisting of three paired divinities: (a) the 'spirits of our grandfathers and grandmothers' we met in the pagan prayers, now turned into manifestations of God (*Allah Taala*), (b) two new parental divinities, and (c) two members of the Holy Trinity, namely Jesus Christ and his/our Father 'who is in Heaven'

119

Figure 6.3. Skrang women sowing the rice in the wake of the men's dibbling (*nugal*).

– but without the Holy Spirit. I will not indulge here in ethno-theological speculations on the binary and transformative nature of much (religious) thought (Leach 1976). Yet I need to stress the *continuity* of this prayer with antecedent prayers, whereby Iban notions of ancestry are preserved.

There is, however, a fundamental political change at work here: it is no longer the farmer's ancestors who are called upon for spiritual help and legal recognition, but rather the divine ancestors of all mankind. Furthermore, it is no longer the *bilek*-family and their closest relations (*kaban*) who perform this most crucial farming ritual, but rather an outside agent on behalf of the new Divinities. A third related development is the sheer *complexity* of such syncretistic notions, a fact that can be overshadowed by the apparent simplification and shortening of ritual practice introduced by the Christian agents. Only trained priests are qualified to delve in the intricacies of the new belief system. All three factors are proof of a power/knowledge shift from the local authority and oral knowledge of the elders to the cosmopolitan authority and literate knowledge of a younger priest. On the larger scale of Sarawak, this shift has been in the making since the arrival of European missionaries over 150 years ago.

Figure 6.4. A Skrang farm hut (*langkau umai*).

Flaws in the Ideological Model

I will now turn briefly to the interdisciplinary field of literacy studies to better situate my argument. Figure 6.5 provides a sample of works on, or related to, literacy organised by topic (cf. Figure 6.6) to give some indication of the rich diversity of this problem area. Its practitioners have addressed three main questions:

1. Is literacy a uniform, unilinear phenomenon?

2. Can literacy be studied independently from its social and political contexts?

3. What are the cognitive effects, if any, of literacy? (Cole and Nicolopoulou 1992)

From the 1980s onwards, scholars in education, sociology, linguistics and other fields began to favour 'ethnographic' and qualitative approaches to the study of literacy. Gradually some scholars developed a perspective opposed to the autonomous model known as 'the ideological model'. In their view, literacy practices are hugely diverse and always entangled with power relations.

They reject any idea of a 'great divide' between orality and literacy and explore instead context-specific oral/literate 'mixes' in a range of societies, the stress being on how ideology guides literacy practices (Street 1993: 7–13). The ideological approach enjoys today paradigmatic status within the anthropological research area of literacy. Given this rarely disputed pre-eminence I will now point at three of its flaws by way of a foundational study: Kulick and Stroud's chapter, 'Conceptions and uses of literacy in a Papua New Guinean village', in Street's (1993) important volume *Cross-Cultural Approaches to Literacy*. This volume introduced the interdisciplinary field of 'New Literacy Studies', together with the ideological paradigm, to British social anthropology. It was here that Bloch first addressed the problem of literacy through his Malagasy data.

Culture	Graff 1987, Wagner 1993
Development	Grillo and Rew 1985, Wagner 1993, Olson and Torrance 2001, Robinson-Plant 2001, Street 2001
Education	Spindler 1974, Hanson 1979, Bourdieu 1984, Freire 1985, Collins 1986, Erikson and Bekker 1986, Varenne and McDermott 1986, Bloch 1993, Camitta 1993, Besnier 1995, Doronilla 1996, Rival 1997, Hornberger 1998, Aikman 1999
Emotion	Besnier 1995
Ethnicity and nationalism	Gellner 1983, Wagner 1983, Fishman 1986, Grohs 1990, Reder and Wikelund 1993
Gender	Radway 1984, Horsman 1989, Yates 1994, Robinson-Pant 2001
Historical evolution	Havelock 1976, Goody 1977, 1986, 1987, Ong 1982, Harris 1986, Barton 1988, Houston 1988
Identity	Lewis 1993, King 1994, Rival 1997, Slater 1998, Sheridan et al 1999
Ideology	Street 1984
Indigenous knowledge	Kulick and Stroud 1993, Rival 1997, Aikman 1999
Indigenous resistance	Bourgois 1986, Grohs 1990, Collins 1998
Power, politics	Spolsky et al 1983, Freire 1985, Grillo 1990, Besnier 1995
Reading	Radway 1984, Boyarin 1993
Religion	Spolsky et al 1983, Smalley et al 1990, Probst 1993
Restricted literacy	Bourdieu 1984, Doronilla 1996
Secrecy	Scribner and Cole 1981, Bledsoe and Robey 1993
Self and person	Besnier 1991, Kulick and Stroud 1993
Social change	Jackson 1975, Thomas 1986, Street 1987, Smalley et al 1990
Social practice	Cook-Gumperz 1986, Prinsloo and Breier 1996, Barton & Hamilton 1998, Barton & Hall 1999, Barton et al 1999, Sheridan et al 1999
Speaking and writing	Shuman 1986, Chafe and Tannen 1987, Sweeney 1987, Finnegan 1988, Chartier 1989, Woolard 1989, Stetter 1997
Trade	Street 1984, Kalman 1999
Witchcraft	Bastian 1993
Writing	Basso 1989, Swzed 1981, Walker 1981, Archetti 1994, Barton & Hamilton 1999, Barton et al 1999, Fishman 1991, Scheridan et al 1999

Figure 6.5. A sample of contributions to literacy studies by subject-matter.

Kulick and Stroud question the notion, widespread amongst both missionaries and their secular critics across the Pacific, that literacy 'constitutes a kind of potent, active force in itself, and that it acts as an 'agent' of 'linguistic, religious and social change' (1993: 31). To these anthropologists, such a notion resonates with the autonomous scholars' thesis that literacy transforms 'cognitive processes, social institutions and historical consciousness'. True to the ideological spirit, Kulick and Stroud, 'rather than stress how literacy affects people, [...] want to take the opposite tack and examine how people affect literacy' (1993: 31).

They argue their case on the basis of field research in Gapun, a small village in the lower Sepik area of Papua New Guinea (henceforth PNG), in 1986–1987. While local children usually attend school for three to six years, Gapun adults use literacy in two broad ways: in relation to Christian teachings, and to aid interpersonal relations, e.g., to write messages requesting assistance, list names, or record deaths (1993: 33). For instance, Kulick once received a note written in the form of a compressed, flowery speech asking for his help towards financing a conciliatory feast. The authors interpret this note as an extension of vernacular forms of oratory – the anthropologist was being 'orated at' rather than written to. In a society where interpersonal relations often verge on conflict, such notes avoid embarrassment as they tread the thin line between asking and ordering (1993: 50–52). Significantly absent from Gapun, certainly when compared to Sarawak longhouses, was the modernist belief that everybody should learn how to read and write (1993: 32–33). Gapun's worldview is millenarian, and modern schooling is seen as a way of one day learning 'the secret of the Cargo'. The only non-religious texts local adults ever read are glossy brochures from U.S. mail order firms.

> Proclaiming triumphantly that they have finally found the 'road' they have been seeking, young men sit down and write brief letters to the addresses they find in the front of the brochures, requesting that the Cargo be sent to them forthwith (1993: 41).

Kulick and Stroud reach the conclusion that Gapun villagers have been 'active and creative in their encounter with literacy', turning it to their own uses. They have 'their own ideas about reading and writing, generated from their own cultural concerns' (1993: 55). This 'ideological' analysis – very close, of course, to Bloch's – is marred on three counts. The first flaw has to do with the authors' notion of 'creativity'. In this connection, it is useful once again to outline Richard Rorty's (1991: 94–95) theory of belief acquisition. As it will be remembered from the previous chapter, Rorty distinguishes between 'paradigms of inference' and 'paradigms of imagination'. Paradigms of inference occur when our logical space does not change, that is 'when no new candidates for belief are introduced', e.g., when we add up a column of figures or run down a flow-chart. Paradigms of imagination, by contrast, include giving new meanings to old words, inventing beliefs, and colligating 'hitherto unrelated texts'. Gewertz and Errington's (1991) PNG ethnography of the Chambri, also mentioned in the previous chapter, offers us a good example of an imaginative indigenous colligation of texts. In terms of Rorty's theory, the elders skilfully managed to prevent the man from introducing 'new candidates for belief' into the local pool of beliefs, thereby protecting their own claims to ancestral knowledge.

We are told of no equivalent manoeuvres in Gapun. As we can glean from Kulick and Stroud's (1993: 35) own description, the place has been caught up since at least the Second World War in a long process of socio-economic and ideological 'involution' (cf. Geertz 1963), a half-century marked by recurrent outbreaks of millenarian activity – in the 1940s, 1950s, 1965–1966, and as recently as 1987. Some Gapun villagers have acquired literacy skills, yet they have turned them to cargo-related and other local uses that offer them few insights into the political economy of PNG and beyond. Unlike the Chambri evangelist, Gapun cargoists operate under a paradigm of inference wherein imported materials and skills, including school literacy, leave the local ideological space largely unchanged. In stark contrast, parents in other parts of PNG do see schools as roads to the wider world. According to Sillitoe (2000: 210–211) many parents are rejecting pilot school projects in local vernaculars (*tokples*) as second rate. They are demanding that their children be taught in English. Like parents in Sarawak (Seymour 1974) and other developing countries, they see an English-language education as their best chance for upward mobility. Meanwhile *nouveaux riches* in Wewak and elsewhere are sending their children to 'international' schools originally built to cater for colonial expatriates. Armed with the cosmopolitan literate knowledge acquired at these schools, some have even won newspaper-run English poetry competitions to celebrate Mother's Day (Gewertz and Errington 1999: 71). Therefore in marginal Gapun, with its 'specialized mythology' (Appadurai 1986: 48) we can only speak of *inferential* creativity, tight ideological parameters and political impotence. Indeed, although Gapun residents suspect that the Catholic clergy and national government are concealing the secret of the cargo from them, 'all the villagers can hope to do is read and reread the texts they possess ... hoping that someday they may stumble onto a clue that will reveal to them the 'true' meaning of the words contained in their books' (Kulick and Stroud 1993: 55).

The second flaw in the ideological ethnography under consideration derives from the authors' impoverished notion of agency. Recall that they reject the popular idea that literacy can be an 'agent' of change (1993: 31). To them, social agency is the sovereign monopoly of humans. Here we can refer to a growing number of studies exploring the agency of non-human entities, including institutions (Douglas 1986), art objects and images (Gell 1998), biographical objects (Hoskins 1998), homes (Miller 2001), television sets (this book, chapter 6), broadcast discourse (Spitulnik 1996), religious beliefs (Boyer 2000), websites (Miller 2000) and even the agency arising from an 'abeyance of [human] agency' during certain ritual stages (Miyazaki 2000). As these studies suggest, we should pay much more attention than we have so far to 'forms of agency that do not necessarily privilege the autonomy of human agents' (Miyazaki 2000: 31). Proponents of the ideological model, then, reject the autonomy of literacy only to exaggerate the autonomy of human agents.

The third flaw concerns geopolitics. Kulick and Stroud are all too eager to contrast their micro-sociological rural data with broad assertions about literacy among 'Euro-Americans':

> Meaning in Gapun is … the responsibility of the listener or the recipient of speech. In this sense, village communicative expectations differ importantly from those common to middle-class Euro-Americans, among whom the burden of successful communication is seen to lie with the speaker, who is expected to strain to 'get across' his or her viewpoints and thoughts to the listener (1993: 54–55).

Contrasts of this type do not help us to understand the geopolitical dimensions of Gapun literacy. In fact they cloud our vision by positing a sharp West-Rest dichotomy rather than comparing the histories of literacy in commensurate regions, say, Western Europe and Melanesia, as well as the distinctive *national* histories that are still unfolding within those two culture areas. Moreover, we are offered a contrast between a small Melanesian village and a vague socio-economic category ('the middle class') spread across two continents. It is more fruitful, in my view, to compare and contrast like with like. For instance, Lewis (1993) has written an insightful essay on the modern history of literacy in the Horn of Africa by comparing Somalia and Ethiopia. In the Gapun case, we would have benefited far more from a comparison with other localities in PNG, both rural and urban. In the current post-colonial order, largely built on North Atlantic principles, two central expectations are the universal provision of school education and the eradication of illiteracy. When certain groups within a state (e.g., Wewak elites) embrace modernist forms of literacy, others negotiate them (e.g., the Chambri), and still others, such as Gapun villagers, reject or are unaware of such forms, this all makes for fertile comparative ground – as well as having urgent practical implications. Literacy may not have greatly altered Gapun's cultural traffic sub-system, but it is undoubtedly central to the growing disparities in the distribution of cultural capital through the PNG system.

The Anthropologies of Literacy and Media

The ideological model of literacy betrays a form of ethnographic reduction-ism that also afflicts other anthropological discourses on near-global institutions, including money (e.g., Bloch and Parry 1989), clock and calen-dar time (e.g., Gingrich 1994), and television (e.g., Abu-Lughod 1997). To be sure, these different problem areas have varied histories but they all share a commitment to celebrating micro-cultural diversity at the expense of geopo-litical and historical comparison. In this respect, the parallel histories of literacy and media anthropology are instructive. While the former was shaped around a rejection of the optimistic technological determinism of 'auton-omous' scholars, media anthropology has reached its own 'ideological' consensus through rejecting what was seen as the *pessimistic* determinism of the Frankfurt School regarding the impact of mass media technologies (see Ginsburg's 1993, 1994 search for a third way).

The reasons for the continued separation of these two anthropological subfields deserve a study in their own right. After all, the points of contact and overlap are numerous, not least having to contend with neighbouring disciplines that have eagerly taken 'ethnographic turns' in recent decades. Consider, for instance, the work on women's popular literature (Radway 1984), Indian cinema turned into Nigerian novels (Larkin 1997), popular cinema and sermons in Ghana (Meyer 2004), teleported texts on Aboriginal television (Michaels 1991), foreign correspondents in Central America and elsewhere (Pedelty 1995, Hannerz 1996), computer software production in France (Born 1997), internet relay chat (IRC) and pornography (Slater 1998), etc. Most of these media ethnographies entail not only a study of orality, liter-acy and textuality, but also of the relationship between textuality and *visuality*. The local oral/literate mixes identified by literacy scholars are often oral/textual/visual mixes of increased complexity as more media technologies are appropriated in local and occupational settings around the world. It is there-fore more pertinent today to speak of 'oral/media mixes' than of 'oral/literate mixes'.

A good example of a thick oral/media mix can be found in Georgina Born's (1997) ethnography of an artificial intelligence (AI) music research centre in Paris. This organisation is constantly buffeted by the conflicting agencies of hierarchical programming codes, intricate musical scores, obsolescent software and hardware, powerful U.S. multinationals, a demanding local management, and a team of post-1968 libertarian programmers. Faced with baroque, poorly documented 'ancestral' programs, the local AI researchers often have to fall back on two ancient human achievements in order to decipher them: orality and sociality. In other words, they have to find veteran colleagues who are willing and able to translate their half-forgotten encoded knowledge into oral discourse. Born faced severe practical problems of her own: not only did she have to translate from the 'corporate culture' of AI experts into that of AI-deprived anthropologists – she first had to attend to the myriad kinds of translations that went on *within* the organisation. These involved at least four 'literacies' – alphabetic, numerical, musical and cybernetic – and a number of specialised ones, notably the many programs and codes used over the decades. It is to Born's credit that she has handled this cybernetic Babel with great dexterity. Her case study suggests nonetheless the need for media and literacy anthropologists to undertake team research in increasingly multi-textual and multi-mediated locales that defy the capacity of any single fieldworker. This could extend, of course, to non-anthropologists. Eric Hirsch's (1994) collaborative work with media theorists on information and communications technologies (ICTs) in British homes has set a worthy precedent in this latter category.

If literacy and media anthropologists are to cooperate in future they should, at any rate, address a major methodological issue downplayed by the

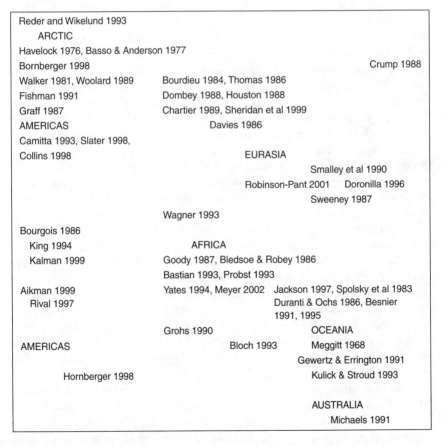

Figure 6.6. A sample of contributions to literacy studies by geographical area.

ideological model: how to define, research, and compare oral/media mixes in commensurate social formations such as villages, social networks, companies and states (cf. Barnard 2000: 57, Gingrich and Fox 2002). It will no longer do to contrast a Melanesian village with 'the Western middle-class'. As a small step in this direction, in Figure 6.6 I sketch out one of the hidden geographical dimensions of literacy studies.

The Geopolitics of Iban Literacy

At this juncture my ethnographic account has to part ways with that of Bloch and other 'ideological' authors. It would not be difficult to rummage through my field notes and find further examples of how the Iban have appropriated literacy in their own, non-Western terms. For instance, I could talk about the young man in the Bintulu area whose services are much in demand as a ghost writer of love letters in poetic Iban. Or I could analyse the letters from a labourer (*kuli*) to his *bilek*-family apologising in formulaic terms for not being able to fulfil his ritual obligations owing to work pressures (cf. Besnier 1993 on Polynesian letters). Or focus on that same migrant labourer's notebook; especially on his use of literacy for a variety of 'traditional' purposes, including the recording of a plaintive poem (*pantun sabana*), a minor rite (*biau pengabang*), home remedies against stomach ache, tuberculosis, poisoning, etc., as well as a variety of charms intended to woo a lover, humble a proud woman, appease an irate wife, break up a marriage, and so on. I could also study the massive annual sending of Dayak Festival greeting cards containing a standardised, neo-invocatory message (*Selamat gayu guru, gerai nyamai*, etc.), or analyse the script of a longhouse quiz show on Iban lore I once attended (chapter 9). Alternatively, I could trace the metamorphoses of segments of Iban discourse as they travel in and out of the oral/aural and textual domains. For example, local legends as they are initially told to Thomas T. Laka, a popular broadcast storyteller, who then records, transcribes, edits, proofreads and reads them out on air so that they can return, in a new form, to the oral/aural domain where they originated – or more precisely, to thousands of clusters of listeners across Sarawak (cf. Spitulnik 1996 on Zambian radio). I could also try to assess the influence of literacy on 'deep' (*dalam*) speech-making, as more and more orators today commit their thoughts to writing before their nervous performances in front of a longhouse microphone (when many literally feel 'out of their depth').

All these instances of indigenisation would merit further study. However, if considered by themselves, in their micro-settings, they may distract us from more pressing 'macro' actualities. More concretely, they may conceal the political truth that Sarawak is, and has been since its inception in the mid-nineteenth century, a state built on an ethnic division of labour and knowledge. Whilst the Iban and other Dayaks form a predominantly poor rural population, most ethnic Chinese are urban and have a much higher average income and level of formal education. The government is, however, in the hands of the Melanau Muslim minority, in rivalry with the Malays who, although the majority at national level, represent but one fifth of the population of Sarawak (Jawan 1994: 189–223).

To sketch out the geopolitics of literacy in Sarawak it is useful to revisit the work of Jack Goody (1987: 3) who carried out field research into orality and literacy in rural West Africa. In the early days, he reports, some people in the region used literacy to communicate with supernatural agents. Being illiterate was not shameful then. Yet with the consolidation of a colonial administration, success in life was increasingly associated with those who 'know book'. In Ghana, legal innovations in the 1930s put pressure on the native chiefs to become literate. The country's first native parliamentarians, elected in 1951, were schoolteachers and clerks, not traditional chiefs. The illiterate were effectively barred from the new corridors of power. The arrival of radio kept the elders informed of developments in other parts of Ghana and beyond, but it could be no substitute for 'know book' (1987: 140–143). To Goody, literacy has had a profound impact on rural identities in West Africa, for 'those who remain behind … begin to see themselves as inferior to those who have learnt book and gone away' (1987: 146).

An akin process unfolded in rural Sarawak. The Iban equivalent of the Ghanaian term 'know book' is the identical *nemu surat*, a phrase frequently used by older illiterate farmers to describe the brighter longhouse youngsters, or the new generations as a whole. By contrast, they themselves 'don't know book': *Enda nemu surat*. With the spread of rural schools across the state that began in the 1960s (Jawan 1994: 172–174), the vast majority of Saribas Iban under the age of 35 have acquired at least basic literacy skills.

Even more important than the vast reach of literacy is the continued role of schools and their central print medium, the textbook, as instruments to separate out young rural Iban into two categories: a 'bright' (*pandai*) minority and a 'stupid' (*beli*) majority. Seymour (1974) observed the process first-hand in Sarawak's Second Division in the early 1970s. He found a gulf between the administration's lofty ideal of the rural school as a tool of national development aimed at the backward masses and the actual practices of teachers and parents. The real goal of the teachers was to prepare a handful of pupils from every class for secondary school. They would openly praise the high achievers and deprecate slower pupils as lazy and stupid (a distinction reproduced by the pupils, as we saw in chapter 5). Performance was largely evaluated on the basis of mechanical, uncritical reading and writing skills (1974: 282–284). Most parents were not concerned about teaching methods or the potential uses of the new knowledge in the local economy. They saw the school as the only possible avenue for their children's, especially the boys', upward and outward mobility (1974: 282) away from what was now described as 'our wretched lives as farmers'.

The life histories of two middle-aged residents of Entanak longhouse confirm Seymour's account of the rural primary school as a manner of occupational sorting office.

Apai Dora ('Father of Dora'), entered school in Betong (Saribas) in 1961, at the age of 10. He used a longboat to paddle to school from his father's longhouse, a journey that could take from thirty to sixty minutes depending on the current. His sixth year of primary was particularly 'tough' (*pedis*), for out of 88 pupils only 17 made it to secondary, himself included. However, he failed his Form 3 examinations and had to give up his formal education.

Sulah is an unmarried paddy farmer in her late 40s. She went to school until Primary 5. In those days, she recalls, there was no piped water or electricity. The main road had already been built, but there was no bus service. There were many boarders, but Sulah was not allowed to board because of Entanak's proximity to the school. All pupils were required to help with the construction and care of a fish pond. They also grew vegetables, for which the teacher would reward them with a dollar every year, and cleaned the school in teams. 'We had to be clean'. The principle guiding many school activities was, she explains, *gotong-royong* (M. 'cooperative undertaking'). Unlike youngsters today, Sulah's generation, she says, were highly disciplined. There was no smoking. The few mischievous (*manchal*) boys were made to roast in the sun (*jemboi*) for hours on end. Literacy was the top priority. 'They made us write a lot. I still know how to'. Lessons were in English or Iban, although Sulah, like most of her contemporaries, never learnt 'deep English' (*Inglis dalam*). She left school at an early age because her mother needed help in their crowded *bilek*. 'Nowadays who wants to do that?'. In those days girls were generally not encouraged to attend school for too long, if at all. Sulah's older sister, Iding, has no schooling. As a girl she was busy helping her mother raise their many brothers. 'My mother wouldn't send me to school' (*Indai aku enda ngasoh belajar sekula*). She now regrets it: 'It's a wretched life in the longhouse if you didn't go to school' (*Merinsa ba rumah panjai 'ti nadai sekula*).

A parallel formative influence was radio. For many Saribas Iban growing up in the 1960s and 1970s, whether at home or as immigrants in an urban area, literate or illiterate, the Iban Section of Radio Sarawak (later RTM) provided a constant source of news about and entertainment from the wider society at a time of far-reaching social, political and economic changes. In those days, the Iban Section had a strong Saribas flavour to it (chapter 3). It was a very powerful disseminator of the developmentalist creed they had learnt at school. This creed maintained that individual development through book learning should serve the common good rather than selfish pursuits. As in West Africa, however, the 'secondary orality' of radio (Ong 1982) was no substitute for knowing book.[3] Chronologically speaking, the third influential post-war institution in the lives of many Iban was *bejalai* or *pegi* (Kedit 1993), a journey traditionally undertaken by young bachelors in search of adventure, employment and valuable artefacts to add to the *bilek*-family heirloom (*pesaka*). When Apai Dora failed his Form 3 examinations, he decided it was time to *pegi*. 'I was not fit for farming' (*Aku enda tan bumai*). In 1970 he worked as a 'coolie' (*kuli*) for a Chinese *towkay* at a sawmill near the divisional capital. From 1973 to 1976, until the age of 25, he worked at building sites in Brunei, where the wages were higher than in Sarawak. On returning to the longhouse he felt he had no choice but to take up pepper growing and farming. In 1983 he left again for Brunei, where he worked as a labourer for another three years, after which he once again returned to the longhouse.

The institution of *bejalai* is gradually turning into the rural-urban migratory oscillations that characterise the unstable economies of most developing countries (Kedit 1993: 152, Goody 1987: 146). As such, it is no longer restricted to men. From the end of the Japanese Occupation, increasing numbers of young women have migrated from Saribas longhouses to other areas in search of waged employment or to join their husbands. Some settled permanently in urban areas, while others returned to their longhouses. Sulah belongs to the latter category. In 1980 Entanak residents lived in small makeshift houses (*dampa*) while they built a new longhouse. In order to raise funds towards the construction costs, Sulah moved to Bintulu for a year to work as a maid for wealthy relations. The following year she moved to Kuching to work for another highly educated branch of her kinsmen (*kaban*). 'They paid a thousand ringgit a month rent. I didn't pay any'. Her starting wages were RM 120, then RM 150, of which she would send RM 50 to her parents through registered mail. In 1982 her ageing parents asked her to return to the family *bilek*. She obliged, but there was 'no money to be made' at Entanak, so she moved out again, on this occasion to Simanggang, to look after an Iban teacher's baby daughter.

Both Apai Dora and Sulah acquired a basic school education that did not equip them for a successful career in the urban centres. Instead, it prepared them for a low-skilled, low-waged cycle of relocations to and from their longhouse *bilek*. Their experiences in the employment of wealthy Iban relations or Chinese *towkay* were similar to those of their semi-educated rural brethren everywhere. They taught them more vividly than any school lesson that wealth and power only come to those with a solid educational background and a supportive social network. They taught them about the growing disparities between the rural poor and the urban rich, and about a middle level (*pangkat*) potentially available to rural Iban who have completed their secondary education: the lower ranks of the government service comprising clerks, nurses, teachers and others. The dream of a 'nice' (*nyamai*) life employment in the public sector has remained a central component of the Saribas ideology ever since the spread of literacy, and has been passed down to the younger generations.

A fourth source of pro-literacy ideas was the growing number of developmental agents operating in the Saribas from the 1960s, including politicians, literate headmen, doctors, nurses, missionaries and catechists. Their messages reiterated a plain, undisputed idea: success belongs not only to the hardworking, it belongs those who are hard-working *and highly educated*. According to Berma (2000), however, in 1990 the Iban remained a predominantly agricultural population (72.7 per cent) with a very high percentage of people lacking any educational qualifications (78.1 per cent) and a negligible proportion of university graduates (0.2 per cent). This discrepancy between ideals and perceived achievement is a continued source of resentment and low self-esteem among the Iban.

Conclusion

Literacy has not transformed the nature of Merina knowledge – it has confirmed it.

Bloch (1998: 161)

Literacy has both confirmed and transformed the nature of Iban knowledge. There is no paradox here. In some social practices, such as Christianised farming invocations, it serves pre-state indigenous purposes (while furthering the aims of an imported organisation, in this case the Church). On other occasions, for instance in a classroom setting, literacy primarily serves to turn rural children into a Malaysian underclass. In the rural areas, parochial 'ideolects' contain folk ideals about literacy partly derived from Western blueprints. These ideals have been routed for generations through regional centres of ideology production (missions, district offices, ministries, radio stations, etc.). They assert that success in life belongs not to those steeped in the oral past but to those who know book. It is only bookish Iban, the belief goes, who can help their brethren catch up with Malaysia's more advanced races. Bloch's 'ideological' theory of literacy is a potent antidote against teleological approaches to literacy. It is good to do ethnography with, particularly in the Austronesian world, and to defend the work of indigenous scholars like Sandin or Besy from overly positivist anthropologists such as Freeman. Yet it can only take us part of the way. By considering only local appropriations of literacy, Bloch and his ideological colleagues fail to map both the uneven distribution of literate knowledge and the consolidation of pro-literacy ideas that characterises most of the developing world (but see Bloch 2003). Goody's autonomous approach remains an essential guide to the second leg of the journey.

Notes

1. The number of pagan-inspired Christian prayers is potentially much greater. The book *Adat Kristian* contains 61 such prayers (*sampi* or *sembayang*). In the Preface, the Catholic Bishop, A.D. Galvin, makes no bones about their mixed provenance, quite the contrary: 'We are happy that this book, *Adat Kristian*, follows both the Iban customary law of our ancestors [lit. grandfathers and grandmothers] and the wording of Chistian prayers' (*Kami gaga ati ka surat 'Adat Kristian' tu nitih ka adat Iban ari aki ini menya, disereta ka dalam leka sampi kristian*). The Bishop also encourages his readers to further adapt the contents of the book to local custom if they feel the need to do so (*Sampi ti dalam surat tu itong ka chunto aja, tau diubah*).
2. Compare this prayer with that recorded by Freeman (1992 [1955]: 282) in the Baleh during *pemanggol* (Freeman offers but the following translated extract):
   Land that is fat, fat in deep layers,
   Luxuriant land, land that is fruitful,
   Soil soft and fecund, land richly fertile;
3. H.D. Lyons (1990: 421) describes a similar ideology in Nigeria, West Africa.

7

MEDIA EXCHANGES

Once you are dead, put your feet up, call it a day, and let the husband or the missus or the kids or a sibling decide whether you are to be buried or burned or blown out of a cannon or left to dry out in a ditch somewhere. It's not your day to watch it, because the dead don't care.

Thomas Lynch (1998: 14)

So we gave [our TV] to the deceased because she still wanted to watch it. Sometimes people dream [of the dead]; that means they're searching [for personal belongings they left behind]. The more you pity the dead, the more things you let them take with them.

Mother of Luta, 1997

In April 1997 I took part in a burial at Entanak Longhouse, my Saribas home base. At dawn, the all-male burial party marched down the longhouse gallery to an uproar of wailing women and the shrill squawking of cocks. The European-style coffin had been fastened onto a long bamboo pole. Half a dozen men carried it. As is customary with death-related practices, it was lowered from the downriver end of the longhouse. The men lifted it onto the back of a lorry and drove some five minutes until they reached a narrow opening in the thick forest undergrowth. The pallbearers lowered the coffin by the pole and followed a man who cleared the way with a bush knife. About a dozen men followed down the slippery trail. Some carried food and cooking implements for the graveyard meal, others the deceased's grave goods (*baya'*): his clothes, his comb and toothbrush, his favourite chair and table, his television. After the men had dug up the grave, the deceased's son-in-law took one of the idle hoes and smashed up the television screen. 'So that he can still watch TV over there', he explained to me. He then proceeded to shatter the rest of the grave goods. Later in the day, once the Christian burial and the meal were over, the television set was placed at the foot of the grave.

Five Stages of Appropriation

In this chapter I wish to focus on the materiality of television and its relationship to nation building among Saribas Iban. To do so, I will employ a modified version of Kopytoff's (1986: 67) 'biography of things' approach. Kopytoff believes the biography of a car in Africa would yield

> a wealth of cultural data: the way it was acquired, how and from whom the money was assembled to pay for it, the relationship of the seller to the buyer, the uses to which the car is regularly put, the identity of its most frequent passengers and of those who borrow it, the frequency of borrowing, the garages to which it is taken and the owner's relation to the mechanics, the movement of the car from hand to hand and over the years, and in the end, when the car collapses, the final disposition of its remains. All of these details would reveal an entirely different biography from that of a middle-class American, or Navajo, or French peasant car.

Partly building on Kopytoff, Silverstone et al. (1994) have developed an intriguing model of domestic media consumption. They distinguish four main overlapping stages in this process:

1. *Appropriation*: how households acquire or purchase their information and communication technologies (ICTs).

2. *Objectification*: how household members transform an anonymous commodity into a familiar object within the 'geography of the home'.

3. *Incorporation*: how they accommodate new ICTs into their daily routines.

4. *Conversion*: how they convert items from the media (e.g., news, images, songs) into discursive materials they can use in their social lives.

There is one fundamental element missing from this scheme: stage five of the process. I shall term this fifth element 'disposal'. How do households in a given society dispose of their media artefacts, say, when they acquire a new video or their TV set is damaged beyond repair? Do they pass them on to poorer relations, resell them, recycle them, destroy them? In terms of Kopytoff's African example, we need to know what happens after the car collapses; we must document 'the final disposition of its remains'.

Below I use the biographical approach to artefacts to examine the social and economic significance of television amongst ethnic Iban in the Saribas area of Sarawak. But rather than produce full biographical profiles of television sets I will concentrate on two phases in their 'careers': (a) how they were acquired and (b) how they were disposed of. One reason for leaving out the three middle phases is to avoid redundancy, as the impact of media technologies on the organisation of time, space and sociality in Saribas longhouses is a problem I address in the next chapter. Another reason is the assumption that in rural societies we can learn a great deal from the critical points at which commodities are exchanged for money, labour, gifts, gratitude or supernatural protection, for it is at these junctures that the group members tell themselves (and at times others as well) what they think they are doing. More importantly for our present concerns, they tell us *who they think they are*. This strategy allows us, therefore, to identify contemporary processes of self-formation within a given social world. In addition, we can learn about the conflicts that may arise when two or more clashing value frameworks impinge upon an exchange. For instance, in an Iban setting, when selecting the burial goods (*baya'*) for a deceased family member to take with her to the afterlife. In turn, these 'border clashes' tell us about the limits and contours of the local self. In sum, this approach integrates the social, relational and active nature of consumption (Appadurai 1986: 31) with the endemic features prevalent in a given locale.

One Working Television Set

Writing in 1951, Derek Freeman (1992: 222) described how, for young Iban men

> going on journeys is the greatest and most consuming interest which life has to offer. The lure of the distant sea and its fabled ports is inducement enough; but added to this are varied opportunities to earn money, and ultimately to purchase a gong, a jar or a shot-gun for one's triumphant home-coming.

Forty years later, the Iban passion for family heirlooms (*pesaka*) seemed to have subsided. Arno Linklater (1990: 45) was commissioned by *Time Life* to write a book about the Iban as a 'colourful, exotic and above all primitive people'. He found that his co-researcher's photographic work was doomed from the outset. This is what they encountered in a remote longhouse in the Batang Ai area:

> Outboard engines and chain-saws hung from posts in the gallery. Their kitchens were stocked with bright yellow plastic buckets, aluminium saucepans and tins of Milo, a syrupy night-time drink. All this could be minimised but not the problem of their clothes. Sarongs had replaced short woven skirts for the women, and the men no longer wore the traditional *sirat* or loin-cloth originally woven from bark. They found cotton shorts more convenient, and from their work at the timber camps and oil-fields, they brought back baseball caps and T-shirts advertising Camel cigarettes and such folk beliefs as 'Love is never having to say you're sorry'.

Let us now return to the burial episode that opened this chapter. At first, I found it hard to believe that the deceased's son-in-law, a construction worker with a family of 16 to support, had so readily given up their only working television so that the departed member could 'still watch TV over there'. Not long before this burial, I had conducted a door-to-door longhouse survey that clearly demonstrated that Saribas Iban *bilek*-families consider television to be their most important belonging, for reasons I explain below.

An obvious answer to the mystery was not hard to find. It was both given to me at a later point by the participants themselves and available in Richards' *Iban-English Dictionary*. Before sending an object to the afterlife the Iban must destroy it,[1] for their Afterworld (*Sebayan*) is a back-to-front realm where things fall upwards, water is carried in sieves and cracked jars, light is dark (Richards 1981: 30) ... and television can only be watched on smashed-up screens. In *Sebayan*, the belief goes, the deceased will be able to make use of the object's 'spirit' (*semengat*) (1981: 336). But the nagging question remained unanswered. Why destroy a valuable television set? Was that not an irrational act, a waste of precious technological resources?

The Anthropological Problem of Value

The 1980s and 1990s witnessed a surge in scholarly interest in the study of consumption and material culture. One important collection of essays, *The Social Life of Things* (Appadurai 1986) challenges what the authors see as dominant Western notions of an atomised, culture-free individual consumer with unlimited needs. In his introduction, Appadurai sets out to overcome the Marxist tendency to define economic relations largely in terms of production by examining more closely the specificities of consumption across historical periods and cultural boundaries. He defines commodities as 'things in a certain situation' (1986: 13) rather than as kinds of things strictly differentiated from those used in gift and barter exchanges. To this anthropologist, what is socially relevant about commodities is not any intrinsic, immutable attribute but rather their exchangeability at various stages in their social careers. In order to understand the shifting social and economic value of commodities, we must study how they circulate in social life, hence the title of the volume.

One of the contributors, Alfred Gell (1986: 110–114), has urged western anthropologists to transcend the utilitarian bias prevalent in their own societies when studying consumption in other cultures. He supports his argument with the case of the Sri Lankan fishermen whose income rose sharply following the introduction of new technologies of refrigeration (Stirrat 1989). They promptly acquired modern toilets and TV sets and had spacious garages built. Alas, they had no running water, electricity or roads with which to enjoy these modern conveniences. Rather than seeing this episode as an example of peasant naïveté or irrationality, Gell finds that their purchases resemble those of wealthy art buyers in the West. They are the creative, collective act of appropriating a radically novel aesthetics, one not previously available locally.

> It is easy to laugh at such crass conspicuous expenditure, which by its apparent lack of utilitarian purpose makes at least some of our own consumption seem comparatively rational. Because the objects these fishermen acquire seem functionless in their

environment, we cannot see why they should want them. On the other hand, if they collected pieces of antique Chinese porcelain and buried them in the earth as the Iban do (Freeman 1970), they would be considered sane but enchanted, like normal anthropological subjects (Gell 1986: 114).

Similarly, it is easy to laugh at the replacement of those pieces of antique porcelain that Freeman came across in the late 1940s with the 'modern' television sets I saw at late 1990s Iban burials. Are the Iban no longer 'sane but enchanted'? Are they no longer 'normal anthropological subjects'?

The difficulty with Gell's post-utilitarianist approach is that it can lead us to the opposite extreme of discarding all potentially utilitarian aspects of consumption in non-Western societies. It also hampers the ethnographic inquiry by reducing the problem of value to a dichotomy: that of utility vs. the absence of it. A more promising approach to artefacts is Miller's (1998: 6–7) view of material culture as 'an endless creative and hybrid world' to which no rigid etic classification can do justice. What is needed, he argues, is an ethnographic 'generality of difference' in the study of artefacts. Those artefacts that matter to participants in the ceaseless construction of self and others ought to matter to researchers as well. In this chapter I focus on artefacts that matter to Saribas Iban, especially television sets. I will not, however, limit the inquiry to those aspects of the value of Saribas Iban media artefacts that would appear to contrast with a supposed Western utilitarianism, for I am doubtful that Gell's contradistinction is a valid one. Instead I will start by opening up the semantic field of the term 'value' (*rega, guna*) in a Saribas Iban context to situate more precisely the subsequent inquiry.

Nine Value Frameworks

In a survey I carried out early in 1997, television appeared to be the most highly valued property owned by Saribas Iban, even above their family heirlooms (*utai pesaka*). I asked adult residents of three longhouses which among all their belongings, both family heirlooms and modern objects, were most useful or important to them (*Di entara semua utai ti dikemisi kita sebilek, lama enggau baru, nama utai ti beguna agi?*). The results indicated a clear preference for television, as shown in Table 7.1.

The follow-up question in the survey was: Why are these particular objects so important to you? Those who had chosen their TV sets gave very similar, concise explanations: they want to know what is happening in the world, keep abreast of development(s), especially overseas. In their written responses three adults made this clear:

TV shows countries other than Malaysia. It also shows both foreign and Malaysian news.

Melissa, 25, handicraft factory worker

138

Table 7.1. Most valued *bilek*-family possessions among Saribas Iban.

Possession	Responses
1. television set	26
2. refrigerator	14
3. earthenware jars *(tajau)*	10
4. land[2]	8
5. radio set	7
6. gas cooker	4
7. vegetable garden	3
motorcycle	3
9. telephone	2
car[3]	2
all heirlooms	2
no preference	2

Sample: 119 *bilek*-families in 6 longhouses (from which 83 interviewees responded to this question).

We can watch the news on TV, watch stories and see countries that are far away from Malaysia when we turn it on.

Apai Dunggat, 45, male farmer

In our family we find that the most useful thing [we own] is [our] TV, because through TV we can know what has happened around the world: the wars, the floods, the burnt down houses and much more besides.

Indai Edut, 28, housewife

These survey responses demonstrate that Saribas Iban, unlike Gell's Sri Lankan fishermen, do indeed value television as an information technology.[4] Such a form of valuation derives from recent historical memory, from a sense of having been left behind by those among their urbanised brethren who are now 'clever and rich' (*udah pandai, udah kaya*). However, this is but one way in which they talk about television, one appropriate to the context of a formal survey conducted by a foreign researcher. That is, they stressed the 'serious' value of television over its entertainment (*hiburan*) value.[5] But I wish to argue that there are at least nine kinds of overlapping value frameworks whereby Saribas Iban estimate the worth of television as an artefact-cum-medium outside the rigid confines of a questionnaire.

1. *Market value (rega)*. Television sets are expensive to purchase, yet, unlike family heirlooms (*utai pesaka*), they rapidly lose market value. The market is controlled by the Chinese diaspora.

2. *Exchange value*. Television sets are important exchange items in the regular flow of gifts (*meri*) and counter-gifts with the living and with the dead; they keep people together.

3. *Status value.* Television sets are conspicuous markers of inter-familial disparities in wealth, prestige and social status (*pangkat*); they separate people.

4. *Utilitarian value (guna).* Television sets are seen as the chief providers of information (*berita*) about more advanced urbanised societies.

5. *Moral value.* Owning a television and watching it regularly provides Saribas Iban with materials to contrast their local custom (*adat*) with the televised lifestyles and morals of other, more powerful ethnic groups.

6. *Aesthetic value.* Television sets can be appreciated for their design and style. The Saribas Iban domestic aesthetics is eclectic: Iban and alien elements are often juxtaposed in the local sitting-rooms (*bilek*).

7. *Historical value (asal).* Television sets, unlike family heirlooms (*pesaka*), are not generally attributed the potentiality to transcend the human lifespan (historical temporality). However, some urbanised Saribas Iban may regard them as 'collectibles' (*koleksi*).

8. *Biographical value.* Television (both as an artefact and as a medium) is routinely used in the construction of a sense of self in relation to others (lifelong temporality, cf. Hoskins 1998). In certain situations, it can therefore be reclassified as a grave good (*baya'*).

9. *Social value.* Television sets routinely provide the time-space coordinates for a new form of *bilek*-based evening socialising (day-to-day temporality).

The main purpose of charting out this vast analytical space is to capture some of the complexity inherent in any ethnographic study of value and exchange. Covering all these dimensions of value adequately is not possible in this chapter. Here I will concentrate on the *exchange value* (no. 2) of media artefacts, and in particular television, although it will soon become apparent that the boundaries between these analytical constructs are fuzzy. For instance, the market value (no. 1, *rega*) of a television set can be an important measure of its significance as a gift (no. 2) when a well-off *bilek*-family decide to give one to poorer relations. In addition, this act of giving might also be interpreted in terms of status (no. 3), utility (no. 4) and morality (no. 5) at different times by different people within the social network concerned. The empirical combinations are endless, and in the ten case studies presented below I can only hope to map some of the socially-regulated paths through which media artefacts circulate and are valued.

Three Methods of Acquisition

I have identified three chief paths through which television sets are acquired and four through which they are disposed of, as shown in Table 7.2. Let us consider first the three major methods of acquisition. One point of entry of

Table 7.2. The socially-regulated paths of acquisition and disposal of television sets among Saribas Iban.

Acquisition	Disposal
1. As a gift from rich relations	1. As a gift to poor relations
2. As a local hire-purchase (*lun*)	2. As a collectible (*koleksi*)
3. As an urban cash purchase	3. As a 'stand-by', broken piece of furniture
	4. As a grave good (*baya'*)

television sets into Saribas Iban homes is as gifts (*meri*) from better-off relations. Many Saribas *bilek*-families cannot afford to purchase their own TV sets. They must rely on migrant kin working in urban areas, timber camps or off-shore oil rigs.

Household A: Thomas, 31, supports a family of 8. He used to earn only RM 420 a month as a conductor with STC, the local bus company. Now he can make as much as RM 75 (ca. U.S.$13[6]) on a good day as a construction worker and occasional carpenter. In 1990 or 1993 a cousin of Thomas' who lives in Kuching presented them with their first, and to date only, television set – a colour Goldstar. Thomas estimates it cost him approximately RM 1000 upfront (U.S.$250).

Household B: This hard-up family of six depend on the erratic earnings of two brothers who currently work in the local building sector. They bought their first TV set, a black-and-white model, in the early 1980s. They had it repaired in Kuching once but it broke down again. In 1995 the head of the household's brother, a carpenter in Kuching, gave them a black-and-white Panasonic imitation. It still works. They estimate it cost him RM 700 to RM 800.

Media theorists, who base their notions largely on studies undertaken in Western countries, have paid little heed to the severe economic constraints in the consumption of media that characterise Third World societies. For example, in late 1990s Afghanistan, radio listening was rationed. Choices had to be made about stations and listening times in order to conserve the life of batteries. Unlike in affluent societies (Tacchi 1998), if the radio was on, it could only mean that it was being listened to (Skuse 1999: 21). Among the Saribas Iban, there is a strong link between income and television or car ownership. In the richer longhouses, often close to a market town or further away but blessed with abundant pepper harvests, most if not all *bilek*-families own a TV set while very few or none own a car. In poorer communities television sets are rarer; and rarer still it is to have them repaired when they break down. When households face hardship owing to a depressed local job market, a poor harvest or the death of the family ricewinner, televisions become luxury items.

In the six longhouses I surveyed in the Saribas area, the percentage of *bilek*-families owning one or more TV sets (usually one) went from 100 per cent at a community next to the market town (*pasar*) to 55 per cent at a poorer long-house some four miles further away from town. Yet these figures can be misleading: at a third, even poorer longhouse with 65 per cent ownership, I found that of the thirteen television sets owned by families there, only four were working – having the other nine repaired was beyond their present means. *Television is a much valued, yet dispensable, commodity.* There are indeed poor families in the Saribas who have no support from relatively wealthy relations and cannot even afford a radio set, let alone a television. Most of them, however, manage to watch it with relations who live nearby, as in the following example:

> *Household C*: A six-strong family of two parents with four children aged 4 to 15. The father, 45, works intermittently as a labourer (*kuli*) for some RM 30 a day and helps with the wet paddy farm at peak periods. They have no family heirlooms and have never owned a TV set. To watch it they often go next door to the mother's first cousin who is married to Thomas (Household A). They used to have a small radio bought when the father was a labourer in Brunei but it broke down 'a long time ago' (*lama udah jai*), so they also have to listen to the radio next door.

A second well-established point of entry for a television set is as a flexible hire-purchase from a prominent local Chinese merchant. We shall call him Mr Chan. A long-time resident and fluent speaker of Iban, Chan set up his own shop in 1982. His father was a fishmonger, whereas he has diversified into furniture, electronic goods, bicycles, and antiques[7] and claims to have customers in virtually every longhouse across the Saribas and Skrang region. He used to travel frequently up the Skrang in search of Iban heirlooms (*utai lama*), but nowadays few of any value are to be found in longhouses. Most of them, he says, are now owned by wealthy urban Sarawakians (as Beavitt 1995 confirms[8]). Moreover, as longhouse residents have become aware of their increasing market value only destitute families are today prepared to part with their heirlooms. When asked about the potential risks of selling haunted jars, Chan is firm: 'No, no, my jars have never harmed anyone' (*nadai kala ngachau urang*).

Chan buys his television sets and other mass-produced merchandise whole-sale in Kuching. For almost 20 years now his customers have been able to hire-purchase (Ib. *lun*, from E. loan) television sets and other costly goods. Thus a television worth RM 1000 can be purchased in monthly instalments of RM 100, sometimes RM 80 or less if the family are facing financial difficulties (*suntok*). Black-and-white sets cost just over RM 300. According to Chan, his customers are happy to buy in instalments. Newly arrived traders are reluctant to offer this service for lack of trust in the local population. Indeed even Chan has suffered from an increase in the default rate. He estimates that one or two out of every ten customers never meet their financial obligations. 'People are not like before. I'm paying so-and-so's wife a visit to embarrass him [into paying up] (*'Ka nemuai bini Sanu, ngasoh iya malu*)'.

Household D. Four generations share this six-strong *bilek*, from a primary schoolboy to his great-grandfather, born in 1901. Aki Nyaru, 58, was the first person in the long-house to own a wireless, a Philips he bought in the 1950s for RM 115. In those days he was a 'leading coolie' [E. term used] in the divisional capital, Simanggang (Sri Aman). The new artefact was an instant success in the longhouse. He still remembers how a dumbfound woman went round the talking box in search of the mysterious speaker, and how their *bilek* was always full of people eager to listen to the Iban-language broadcasts. In 1977 he found local employment as a *kuli* with the Public Works Department. Two years later he started paying Mr Chan for a black-and-white television in irregular instalments. Two or three years after the longhouse had cele-brated its 1988 *Gawai Antu*, or mourning feast, he replaced it with a Sharp colour TV which he also paid Chan for in variable instalments of about RM 100 a month totalling some RM 2100. He believes local life has generally improved over the years. For instance, 'in the old days you couldn't buy on hire purchase'. No longer a labourer, these days he taps his own rubber trees and farms wet paddy. The family live on his son's considerable wages as a lorry driver, up to RM 1800 a month with overtime.

Household E. Stella, 28, and her husband Edut, 36, live with their daughter in a small house on stilts they built beside the longhouse. He is a mechanic with the local bus company. She does some farming and describes herself in English as a 'housewife'. They bought their first television and video in 1990 on hire purchase from Chan, RM 700 upfront and the remaining RM 400 in four monthly instalments. When it broke down Chan himself repaired it. In 1994 they decided to buy a Panasonic television and video set. This time the method of payment was 'more comfortable' (*nyamai agi*): Edut's employer paid directly to Chan by deducting RM 100 from his salary every month.

Chan's business activities illuminate two aspects of local media acquisition. First, they shed light on the middle-income section of the longhouse popu-lation, that is families with one regular wage earner employed locally, almost always a man working for a construction firm, the bus company, the police or the Public Works Department (now JKR). There is a marked sexual divi-sion of labour in longhouses lying close to the market town. Unlike more remote communities devoted exclusively to rice farming and cash cropping in which many everyday tasks are shared by men and women, here in longhouses within the market town orbit, men generally work for wages while women combine farming and domestic chores. These wages allow families to hire-purchase television sets, refrigerators and other costly commodities, making them ever more dependent on the vagaries of a local job market that relies heavily on developmental funds from the state government in Kuching, that is on political patronage.

Second, trade in television sets and other media devices is in the hands of the Chinese diaspora – and so is the private sector that employs thousands of Iban labourers-cum-consumers across Sarawak. Chinese entrepreneurs have to understand their customers' beliefs and needs if they are to prosper. In the account presented earlier Mr Chan reveals his knowledge of both pagan thought and of the uses to which the notion of *malu* (shame) can be put in an Iban setting. Kopytoff (1986: 88–89), following Curtin (1984), has stressed the importance of trade diasporas for the history of world trade. These groups have 'provided the channels for the movement of goods between disparate societies' acting as a cushion against the impact of the world economy upon small-scale societies. In terms of the 'double articulation' of television in culture and economy (Silverstone et al. 1994), it is important to note that Malaysia's Chinese contribute little to television's contents – a role largely in the hands of Malay producers of official culture in the capital, Kuala Lumpur. The crucial role of the Chinese merchants is to buy and sell the hardware through which the mediated quasi-interaction (Thompson 1995) of rural Iban with Malay(sian) culture producers takes place. Malaysia's ethnic division of capital (cultural vs. economic) into Malay and Chinese fields of power relations, is therefore reinforced by a parallel division of labour in the production and distribution of media contents and artefacts.

With the continued monetisation and urbanisation of rural Sarawak, however, it is likely that informal verbal arrangements of the kind Chan has established with his longhouse customers will be increasingly replaced by more impersonal, inflexible written contracts (i.e., mediated interactions [Thompson 1995]). In fact, a rival company already uses quite a different strategy with defaulters: they recover their goods by force. In other words, the nature of commodity exchanges in the Saribas is changing as its economy becomes more firmly locked into the wider national and world economy. What is unlikely to change in the near future is the national media's ethnic-based double articulation.

There is a third point of entry for television sets: as commodities purchased by Saribas migrants for their own uses – that is, not as gifts. The migratory flow of rural Iban is by no means one-way; many migrants return to their longhouses when economic circumstances in their home areas permit it, or to retire. Once they have decided to settle back into their home communities, they bring their television sets, refrigerators and other household goods along with them.

Household F. The longhouse headman, 46, is married with three children. They all share a spacious *bilek* with his mother, his sister and her two daughters – a nine-strong domestic unit. The headman is a driver with the local bus company. His wife, 30, works as a farmer and housewife. His late father was a business associate of Chan's, trading mostly in Skrang heirlooms and Kalimantan cattle. This connection allowed his father to hire-purchase from Chan one of the longhouse's first television sets. He began payment for a 14″ black-and-white National set in 1982 at the reduced rate of RM 450. In those days Entanak longhouse did not yet have a regular electricity supply, so their television ran on a car battery costing RM 90. The headman's sister used to work as a teacher in Kapit, far in the interior of Sarawak, where she bought an 18″ colour National television for RM 800 in the 1980s. Living conditions in Kapit were hard, and after a few years she decided to return to her Saribas *bilek* bringing back, among other objects, her colour TV set. It replaced her father's obsolescent set which they gave to relations in a poorer longhouse 8 miles from town. She now works locally as a clerk and earns some RM 1000 a month. In 1996 she bought a Sony television on a trip to Kuching for RM 1200 upfront. A year later, she bought a video. She also owns the only car in the longhouse.

This example shows that we should be wary of fetishising that most visible of visual media artefacts: television. It is no secret to rural Iban that increased employment opportunities and financial security are open to the better educated among them. The latter's acquisition of expensive commodities over the years provides other families with what to them is tangible proof that education is the best avenue to wealth and security. When talking about relatively wealthy relations, Saribas Iban often refer to their early educational successes. For instance, a local teenager who is now studying at an American university on a Malaysian government scholarship, is well-remembered as a studious boy who was 'always reading books in his *bilek*'. In the minds of Saribas Iban, the school's print media are the means to the future acquisition of electronic media and other advanced technologies. The true significance of the headman's sister's purchases lies in the 130-year long Saribas association of literacy with tangible material wealth. Pringle (1970: 201) says of 1860s Saribas Iban (Dayaks) that their conversion to Christianity 'was linked to [an] interest in education, and undoubtedly to the conviction that writing was somehow the key to European power'. An early European missionary related the following incident:

> A party of Saribas Dayaks going on a gutta expedition asked for a copy of the first Dayak reading book, because one of them could read, and thought he would teach the others in the evenings when they were not at work. And this is indeed what did happen, and when the party returned most of them were able to read. The Saribas women were just as keen as the men, and many of them have been taught to read by some Dayak friend. I have myself noticed, when holding services for some Christians in villages in the Saribas, how many of those present were able to use the Dayak Prayer-Book and follow the service and read the responses (Gomes 1911: 107, quoted in Pringle 1970: 201).

Four Methods of Disposal

At the time of field research (1996–1998), wealthy families in the Saribas and other rural areas of Sarawak had owned and replaced television sets for almost twenty years. Over the years, four standard ways of disposing of old sets have emerged. One possibility is to present it to relations who cannot afford to purchase or repair their own set, as in the above example from the headman's *bilek*-family (Household F). What kind of an exchange is this? According to Appadurai (1986: 12) anthropologists have tended to romanticise the difference between a gift and a commodity exchange as being representative of small-scale and industrial societies, respectively. He prefers to understand commodities not as special kinds of goods but as 'any thing intended for exchange' and reminds us, with Bourdieu (1977), that gifts are also 'economic calculations' yet with in-built lapses of time that may conceal their true nature. To him, as we said earlier, commodities are 'things in a certain situation', that is things whose most salient feature at certain times in their social lives is their exchangeability. The main difference between gift and commodity exchanges is that the former are generally person-centred, social exchanges whereas the latter are object-centred, relatively impersonal and asocial (Appadurai 1986: 12–13). According to this perspective, giving a television set to relations in another longhouse is therefore a self-interested, yet personal, form of economic calculation. This corresponds to the evidence I have gathered. Peter Kedit (1993: 136), an Iban anthropologist, describes how urban-based Iban still

> maintain ties with their rural communities and help them solve problems in such activities as farming, funerals or festivals. Their original home is a place of sentimental value with fond memories of childhood. But it also has economic value because land holdings are still owned by their families and they have rights to them.

The phenomenon is not merely one of a flow of gifts from urban to rural Iban, or vice versa (see Sutlive 1989 on rural Iban support to Sibu squatters), nor is it limited to money given for farming and feasting. In addition, there is a growing *intra-rural* flow of used televisions and other costly commodities-turned-gifts that reflects economic asymmetries derived from an unequal access to waged employment. Giving a television set is both an act of kinship solidarity and an unambiguous statement about the relative position of each *bilek*-family in the race to modernity. Gell (1986: 112) argues that 'very recognizable forms of consumption' studied by anthropologists, such as eating, drinking or sharing the pipe should not mislead us into thinking that 'consumption equals destruction'. Even ephemeral goods such as the food served at a feast 'live on in the form of the social relations they produce'. He sees consumption as 'the appropriation of objects as part of one's *personalia* – food eaten at a feast, clothes worn, houses lived in'. Be that as it may, in the Saribas Iban case we must make a distinction between the materiality of television sets and that of ephemeral goods. Television is having an enormous impact on the organisation of time and space in the more economically advanced Saribas longhouses (chapters 8 and 9), while foodstuffs and beverages of European origin (e.g., French cognac) readily fit into existing temporal and spatial structures.

A second option available to rural families is to keep the old television set at hand. Some families store them away in the loft (*sadau*), others in the main living area of the *bilek*. As the following case study shows, a long acquaintance with the obsolescence of modern technology, together with influences arriving from the urban areas, is gradually allowing some television sets to inch their way into the new category of 'collectibles' (*koleksi*).

Household G. Three generations share this wealthy *bilek*. Indai Rita, 33, is married with two children. Her husband works as a well-paid lorry driver along the logging tracks of the interior. Her sister, 30, also has two children and is married to a laboratory technician who lives in a small town a four-hour drive away. Their father, Emmerson, 56, is a retired policeman. He joined the Police Field Force in 1963, the year Sarawak joined Malaysia, and was soon involved in skirmishes with the Indonesian army along the border. In the 1970s he took part in anti-communist operations in the Rejang and in 1983 he fought off Ilanun pirates who were raiding Sabah from bases in the Southern Philippines. Transferred back to his native Saribas in 1996, he was promoted from corporal to sergeant before retiring. These days he looks after a large pepper garden with his wife, a profitable activity owing to prevailing high market prices. They first acquired a television in the late 1970s, a black-and-white model Emmerson bought while he was based in the divisional HQ which they brought back to the longhouse in 1996 as a 'collectible'. It is now gathering dust at the far end of the *bilek*, next to their family heirlooms. 'It's part of our collection (M. *koleksi*)' says Indai Rita, laughing, 'Who knows, one day it may fetch a high price as an antique!'. The television they currently use, a 16″ colour Singer, was hire-purchased by Indai Rita's sister for over RM 1000 in the late 1980s. 'It's an old Malaysian model. Nowadays there are lots of models to choose from: Panasonic, Fischer, Toshiba, you name it … I reckon the one at Beng's coffee-shop is at least 36 inches. Now the screen at the laser-disc shop,[9] that's even bigger'. The family have built a small house by the pepper garden where Emmerson spends most of his time. There he has a 20″ colour Toshiba he hire-purchased in the mid-1980s here in the Saribas.

This case study brings us to the relationship between contemporary Iban identity and temporality. It captures the long-term repercussions of one of the few career avenues open to young Iban men after independence in 1963: the security forces. Many Iban families were built 'on the move' as the head of the household was posted to different Sarawak localities in accordance with the security needs of the new nation. For both parents and offspring, the construction of a sense of self and family took place alongside the army's construction of a united Malaysia. Commodities played, and still play, an important part in this parallel process of family and nation building. Indai Rita enjoys demonstrating her technical sophistication through a code consisting of the television's size, price and brand. In doing so she is indirectly proving her competence in matters modern as well as her family's urban credentials. Indai Rita is well aware of her cultural ambiguity as a young, formerly urban woman now living in a longhouse. Often during our frequent conversations in the longhouse gallery, she would pepper her remarks with English and Malay terms and laugh at the odd juxtapositions created. She was particularly fond of ironies and wordplays involving both rural/Iban and urban/Western notions.

Indai Rita's remark about their old TV set being part of their *koleksi* (a Malay term few rural Iban would use) of family heirlooms made us laugh because it was an insightful way of bridging two distinct classes of things (traditional heirlooms vs. modern goods) by means of a single, non-Iban word. After all, humour and insight alike are based on the meaningful reunion of two disparate items of common knowledge. Miller (1994: 396) argues that through artefacts 'we give form to, and come to an understanding of, ourselves, others, or abstractions such as the notion of the modern'. In an indirect way, Indai Rita tries to understand the modern by joking about the historical process whereby some items from the class 'new things' (*utai baru*) may come to be considered 'old things' (*utai lama*). There are a number of historical precedents. For instance, shotguns and rifles, known as *senapang* (orig. Dutch *snaphaan*) have been treasured as family heirlooms (*pesaka*) for over a century now.

A third television disposal method is what we might call 'non-disposal', or a 'stand-by position'. In poor Saribas longhouses which have suffered the ravages of a depressed rubber market and consequent outmigration of the younger population, it is common to find television sets that ceased to work many years previously still taking pride of place in a quiet *bilek*. Usually they are covered with a cheap embroidered cloth awaiting the return of a young migrant who will, it is hoped, see to it that it is repaired. This event may take years to materialise, if it does occur at all. It is one thing to acquire a television set or refrigerator in an urban area. Quite another problem is to have them repaired when they break down and the only person left in the *bilek* is, say, an elderly widow. In poor communities devoted to farming and some occasional low-yielding rubber tapping, the attitude of the largely elderly population is one of having to 'make-do' with whatever resources are available at the time.

This chapter opened with the fourth socially-regulated path, namely the disposal of the television set at the grave:

Household I. Indai Luta is a wet-rice farmer and housewife in her mid-40s. She is married with three adolescent children. Her husband is a driver with the local bus company. In the mid-1980s he hire-purchased their first television set, a RM 400 (new) black-and-white Japanese model, at Chan's. Every month RM 30 to 50 would be deducted from his salary. A decade later, Indai Luta's mother '... took it [to the afterlife] with her. She used to enjoy watching TV ... We Iban have many kinds of heirlooms: jars, shallow gongs, deep gongs, old china plates ... But nowadays there aren't any old things left so we give them TVs. You see, things wear out all the time, so we give them away [i.e., to the dead person]. It's a shame to throw things away when people die. So we gave [our TV] to the deceased because she still wanted to watch it. Sometimes people dream [of the dead]; that means they're searching [for personal belongings they left behind]. The more you pity the dead, the more things you let them take with them'. Some time after Indai Luta's mother died, they hire-purchased a new television set, once again at Chan's. This one was a new 14″ colour Panasonic paid in monthly instalments of RM 50 for a total of RM 1200.

Household J. With 16 souls, this is by far the largest *bilek*-family in the longhouse. Apai Laka, 47, is a construction worker. He lives with his wife, 26, their three children, his mother-in-law, his wife's seven siblings and their three offspring in a rather small *bilek*. Apai Laka's father-in-law bought the family's first television in 1983, a colour model with a dangerous propensity to heat up (*'ka angus*). In 1987 he decided to replace it with another colour television. He remained a keen viewer for many years. Unfortunately in 1997 he was taken seriously ill. Some blamed it on an evil spirit, others on poisoning, still others mentioned the word cancer (*kenser*). He died in a Kuching hospital and was brought back to the longhouse for a syncretistic funeral. His family have at present no functioning television, for 'the deceased took it with him' (*udah dibai urang mati*) to the afterlife. With 16 mouths to feed, Apai Laka can ill afford the RM 100 needed to repair the old set.

We can now retake the questions that opened this chapter. Why destroy a valuable television set? Isn't that an irrational act, a waste of precious technological resources? After all, the survey results I presented earlier show an undisputed preference for television, whose purchase requires a considerable financial sacrifice for most Saribas families. Part of the answer is contained in Indai Luta's explanation: the dead will come back to search for their goods unless their relations 'pity them' (*sinu ka sida*) at the burial. Despite a long period of missionary activities and the proven advantages of a Christian name and education, Saribas Iban are notably sceptical about the efficacy of purely Christian practices. Anglican priests from other Iban areas of Sarawak have decried for generations the obstinate unwillingness of Saribas Iban to overcome their 'pagan fears', in particular the fear of spirits (*antu*). As one priest put it to me, punning on the Malay word for democracy: 'Saribas Iban live in an *antukrasi*, not a *demokrasi*'.

To answer the question fully, we have to examine critically the expression 'valuable television set'. Valuable for whom? In what context? At which stage in the life of the person and the object? A narrowly utilitarian answer would miss the point of why such goods should matter to the dead – and, more importantly, to the living. They matter to both the living and the dead only if they have become 'biographical objects' (Hoskins 1998), that is objects with which the dead had made sense of their lives. Television sets, unlike family heirlooms, were not purchased to transcend the mortality of their users. Nor were they purchased to accompany them to the afterlife, yet some sets do become so closely associated with the life of a person that they enter an irreversible state of 'decommoditization' (Kopytoff 1986: 65) as part of a set of grave goods (*baya'*) that will eventually achieve immortality. Commodities, we said earlier, following Appadurai (1986: 13) are 'things in a certain situation'. Thus in most societies women reach the peak of their commoditisation at marriage, while paintings do so during an auction (1986: 15). Television sets smashed up at an Iban burial have reached the lowest monetary value as worldly commodities, and yet they are at their highest value in the exchange system binding the dead and the living. The conflict between two bordering exchange systems is, of course, accentuated when the television set is still in good working order. In such cases, the 'degree of value coherence' (1986: 15) is high: it is valuable for both the living and the dead.

The nature of television does not make it an ideal grave good, especially in crowded *bilek*-families with stretched financial resources. As I explore in chapter 8, watching television is a deeply social event in a Saribas Iban long-house. It is the main technological support (with electricity) of a new, *bilek*-based form of evening sociality. By contrast, radio, although often also a shared medium in the longhouse gallery or farm hut, is less problematic an afterlife-bound artefact, for its small size and low weight allow for its lifelong association with a certain individual carrier. Furthermore, its low cost relative to television minimises the economic loss to the survivors. In a word, radio sets make less problematic grave goods. Indeed their sad broken entrails are a common sight at Saribas Iban graveyards.[10]

Conclusion

At the outset I asked the question, how Saribas Iban social identities may be (re)produced through the exchange of television sets for money, credit, gratitude, supernatural protection or some other form of social or economic currency. The biographical approach to artefacts has illuminated two main kinds of reproduction.

First, television sets are central to the ceaseless exercise of comparing and contrasting how a certain ricewinner or household are doing in relation to their rivals 'along the path to prosperity', to use a well-worn governmental slogan on Malaysian television. Yet these artefacts are not sufficient in themselves. Ultimately, what really matters is the kind of economic activity which made the purchase possible. A civil servant's TV set speaks of literacy and financial stability; that of a timber-camp lorry driver signals physical risk and financial uncertainty. In other words, television sets are caught up in a Malaysian system of 'commensurate differences' (Gewertz and Errington 1991), a common market of social distinction linked to achievement and consumption (Bourdieu 1984).

Second, television sets (or their absence) tell people whether certain wage-earners are fulfilling their duties towards less fortunate *bilek*-family members or relations, dead or alive. A good son will bring back to his parents' household a new television set as soon he has earned enough money in an office, building site, oil rig or timber camp. Similarly, a dutiful wife will allow her departed husband to take their television with him to the afterlife. These exchanges/gifts (*pemeri*) reproduce the moral economy of the household as well as the qualities of personhood associated with it, such as continuity (*nampong*), respect (*basa*) and compassion (*kasih*). Television sets are therefore bound up with a parochial 'dialect' of the Malaysian ideology which favours a balance between development (*pemansang*) and custom (*adat*) – or, in the context of the *bilek*-family, a balance between individual acquisition and the long-term reproduction of the family line (cf. Bloch and Parry 1989). This balanced representation of the ideal Iban person is routinely reproduced through a variety of means and agents, including school essays, longhouse speeches, gossip, and the material exchanges themselves (chapter 5).

Notes

1. Hoskins (1998: 21) reports that the Kodi of Sumba, in Eastern Indonesia, break some of the deceased's 'significant possessions' on the grave. She does not, however, attempt to explain this practice.

2. It is quite possible that many respondents did not consider land as a 'thing' they owned (*utai dikemisi*), hence its relatively low valuation when I asked respondents to enumerate valuable things rather than provide them with a pre-set list of them. Richards (1981: 158) defines the term *keresa* as '1. Belongings, chattels, possessions, *kerekesa*, esp. those passing by inheritance and of ritual family (*bilek*) worth, incl. *jukut* (precious objects), *utai pesaka*. Property in land and things fixed to land is separately named and described (e.g., *kebun getah, kayu' buah*), and is excluded from *k.* because traditionally it was free and plentiful and had economic rather than ritual value'. On the other hand, stories abound of Iban in the Saribas basin selling their land to Chinese speculators at very low prices in order to fund costly rituals such as Gawai Antu and/or buy TV sets and other goods.

3. Very few rural Iban can afford to buy and maintain either a car or a telephone, which may explain their low valuation given that respondents were asked to value their actual, not their *desired*, possessions.

4. Lull (1990: 170ff) reports strikingly similar reasons for watching the news among viewers in China.

5. Respondents to Lynd and Lynd's 1920s functionalist study of *Middletown* (1929), in the United States, mentioned two main uses of media, namely leisure and 'getting information' (Peterson 2003: 27–30).

6. The Malaysian *ringgit* (RM) was pegged at RM3: U.S.$1 before the 1970s. Since the adoption of flexible exchange rates in the early 1970s, it fluctuated within the range of RM 2.4–2.7 to the U.S. dollar (Gomez and Jomo 1997: xiv) until the sharp devaluation in September 1997 when it was again pegged to the dollar. The rate remained RM 3.8 to the U.S. dollar until the peg was removed on 21 July 2005.

7. Including brass (*temaga*), glazed earthenware jars (*tajau*), gongs (*tawak*) and round metal stands (*tabak*).

8. Beavitt (1995: 15) links the 1990s boom in the antique (*pesaka*) business in Sarawak to the steady growth of the tourist industry. He perceives an unending quest for 'authentic' ethnic objects among foreign tourists and urban Sarawakians alike.

9. These micro-cinemas became popular with young people across Sarawak in the 1990s. The state-controlled press has repeatedly denounced the screening of illegal pornographic films and their misuse for indecent behaviour.

10. Another factor favouring their presence at graveyards is that radio sets have been bought and sold in rural Sarawak since the mid-1950s, while television sets only began to spread widely in the 1980s.

8

CLOCK TIME

There is no fairyland where people experience time in a way that is markedly unlike the way in which we do ourselves, where there is no past, present and future, where time stands still, or chases its own tail, or swings back and forth like a pendulum. All these possibilities have been seriously touted in the literature on the anthropology of time … but they are all travesties, engendered in the process of scholarly reflection.

Alfred Gell (1992: 315)

Clock-and-calendar time (CCT) may not make the world go round, but it regulates the daily rounds of most people and mobile cultural forms across the world. It is the visible hand of market, state and civil society alike. Its small set of symbols is easily acquired and communicated, for unlike more elaborate codes (e.g., those of art works, Bourdieu 1993), CCT leaves little room for ambiguity. Its material supports (clocks, wristwatches, calendars, diaries, radio sets, television sets, email messages, etc.) are virtually everywhere. CCT has invaded and helped to shape countless economic and technological niches, from offices to farms to the Internet. Technological change has brought us new time machines, such as digital wristwatches, yet they all display the same old representational system. CCT is a cultural pandemic (cf. Sperber 1996) and there are no reports of successful resistance to it. Indeed chronoclasm – which we could define as the intentional destruction of clocks and other time machines[1] – is a very rare phenomenon, while iconoclasm has a lengthy history, notably in the Near East and Europe (Goody 1997).

The low world-historical incidence of chronoclasm (once practised, for instance, by the Taliban) in relation to iconoclasm would merit comparative study. In this chapter, however, my aims are far more circumscribed: to describe the link between the day-to-day uses of CCT among Saribas Iban and the ongoing building of a Malaysian nation (I shall broach the festive uses of CCT in the next chapter). The Saribas Iban case study is but one ethnographic instance of how CCT has colonised the lifeworlds of populations that in previous centuries, or even decades, had no use for it (Thompson

1967, Zerubavel 2003, Rantanen 2005). It demonstrates the extraordinary success, resilience and stability of this media form far away from the North Atlantic countries where it took on its standard form. More germane to the argument I am pursuing in this book, CCT is one of the strongest cultural bonds uniting Malaysians of all ethnic groups and walks of life across the South China Sea.

The Anthropology of Time

Before presenting the ethnographic materials, I shall try to remove some of the hurdles that could lie ahead of the anthropological study of CCT, hence of contemporary time and nation building. The first obstacle is well known. In his *Time and the Other*, Fabian (1983) explores how anthropologists have distanced themselves from the people they study. He reveals in the discipline a 'persistent and systematic tendency to place the referent(s) of anthropology in a Time other than the present of the producer of anthropological discourse'. He terms this professional malpractice 'denial of coevalness' (1983: 31) (in chapter 2, we saw examples of a related problem, 'synchronic essentialism', in the work of some Borneo anthropologists).

The second hurdle is the anthropological practice of using a stereotypical backdrop of 'Western time' in the study of time in other societies, as the sociologist Barbara Adam (1994) has shown with reference to classic studies by Whorf (1956), Evans-Pritchard (1940), and Lévi-Strauss (1972 [1963]). Whilst she convincingly puts the case that there is far more complexity to social time in Western countries than has been acknowledged by anthropologists, Adam offers no advice on how to study time beyond the heartland of sociology, viz. the North Atlantic region (see also Adam 1995).

The third obstacle is the anthropological tendency to ignore the irreversible global spread of CCT ever since the industrial revolution transformed Britain and other North Atlantic countries in the eighteenth century. The two chief anthropological explorations of time to date, Gell's (1992) *The Anthropology of Time* and Munn's (1992) 'The cultural anthropology of time', both broach the industrial revolution but do so in passing. Thus, Gell (1992: 106–108) sets out to reject the crude distinction between 'primitive' and 'modern' time notions implied in Piaget's approach to cognitive growth, in which members of industrialised societies are seen as being 'steeped in the ideas of classical mechanics'. Foreshadowing Adam's argument, Gell stresses the varied embedded social contexts in which modern English speakers use non-metric notions of time to discuss events and organise themselves, e.g., 'in a jiffy/a flash/two ticks/half a mo'. Citing the work of Le Goff (1980), Thompson (1967) and Attali (1982), Gell concedes that clocks 'facilitated certain important historical transformations in the productive basis of industrial society'. Yet for him the mass daily flow of people in a modern economy is 'not produced by individuals co-ordinating their activities on their own behalf, but *simply* by individuals following a socially established schedule' (1992: 108, my emphasis). The problem with Gell's use of the word 'simply' is only apparent as we read on:

> This schedule can be modified in marginal respects, by flexi-time arrangements, or by such *ad hoc* procedures as leave-taking, absenteeism or working late at the office. But these individually determined rearrangements always take place and acquire their significance against a background of established expectations as to the symbolic character of the hours of the day. The hours between 6 p.m. and 7 a.m. are not 'working hours'. Work undertaken during non-working hours is not at all the same, for all that it may involve the same *activities*, as work undertaken in working hours. The time-divisions marked on the clock-as-schedule, as opposed to the clock as measuring-device, are points of inflection within a symbolically structured day (1992: 108).

In his eagerness to blur the distinctions between the West and the Rest, modernity and tradition, Gell draws our attention to the 'symbolically structured' character of all human activity, whatever the historical period, cultural setting or technological resources. For Gell, CCT has failed to turn us Westerners into 'watch-dependent denizens of Megalopolis' forever attentive to 'the little slave-drivers we wear attached to our wrists' (1992: 108). We still live as richly symbolic lives as those of people in pre-industrial societies. On the other hand, he also says that individuals can only alter the social schedules of modern economies 'in marginal respects', e.g., through leave-taking or absenteeism. Gell's notion of clock-as-schedule is potentially a very fruitful one, but he does not follow its implications through. Perhaps the most important of these is the *irreversibility* of adopting the clock-as-schedule (in my terms, CCT) system. Once in place, the system can be easily sustained whatever the ebbs and flows in the social and economic fortunes of a given territory. In many important respects, human agency in modern economies is bound up with the social agency of CCT.

Nancy Munn's (1992: 109–111) invaluable review essay suffers from a similar shortcoming to Gell's book. In the sixth section she examines how certain 'calendric and related time shifts' reach into 'the body time of persons' by grounding them and their daily activities in 'a wider politico-cosmic order'. The three historical examples she gives are, in this order: the Gregorian calendar introduced by missionaries into the Solomon Islands, the secular calendar of the French Revolution, and the spread of industrial time in nineteenth century United States. As well-chosen as they are, these examples exhibit a common social/cultural anthropological feature: they are not presented in any coherent world-historic frame. We do not get a sense of scale, or an idea of how those 'wider politico-cosmic orders' may have inter-locked with other orders as the European powers and the United States expanded beyond their shores. What came first, missionising in the Pacific or the French Revolution?

How did U.S. economic and military expansion in the twentieth century transform time notions and practices in the Pacific, including the Solomons? How do these three country-specific 'time shifts' fit into the common history of humankind? We are not told, and are left pining for a world-historic frame of analysis such as Wolf's (1997) *Europe and the People Without History.*

The fourth obstacle to overcome, closely related to the previous two, is the anthropological tendency to romanticise non-industrial societies. Take Gingrich's (1994: 169) contention that non-western conceptions of time and space are not abstract but 'concretely embedded within the totality of sociocultural cosmovision'. Building on his fieldwork among the Munebbih, a tribal group from Yemen, Gingrich contrasts the written almanacs of urban Arabs with the Munebbih 'orally transmitted star calendar'. The former are of no use in the tribal society whose calendar is 'fragmentary, irregular and interrupted'. Among the Munebbih, time is an experience 'deeply rooted in bodies and emotions' (1994: 175). During the unnamed period between the time-span of the white stars and that of the black (firmament) stars, people experience private feelings of insecurity, danger and lurking evil. It is, in Gingrich's evocative phrase, 'the social time of silent fears' (1994: 173). Unfortunately, there is no adequate consideration here of the role of the state in the everyday and ritual life of the localities studied. Are the Munebbih magically exempted from the moral-temporal order imposed by the Yemeni state? Have they somehow managed to preserve their 'social time of silent fears' entirely separate from the various CCT schedules of the civil service, school system, army and economy? Is their experience of time so 'deeply rooted in bodies and emotions' that it cannot be touched by the mass media and their CCT-guided programming?

A brief reference to another Yemeni source is required here. Towards the end of her 1978–1979 fieldwork in the Yemeni valley of al-Ahjur, the anthropologist Najwa Adra (1993) witnessed the arrival of television. She had hoped to record traditional oral narratives during the long nights of Ramadan, but the local people preferred to spend that time watching a Kuwaiti epic through the new medium. Television had an immediate impact upon social life, and not solely during the month of Ramadan. It also altered everyday work and rest patterns, as most people would now stay up watching TV until the electric generators were turned off at 11 p.m. 'and consequently had a hard time getting up in the morning' (1993: 259). Adra's account casts doubts on Gingrich's, for even if the Munebbih were an extreme case of chronic insulation from the effects of CCT, this insulation would have to be explained. In any comparative endeavour – and anthropology aims at being one – the *absence* of an otherwise widespread social phenomenon, such as television viewing or, say, gender inequality, demands as much of an explanation as its presence (Goody 1997). As Adra (1993: 256) makes clear, Yemen has in fact exchanged or imported cultural forms related to trade, farming, cuisine, clothing, and other domains for no less than 2,000 years.

Adra's ethnography brings us to the fifth obstacle – the gulf between the anthropological study of time and that of media. Both Gell and Munn make passing reference to clock-and-calendar media, albeit always as part of their essentially ahistorical accounts. It is no surprise to find that they overlook the history of media technologies and practices and how these may have contributed to time/calendrical shifts around the world.[2] In turn, those few anthropologists who have carried out any significant field research into media such as radio or television, have told us little about the concomitant spread of CCT. This is regrettable, as in the pending comparative study of media forms, CCT would seem a much stronger early candidate than far more complex forms such as soap operas or chat shows. As a media form it has the advantage of being simple, constant, near-universal, and easily translatable. We could therefore study this form both in its own right and also as a way of honing our comparative skills before broaching thicker genres (for early ethnographic, non-comparative studies of TV soaps, see Mankekar 1993, Rofel 1994, Miller 1994).

The sixth and final obstacle I will consider is more recent. We might call it 'temporal hypochondria', that is an abnormal anxiety concerning the cross-cultural legitimacy of 'our' notions of time. Thus Hobart (1997) has taken Geertz to task for denying the Balinese both agency and a sense of history. In Geertz's account (1973: 393), Balinese calendars are 'clearly not durational but punctual … Their internal order has no significance, without climax. They do not accumulate, they do not build, and they are not consumed'. According to Hobart (1997: 4), this interpretation deemphasises the importance of the Balinese solar-lunar *saka* calendar, and the fact that Balinese people use well-known events such as volcanic eruptions, wars or plagues to single out periods between events. By basing his analysis on his own reading of formal calendars, Geertz is assuming that there is 'a meaning which may be extrapolated without regard to the understandings and purposes of the agents and the subjects of actions' (1997: 4). Although one can sympathise with his post-interpretive approach, Hobart expends too much energy revealing Western academic presuppositions about time as a 'linear and irreversible' reality and not enough on more pressing actualities; for instance, on the use by the Indonesian state of precisely such 'linear and irreversible' CCT notions through various media (including textbooks, radio, television, and shadow plays) to spread and consolidate its rule over the Archipelago. Consider the following mid-1970s lament by one of Soeharto's New Order scholars:

> … irrationality, work methods which ignore economic criteria, dependence on one's family due to [a] lack of self-confidence, a low valuation on time, working without a plan, absence of an orientation towards the future, an avoidance of directness which obstructs communication and so on (Wibisono 1975: 59).

He is not referring to British academics from the pre-audit culture era (Strathern 2000), but rather to Javanese peasants. What solution does the Indonesian scholar propose? To train more puppeteers who can modernise the rural masses, including their time-management skills, through the medium of *wayang* (shadow puppet plays).

A second missing link in Hobart's analysis is the uses of CCT by ordinary Balinese and other Indonesians in addition to, and/or competition with, indigenous ways of social scheduling. As in the Yemeni case, its absence or social *insignificance* would also require an explanation. To judge by a 1990s sojourn of mine in Bali, CCT is already a busy mass agent on the island. My first ever Balinese experience, after a gruelling bus journey across Java, was watching a World Cup final on television surrounded by a mesmerised crowd who, unlike me, supported Brazil. Despite the drivers' best efforts we had failed to reach our destination before kick-off, so we made an unscheduled stop at a small bus station. CCT waits for no man, and the locals knew it full well, for the best squatting spots in front of the television were already taken.

I have made explicit six shortcomings in the anthropological study of time – namely the tendency to deny the natives coevalness, caricature 'Western time', overlook the irreversible global diffusion of CCT, romanticise non-industrial societies, neglect the time-media bond, and exhibit a postcolonial fear of misrepresenting 'the Other'. In the remainder of this chapter I wish to demonstrate the consolidation of CCT among Saribas Iban and its relationship to nation building.

Media and Daily Life

New information technologies are not immediately assimilated into the domestic sphere. Their incorporation may demand a great deal of adjusting and negotiating among family members, as particular technologies may clash with the moral, spatial and temporal structuration of the family group (Silverstone et al. 1994: 1–11). Thus in Australia radio was seen at first, in the 1920s, as an intrusive guest for it 'timetabled family activities and challenged domestic rituals'. Over the years it was gradually naturalised, helping to normalise a regimentation of time and space demanded by the new industrial order (Johnson 1981: 167).

Saribas Iban have listened to the radio on a regular basis since the 1950s. To understand its naturalisation over the decades we need to recall its early days. Grandfather-of-Nyaru,[3] now aged 61, then a so-called 'leading coolie' in a provincial town, was the first person at Entanak Longhouse to own a wireless receiver. He remembers well how an astonished woman went round the set in search of the invisible speaker, and how extremely popular his set was. This is how the wife of an official of the British Colonial Service described the arrival of radio in a remote Iban (then Dyak) longhouse in 1954.

> There were some children playing at the landing-place of the long-house as we arrived. They greeted us and some of them ran off and told the headman or Tuai Rumah, an old friend called Garu … I had come up-river from Sibu, the Divisional capital, with Philip Daly, the Programme Director of Radio Sarawak who was on a trip to demonstrate wireless receivers to a community of Dyaks who were not familiar with them and to make recordings of their songs and stories …
>
> … The orchestra sounded charming on the river bank and the ever-conscientious Philip and his engineer, Mr Chung, immediately set to work to take a recording. The Dyaks were very curious and it was a matter of some difficulty to explain to them exactly what was being done. The music was played back to them and this created great enthusiasm. Once they understood what was wanted they were extremely pleased with the idea and did everything possible to help.
>
> This is typical of the Dyak mentality. Although a relatively backward and unsophisticated people they are quick to grasp new ideas (Morrison 1954: 390).

But how did Iban listeners integrate radio into their day-to-day lives in the early days, after the initial excitement had died down? For lack of hard ethnographic data, let us consult a well-placed Iban source: the rural officer, broadcaster and author Andria Ejau. In the extract that follows, taken from his morality novella *Dilah Tanah*, the residents of a remote longhouse have all gathered at the headman's section of the gallery (*ruai*) to settle a land dispute between a man called Biul and the resident shaman. The community's only wireless (*wailis*) has been turned on:

> … Realising that everybody was there, Biul tried to address the gathering.
>
> 'Hang on, we're still listening to the news,' said Enchelegi, the wife of Shaman Ula.
>
> Not a word could be heard, even coughing was forbidden. The little ones who were whispering on the fringes were promptly scolded by Ensingut. The news was unusually long that evening. One of the reports said that the longhouse at Batang Kara Tunsang had burnt down the night before. … (Ejau 1964: 21, my translation)

In the early days of radio, when receivers were expensive, their reception poor, money rare, and news scarce owing to the difficulty and expense of transport, listening to this medium in rural Sarawak was a collective activity undertaken in the longhouse gallery (*ruai*). Listening etiquette was markedly stringent, and 'even coughing was forbidden'.[4] The same applies to television which began to percolate from the urban areas in the 1980s. A North American acquaintance who knows the Iban well was shocked on a recent trip to Sarawak when an old Iban friend ignored his attempts at conversing while a Bombay musical was being shown on television, in glaring breach of traditional norms of longhouse hospitality. In a parallel example, Pace (1993: 196) describes Gurupa, a remote Brazilian community where television was still a novelty in the late 1980s and 'viewing etiquette' was characterised by a fixed collective gaze upon the screen, still bodies and the absence of talking. He recounts how on one occasion two distinguished guests from Sao Paulo – where television had been available to the well-off for several decades – visited the mayor of Gurupa during prime-time. To the high-status visitors, 'television etiquette required no strict rules on silence, and they proceeded to converse throughout the programme'. Their hosts, however, were trapped in an 'uncomfortable bind' and responded with 'constant fidgeting in their seats, unable to watch television nor properly entertain their visitors'. Going back to the Iban anecdote, it appears that after all it was the Westerner who was breaching his host longhouse's newly established viewing etiquette!

Women and Clock Time

Today radio sets are very common in the Saribas, with many *bilek*-families owning more than one set, and there are alternative sources of information available, notably television. Radio has long become an integral part of day-to-day life among Saribas Iban, especially women. There is a marked sexual division of labour in Saribas longhouses near the market town. At Entanak Longhouse most men work as low-skilled labourers in the construction sector, for the Public Works Department (JKR), the bus company, and the police. By contrast, most women alternate farming with household chores. There is also a good proportion of children of school age, as well as of people over the age of 65 who seldom leave the longhouse.

> *Door 18.*[5] Mother-of-Michelle is in her 50s. She usually gets up at around 5 in the morning, prepares the family breakfast (coffee and rice or biscuits), cooks some more rice for lunch, sweeps the *bilek* and sees her grandchildren off to the nearby bus stop at 6.30. Soon afterwards she leaves for her paddy farm, taking her farming implements, a small radio and a pot with boiled rice and some greens or meat. At around noon she takes a lunch break in the farm hut and listens to the midday radio programme (*Ngela Tengahari*) on RTM's Iban Section. She enjoys in particular the personal messages (*jaku pesan*). In the afternoon she farms again, returning to the longhouse at around five. Now that they have television they hardly ever listen to the radio in the evening. 'We no longer have any elders [at Entanak Longhouse]', she says. 'In the old days people would chat in the gallery because there was nothing to see in the *bilek* (*laban nadai utai dipeda dalam bilek*).

Radio sets are today inexpensive and easily portable. Many Saribas Iban women either keep a small set in their farm hut or carry one with them in their farming baskets (*sintong*). Some have it on while they work in the fields, most during their lunch break in the hut (Figure 8.2). This extract also

Figure 8.1. Low-lying paddy farm (*umai tanjong*) by the Saribas river.

illuminates a fundamental change that began at Entanak and other longhouses in the 1980s: the shift of evening social interaction from longhouse gallery to family apartments (*bilek*). All human beings and societies construct their views of the past in the present (Adam 1994: 509). Mother-of-Michelle looks back at the not-so-distant 1970s, when the longhouse gallery was still busy at night, and offers a presentist explanation for its current bareness: in those days 'there was nothing to see in the *bilek*'. I encountered this version of the past as the 'absence-of' (*nadai*) many a time in rural Sarawak. The past is portrayed as the time when people had no electricity, no piped water, no roads, no schools, and so on – a not-yet-modern time (*bedau moden*). For instance, an Entanak man in his 30s who is very fond of action videos told me that his grandparents were quite happy to attend shadow plays (*wayang kulit*) because in the old days 'they didn't know any better' (*nadai nemu utai bukai*). Another man in his 40s described the institution of *randau ruai* (evening chats in the gallery) as 'the entertainment of our ancestors' (*hiburan urang kelia*) in the days when there was no television *as yet* (*bedau*). But what distinguishes Mother-of-Michelle from both men is not her presentist view of the past, but rather the fact that as a woman and a farmer – not a labourer – *it is radio*

160

that structures most of her daylight life, while television viewing is reserved for the evening. The following case study brings this point out even more clearly:

Door 10. Mother-of-Dora, 32, is a farmer and a housewife. She is married to the head-man and has three children aged 8, 6 and 3. Every morning she rises to RTM's Iban Section. Her mother-in-law looks after her infant daughter when she is away farming. Mother-of-Dora is a very keen radio listener. She usually listens to part of RTM's mid-day programme and to the 1 to 2 show on CATS, the new commercial station, while having lunch and cooling off in the farm hut. She enjoys the news, songs and personal messages. Sometimes she listens to the Malay Section as well. After completing her farming work she returns to the longhouse at around 5 to look after her children and prepare supper. From 6 to 6.45 she listens to RTM Iban in the kitchen, including the news at 6.30 from Kuching and the debates. In her view, one recent improvement has been the opening up of the telephone lines to listeners who can now pass on urgent messages to their relations in remote longhouses or take part in debates of all kinds. 'The RTM people used to do all the talking, they wouldn't let any outsiders [partici-pate]. Now [the listeners] phone in every single day. It started this year, for example to talk about new longhouse projects'. In the evening Mother-of-Dora watches TV with the rest of her *bilek*-family. Although there are more Iban radio programmes now than ever before, she thinks traditional songs are losing ground to pop songs, and radio in general stands no chance against the advance of television.

Figure 8.2.   Inside a Saribas farm hut (*langkau umai*), this girl waits for the adult farm-ers to return from the fields. During lunch breaks farmers will often be accompanied by the sound of a radio.

Mother-of-Dora's day-to-day life offers us a variation on the same theme of daytime radio vs. nightime television structuring. Like other Saribas Iban women, she is keenly aware of the predictable broadcasting schedule, and uses it to guide her farming and *bilek* chores. What struck me about Iban farmers in the early days of fieldwork was their confident, matter-of-fact handling of CCT. I had expected a widespread vagueness about time of the sort we European visitors associate with Southeast Asians in general and peasants in particular, such as Indonesians' proverbial *waktu gumi* (literally, 'rubber time'). In stark contrast, Mother-of-Michelle exemplifies a high degree of temporal structuring built upon what we might call the 'chronographic' dimension of radio and television. In addition to the linear (throughout the day) and cyclical (from day to day) guidance provided by these two media, she values simultaneity, that is the newly-found ability of broadcasters and listeners to partake in a debate (*randau*) or hear an important announcement at the same time from distant places. Simultaneity becomes more valuable during certain seasons, notably in the March-May period punctuated every year by the paddy harvest and subsequent build-up towards Gawai Dayak, the much awaited pan-Dayak festival of 1 to 2 June. The Festival was conceived by urban Dayak intellectuals and officially launched in 1965. Today it is firmly established and hugely successful. In chapter 9 I suggest that this public event is, among other things, a celebration of the Dayaks' symbolic CCT parity with the two dominant 'races' (*bansa*) of Malaysia – the Malays and the Chinese. As Andria Ejau, the indigenous broadcaster and author I quoted earlier, puts it through one of his fictional characters, a native chief speaking to a longhouse audience:

> ... so following the wishes of the Dayak people, every first of June from the year 1965 onwards would be officially recognised as [Gawai Dayak Day]. Ever since that day our people has been on a par with other peoples, for all men to behold. Ever since there have been two days out of 365 in every year for all other peoples to pay their respects to us, two days of public holiday (Ejau 1968, my translation).

At this critical period of farming completion and housework followed by celebration, knowing that others are, to paraphrase Anderson (1991: 23), steadily marching along the same path, is a reassuring feeling for farmers like Mother-of-Michelle. Besides structuring women's daily lives and synchronising them with that of other women, men and children (both locally and throughout Sarawak's sole time-zone) radio provides listeners with a source of (auto) biographical and historical reflection, for instance on the fate of Iban traditions as pop music gains airtime and television attracts ever-larger audiences. A third case study draws our attention to yet another temporal dimension structured by radio and television: national calendrical time.

Door 20. Mother-of-Tina, 23, is a housewife. She is married to a bricklayer and has two young children whose care prevents her from doing farming work. She tells me she listens to Iban radio several times a day, roughly from 7 to 9 a.m., from 12 to 2 p.m. and from 6 to 7 p.m., mostly in her *bilek*. However in the middle hours of the day, when the sun-beaten iron roof makes the stifling *bilek* air unbearably hot, she joins other women and elderly residents in the cooler gallery. Leaving the door open, she can still listen to the radio from there while she knits or sews and her children sleep in their hanging cots. Her favourite programmes are *Selamat Pagi Malaysia* (Good Morning Malaysia), the news, songs and the weekly Iban folk stories (*pengingat tuai*). In the evening she watches television with her eight-strong *bilek*-family, including her husband and parents-in-law. She enjoys the news and the commercials. They usually turn off the television at around 9.30 and go to sleep.

When people talk about their favourite programmes, they are not simply telling us about their personalities and cultural influences; they are also talking about how they structure their day-to-day social time and space, and about a specific articulation between personal, local and national space-time. The radio programme *Selamat Pagi Malaysia*, like *Good Morning America* and its other overseas precursors, addresses the whole nation simultaneously, morning after morning, in the national language.

A second aspect of Mother-of-Tina's media-related practices is the combined effect of four post-war technologies upon the longhouse 'soundscape', namely corrugated iron roofs, radio, electricity and television. The replacement of leaf-thatched roofs (*atap daun*) made of local materials with mass-produced corrugated iron roofs has had the unintended side-effect of making the longhouse hotter, leading to the routine afternoon migration of people from family room (*bilek*) to gallery to escape the oppressive heat – a shift which mirrors the impact of electricity and television upon evening patterns of spatial use in the opposite direction, that is from gallery to *bilek*. In addition, the sound emanating from *bilek* radios onto the shared gallery has altered the afternoon soundscape. Some sections of the gallery are fairly quiet, particularly at peak farming periods, for they correspond to *bilek* whose women spend their afternoons on the farm. Others are loud, especially when two or three women have their radios on. Writing about Gerai Dayak longhouses in the Indonesian province of Kalimantan Barat (West Borneo), Helliwell (1993: 51) reports that the permeability of the partitions between neighbouring family rooms (*lawang*) allows 'an almost unimpeded flow of both sound and light between all the apartments that together constitute a longhouse'. The Gerai Dayak longhouse, she adds (as we saw in chapter 2), is a 'community of voices'. Gerai voices 'flow in a longhouse in a most extraordinary fashion; moving up and down its length in seeming monologue, they are in fact in continual dialogue with listeners who may be unseen, but are always present. As such they create, more than does any other facet of longhouse life, a sense of community'.

In Saribas Iban longhouses walls are also thin and permeable to the human voice, yet during the day another familiar strand is woven into the invisible fabric that crosses through the thin walls and along the gallery: the voices and music from the radio. Together they web a distinctive kind of parochial temporality, the here-and-now of a hot, sleepy longhouse in the middle hours of the day (*ngela tengahari*). In the evening, this *ruai*-based community of mediated and unmediated sounds moves back to the family rooms (*bilek*), where it disperses into clusters of loud electronic sounds and flickering lights that allow for little inter-*bilek* communication. This web of temporality extends beyond the longhouse to the local schools and workplaces, and beyond them to other state agencies and private firms across Malaysia. One of the key underpinnings of the Malaysian culture area is precisely this lived-in synchronicity. Indeed, one of Mahathir's chief nation-building legacies is his creation, early in his premiership, of a single time-zone for the entire country (Rashid 2004).

Men and Clock Time

Now to men's labour-dependent activities. If most women structure their days with radio, men's days are already pre-structured by the demands of an inflexible workplace. The following example illustrates, perhaps in an extreme form, the contrast between men and women:

> *Door 4.* Father-of-Ross is a policeman in his early 50s. His wife and daughter-in-law work together on a low-lying paddy farm (*umai tanjong*) by the Saribas river. He met his wife in the state capital and was then posted to provincial Sri Aman where their three children were born. In 1987 they moved into Entanak Longhouse to prepare for the following year's major bardic ritual, *Gawai Antu*. They have lived in the area ever since, for the past few years in a detached brick house they built opposite the longhouse. Father-of-Ross works in shifts (*sip*), either on Shift A (from 7 a.m. to 3 p.m.), Shift B (from 3 p.m. to 11 p.m.) or on Shift C (from 11 p.m. to 7 a.m.). He has one day off a week. In the office he sometimes listens to Malay-language broadcasts and checks the football results in the Malay papers. If he is not working in the evening he will usually stay at home listening to the radio. Most evenings his teenage son and daughter watch television at a cousin's *bilek* in the longhouse (door 12, see below). It is Father-of-Ross' own television but they cannot watch it at home because they have yet to be supplied with electricity. Occasionally he will join his wife, children and cousins at door 12. At other times he watches television with his sister who lives fifteen doors downriver. Either way a glass or two of distilled rice wine (*chap langkau*) are always good to relax with (in colloquial Ib. *rile*).

Where women's daily, seasonal and yearly cycles are structured primarily through farming, those of men are structured through the waged workplace. Father-of-Ross's shift-based schedule is a non-ecological application of CCT to the organisation of labour – it knows neither ecological niches nor seasons. By contrast, his wife's annual organisation of farming work follows the cycle of wet and dry seasons (*maia landas* and *kemarau*). Moores (1986, in Morley 1992: 258) maintains that radio brought the 'domestication of standard national time' to families around the world. This excerpt shows how in the Saribas Iban case (and probably in many other rural areas of Southeast Asia as well), this point is far more relevant to women's apprehension of CCT through radio than to men's utter dependency on the rigid temporal demands of the workplace, in which radio does not play a central role. Radio does not only produce and reproduce a synchronised Malaysian polity, it also helps women coordinate their freelance activities with those of their men and children whose day-to-day life is organised for them by their institutions. In other words, it sustains the social organisation of a local community over time and space. It is only in the evening that CCT is jointly 'domesticated' in the family *bilek* by stable clusters of television viewers drawn from all four socio-economic segments of the longhouse population (men, women, children and the elderly), as in the following instance:

> *Door 11.* Father-of-Juna, 43, has been a local bus conductor for 18 years. His wife is a farmer and a housewife. He works six days a week, including Sundays. He rises at 5.30 and leaves for work at 6 as the first Iban programme comes on the radio. At 11.30 he returns from the market town bringing greens or fish to supplement their lunch. If his wife is away farming, he eats with his elderly father. At around 12.30 he goes back to work. The last bus (Ib. *lasbas*) he inspects departs at 3.20 p.m. and returns to town over an hour later. Occasionally he will listen to the news at 7 on the Iban Section. Father-of-Juna used to be a keen radio listener. He was particularly fond of traditional Iban oral and musical genres, even if often he could not grasp their 'deep meaning' (*jaku dalam*) [cf. chapter 2]. Nowadays he prefers television, especially the 8 o'clock evening news on the first channel, which he watches with his father, wife and children. The institution of *randau ruai* (evening chats in the gallery) was the only form of entertainment available to Iban in the old days (*hiburan urang kelia*), he says. Today things have improved, for they can enjoy watching people from other countries ('*rindu meda urang ari menua tasik*').

Moores (1988: 35) has argued that capitalism 'tabled' time, dividing weeks and days into 'units of work and leisure'. Among rural Iban, this division is captured verbally in the adoption of two standard Malay words into everyday Iban: *kerja* (work) and *hiburan* (entertainment). *Kerja* is normally used to signify waged employment as opposed to unwaged activities within the longhouse sphere, all labelled *pengawa'*, including ritual and farming practices. It is therefore a term more commonly associated with men. *Hiburan* was often used by informants when I asked them about their reasons for watching television or about their favourite programmes. Father-of-Juna's above usage of *hiburan* is interesting in its dual temporality: on the one hand, it charts out the daily and weekly stretch of space-time when he is free from work commitments and able to watch television, on the other it separates him and his generation from the material lackings of previous generations, a view of history I earlier termed 'presentism'. At electrified Saribas longhouses, the *bilek*-family's central marker and conveyor of *hiburan* is television. Echoing the etymological roots of this medium (lit. 'vision from afar'), Father-of-Juna and many other Saribas Iban I talked to often justified their interest in television by explaining that it enables them *to see people in distant countries*, especially white people, deemed far more modern and wealthy than the Iban (see chapter 7). They use television therefore as both a way of 'broadening their horizons' and seeing the future. At the local level, television compresses the space-time paths of Saribas Iban by fomenting the clustering of social life away from the gallery and into family *bileks* every evening at around 8 o'clock. At the cognitive level, by contrast, it *expands* those paths by imaginatively transporting viewers to distant lands and times. The two levels are routinely naturalised and blended in bodily movement, conversation and play.

Prime Time, Prime Place

Scannell and Cardiff (1991: 319) have argued that both radio and television have over the decades made the British nation 'real and tangible through a whole range of images and symbols, events and ceremonies relayed to audiences direct and live'. Following Giddens (1984), Scannell (1988) has distinguished three intersecting temporal planes in the structuring of broadcasting: clock time, life time and calendrical time. Through calendrical time, discrete events in the life of the British nation previously separated in time and space, such as the FA Cup Final, the Last Night of the Proms and the Grand National are now 'woven together as idioms of a corporate national life'. I find this separation of CCT into 'clock time' and 'calendrical time' unhelpful, as it obscures the interdependence of these two strands of temporal-numerical code in modern scheduling practices. Also problematic is the insertion of 'life time' as a comparable temporal plane. It is more fruitful, in my view, to study the biographical-historical uses of the CCT code by broadcasters in different countries. Thus the importance of television in this continuous process of temporal and symbolic weaving has also been noted in Brazil. The remote Amazonian town of Gurupa relies for its electricity supply on a costly diesel generator controlled by the municipal authorities who restrict its operation to a few hours in the evening. However, during daytime broadcasts of events considered vital to the nation – what Dayan and Katz (1992) would call 'media events' – such as a presidential funeral or a football match involving the national team, this rule is relaxed so that the local population may partake of them (Pace 1993: 1997).

In the daily life of Saribas Iban longhouses the more important 'idioms of a corporate national life' also include great media events. They are routinely woven together through the 8 o'clock news on RTM's first channel and its neighbouring slots. This is an example from my field notes:

Entanak Longhouse, 18 June 1997. I watched TV1 with Grandmother-of-Kalong. At 7.30 p.m. they started showing *Emosi* (Emotion), a dull Malay horror drama. Grand-mother-of- Kalong kept filling me in on the various kinship relations binding together the characters. The 'drama' was interrupted by the Muslim call to prayer, featuring new footage of the Malaysian team who recently climbed Mount Everest and some aerial shots of Kuala Lumpur's modern architectural wonders. The slogan 'Let us follow the path to prosperity' was presented in three languages: Arabic, Malay and English. At 7.52 we watched another promotional video, this time on PM Mahathir's Vision 2020 project, aimed at turning Malaysia into a developed nation with a strong national cul-ture by the year 2020. The video appeared to stress the compatibility between Islam, science and technology. It was followed by a panel with the countdown to the 16th Commonwealth Games, to be held in Kuala Lumpur in September 1998.

There followed a second Vision 2020 clip in a karaoke-like format. Five attractive young women clad in traditional dress, each one representing a major ethnic group (Malay, Chinese, Tamil, Kadazandusun and Iban) sang the catchy 2020 song hand in hand. Subtitles had been added, presumably to entice the audience to join in and make the song more memorable. There followed a clip urging drivers to control their speed on the motorway. Then came a third 2020 song promoting cooperation (*kerjasama*) among the nation's many groups. A torrent of pleasant images flooded the screen: there were vibrant cultural shows from Sarawak and other states, glistening robot-operated factories, homes for the elderly and the disabled, healthy-looking school-children, and more. Finally, the news at 8 began. The first item was PM Mahathir's three-day visit to the Lebanon. A sharp increase in sales of Malaysia's national car, the Proton, was expected as a result of this historic visit. Then came a second encouraging report ...

We can break up this barrage of federal government propaganda into nine items:

1. Urban Malay serial (aborted)

2. Muslim call to prayer combined with pro-development slogan

3. Vision 2020 propaganda clip: Islam, science and technology are in harmony

4. Countdown to Kuala Lumpur Commonwealth Games (a future media event)

5. Vision 2020 propaganda clip: the five major ethnic groups are in harmony

6. Motorway safety propaganda clip

7. Vision 2020 propaganda clip: all ethnic and social groups are in harmony

8. News at 8: first cabinet propaganda news report

9. News at 8: second cabinet propaganda news report ...

In Chapter 5 I analysed prime-time television in connection with Saribas Iban sustainable propaganda. Here I wish to tease out a number of interrelated spatial and temporal factors. First, prime-time television is highly structured and predictable. Saribas Iban viewers often remark on how they can get to see distant, more advanced countries through television. What they systematically fail to mention is the temporal-ideological framing of such news reports, a taken-for-granted, naturalised, invisible component that 'goes without saying'. Anderson (1991: 33) has discussed the arbitrary juxtaposition of items on the front page of a newspaper. They are linked through the date at the top, signifying 'the steady onward clocking of homogenous, empty time'. On Malaysian television, the randomness of world news affairs is routinely organised around CCT to serve a stable representation of the world in which the nation is steadily progressing 'along the path to prosperity'.[6] Items 8 and 9 above may be news to the viewers, but they are still designed to support an unchanging unity-in-diversity national ideology. Second, Malaysia's RTM repeatedly broadcasts the theme of a common national *future* that will transcend current religious, linguistic, ethnic, regional, economic and social divides by the year 2020. Saribas Iban viewers may or may not be confident about the attainability of Mahathir's Vision 2020. In either case, and owing to relentless broadcasts on radio and television, they all believe that their future has already been charted out on their behalf by leaders in far-off Kuala Lumpur. No alternative national future is ever broadcast.

This monofuturistic orientation of the state media has percolated into all spheres of Saribas Iban life. For example, local children often sing or hum to the catchy 2020 song. Numerous other instances could be given. Thus I once overheard an inebriated man loudly question the ability of the Iban people to achieve the 2020 dream. At a wedding, a local official encouraged the attendants to strive to achieve Vision 2020. On a trip upriver I met an Iban man who had a 2020 tattoo on his arm.[7] On another occasion, a young man proudly told me about the Commonwealth Games to be held in Kuala Lumpur in September 1998 in which 'all countries in the world' would participate. Characteristically, he knew the exact CCT and geographical indexes, but little about the historical and political significance of this media event. A fourth man had followed closely on television the Malaysian team's Everest climb, and wished an Iban had been represented. These examples are proof of how radio and television not only weave together a national calendar, but also of how they promote the government's CCT orientation through repeated national success stories in the fields of diplomacy, sport, technology, business, etc.

Conclusion

I have identified some of the limitations of the anthropology of time and stressed the comparative potential of clock-and-calendar time. The focus was on the regulated ways in which Malaysia's quotidian order is sustained in Saribas longhouses. Rural Iban live not only in longhouses, they also live within a synchronised modern state (Anderson 1991) – the dominant 'culturally organised lived-in world' of our era (cf. Rival 1997: 147). In the Malaysian culture area, there is no vernacular Iban time to repair to, just as there is no Iban ideology separate from the state ideology. In fact the two media forms, nationalist ideology and modern time, support one another across Malaysia's unified time-zone. To dispel, once and for all, any lingering romanticism attached to indigenous time, Gell's (1992: 315) words on the anthropology of time deserve to be quoted again:

> There is no fairyland where people experience time in a way that is markedly unlike the way in which we do ourselves, where there is no past, present and future, where time stands still, or chases its own tail, or swings back and forth like a pendulum.

Notes

1. The term 'chronoclasm', as it is normally used, bears no homology to iconoclasm. According to Genrikh Altov, chronoclasms are 'paradoxes arising from interference in preceding historical events'. The term is attributed to Wells who used it in his novel *The Time Machine* (1996 [1895]), and has also been used by Wyndham and Asimov (www.altshuller.ru/world/eng/science-fiction5.asp).
2. This silence has also been noted by Mark Peterson (2003: 248n).
3. I am again following the Iban practice of calling someone by the name of his or her child or grandchild, e.g., Grandfather-of-Samuel is the English translation of *Aki Samuel*, while Mother-of-Nuing stands for *Indai Nuing* (see Steinmayer 1999: 110).
4. John K. Wilson, the Scottish development officer introduced in chapter 3, played a pivotal role in spreading the new radio technologies in the Saratok area, northeast of the Saribas. In the mid-1950s, a grant from the Nuffield Foundation allowed him to purchase a number of radio telephone sets. Notice the element of CCT precision: 'Through those radios, Saratok used to relay important messages to all [development] centres and to all longhouses at certain times each day. Indeed each day at ten thirty, everyone stopped what they were doing to come and listen in. Why not? There might be a message for them or for someone in their longhouse' (Wilson 1969: 163).
5. I am assigning random 'door' (*pintu*) numbers to all *bilek*-families in order to facilitate their cross-referencing (e.g., between doors no. 4 and no. 12).
6. In Thailand the most popular daily segment is the news on channel 7, in which the nation is outlined as 'an island in a sea of nothingness' (Hamilton 2002: 162–163).
7. Already in the 1940s, Derek Freeman observed the penchant for promotional tattooing shown by well-travelled Iban men whose bodies were 'as thickly covered with tattooing as is a globe-trotter's portmanteau with labels; and both customs have the same intention: the advertising of achievement … One young man of Rumah Nyala had tattooed on his forearm the proud words: '*Suda kerja di Singapora*' ('Have worked in Singapore') (Freeman 1992 [1955]: 223).

9

CALENDAR TIME

> Ever since that day [on 1 June 1965, when the Dayak Festival was officially launched,] our people has been on a par with other peoples, for all to see. There are now two days out of 365 in every year in which all other peoples pay their respects to us, two days of public holiday.
>
> Ejau (1968), my translation

No visitor to Sarawak can leave without being invited to Gawai Dayak, the Dayak 'Harvest Festival'. The Festival is held across Sarawak every year on 1 and 2 June. In 1997 I was at Entanak Longhouse, my main fieldwork base, during Gawai. The following rite of passage, seemingly minor, helps us to broach the close relationship between Gawai and nation building. At 11.56 p.m. on Gawai's Eve, the master of ceremonies announced through the PA system the imminent 'countup'[1] to the Gawai holiday. Taking up their positions along the outer wall of the gallery – the place of honour – the elders filled their glasses with Gawai rice wine (*ai pengayu*), as indeed did all other revellers. Ten seconds before the stroke of midnight, the collective countup began: *Satu, dua, tiga* ...(One, two, three ...) until we reached a jubilant *Sepuluuuhh!!!!* (Tennnnn!!!!). This was immediately followed by the customary cheer of joy (*babababababaaa-uuuuuuhhhh*), a deafening salvo from a nearby veranda, the Gawai Dayak toast, and the collective exchange of greetings and handshakes. It was then that the revelling began in earnest, with taped pop being played at full blast all through the night.

Before I can explore the nation-building significance of this midnight rite – perhaps not obvious at first sight – I must sketch out the origins and spread of Gawai. The idea of Gawai Dayak was first publicly floated on Radio Sarawak in the 1950s. It was then widely discussed in Sarawak's coffee-shops and longhouse galleries. The British colonial authorities resisted the idea, fearful that it may lead to Dayak political demands. Anthony Richards, an expert in Iban lore and language, was amongst those who vehemently opposed the idea. Yet urban Dayak intellectuals gainsaid their rulers. They argued that

170

an officially sanctioned Festival would allow the Dayaks to reciprocate the hospitality of the two other major 'races' in Sarawak, who opened their homes to them during Chinese New Year and Muslim Hari Raya. It was only in 1965, though, two years after Sarawak had achieved 'independence through Malaysia', that 1 and 2 June were declared a public holiday by the then chief minister, who was a Dayak (Undau 2001).[2]

In chapter 3 we met two of the influential men behind the early diffusion of Gawai. One was Michael Buma, a well-known Iban broadcaster and educationalist[3]. Another was the Iban broadcaster and author, Andria Ejau, who sought to spread Gawai by means of radio programmes and morality novellas (*ensera kelulu*). In the opening scenes of one such novella (Ejau 1968), probably based on a radio drama, a government-appointed native chief (*Pengulu*) is visiting a remote longhouse. He has come to tell his followers about Gawai. On the eve of 1 June, he explains, all Dayaks will be celebrating the new festival at the same time. Perfect timing will be of the essence, since at the stroke of midnight they will all raise their glasses, filled with specially brewed rice wine (*ai pengayu*) to welcome the New Year. The chief then explains to his puzzled listeners what is meant by the term 'Dayak', listing no less than 18 groups and comparing their linguistic diversity to that of the Chinese. It is only now that the Dayaks have recognised themselves as one race (*bangsa*), he adds, 'because schooling arrived to us late' (*laban sekula laun datai ba kitai*). He concludes his allocution by outlining the wider political significance of the new festival. I have translated his exact words at the top of this chapter.

Ejau's native propaganda betrays Gawai's quintessential modernity. He links the festival to three salient concerns of modern nation builders, namely nationalised ethnicity, public visibility ('for all to see') and synchronicity (the dream of perfect timing, cf. Anderson 1991). In all three respects, Gawai has been a resounding success, as every year hundreds of thousands of Dayaks return to their longhouses and villages *in time* to celebrate it, and they do so loudly and visibly. In other words, it exhibits 'the characteristics of most Malaysian festivals' (Boulanger 2000: 50). In contrast Christmas is a low-key event, a sober family affair not celebrated by all Dayaks.

How did Gawai spread from its urban place of birth to the rural areas? Human geographers working on the diffusion of innovations and epidemic diseases have identified two main types of spatial diffusion: contagious (owing to geographical proximity) and hierarchical (top-down, from urban centres to sub-centres). Purely contagious spreads are generally much slower than purely hierarchical ones, but the swiftest spreads are a combination of both. For example, the spread of measles in Iceland occurred through a combination of both routes: there was hierarchical diffusion from the capital to provincial centres as well as contagious diffusion around the capital in Southwest Iceland (Cliff et al. 1981). Since the term 'contagious' has undesirable connotations when applied to cultural diffusion (Ingold 2000b, Debray 1997), I shall use instead the terms vertical diffusion (top-down, hierarchical) and horizontal diffusion (among neighbouring entities, e.g., two longhouses).

It is likely that Gawai spread rapidly in the early years, and that it did so both vertically and horizontally. From Kuching it probably spread vertically to Sibu and other provincial centres, and horizontally to Kuching's outskirts. At lower hierarchical levels, similar processes must have unfolded; that is, from the provincial centres a mix of vertical (to smaller market towns) and horizontal spreads (to their own surrounding longhouses) probably took place. In smaller towns, it is likely that district officers held meetings to disseminate the Gawai script amongst native chiefs and headmen, as they regularly do with top-down innovations. There are reports, however, of remote areas in the interior of Sarawak where pre-Gawai harvest festivals are still the norm (Langub and Belawing n.d., Boulanger 2000: 55).

We can plausibly assume that the more educated longhouse members (many living in towns) were vectors in the early diffusion of Gawai through their funding, organising committees and informal means of persuasion. This was certainly the case in the Saribas (Layar) longhouse where Véronique Béguet carried out fieldwork in 1991 and 1995–1996.[4] As well, Radio Sarawak must have played a part in the spreading of Gawai by reaching all Dayak strata, from the capital and provincial elites to longhouse dwellers. As we saw in chapter 3, Radio Sarawak has been the main public site of Iban and Dayak cultural standardisation since the 1950s. Gawai – co-invented by broadcasters – became part of this modernising project since its inception. This medium also allowed Gawai organising committees to renew their festive programmes, selecting those items (games, songs, rites, etc.) that suited their local agendas and the fashions of the day. In the now distant 1980s, for instance, Michael Jackson was a popular choice among Gawai 'disco' dancers. During my late 1990s fieldwork, Malay and Iban *joget* and Indonesian *dangdut* numbers were all the rage.

In this chapter, I outline, by means of Gawai Dayak, a theory of media ritual in a world of states and clock-and-calendar time. To this end I first revisit the two Gawai I have attended to date, one in a smart Kuching ballroom in 2001, the other at Entanak Longhouse in 1997. I then question the popular idea – common in media studies – that watching television or reading the morning papers is a manner of 'ritual'. I also take issue with recent anthropological studies of ritual for failing to define the term and for blurring ritual with performance. Both media studies and anthropology are ahistorical on the subject of media and ritual; they do not address the question of cultural change. To address it, I adapt Couldry's (2003) theory of media ritual to Malaysia's nation-building project. This theory is compatible both with previous anthropological theories of ritual (e.g., Parkin 1992, Turner 1982) and with the Iban ethnographic record (Sather 1993), although it, too, fails to pass the diachronic test. I am arguing that Gawai is an ethnic festival saturated with media

Figure 9.1. A local television cameraman films the Dayak dancers, who are lined up to welcome the dignitaries.

Source: courtesy Samuel W.F. Onn.

rituals, i.e., rituals designed to provide remote access to a modern country's centres of power and knowledge. These claims of access, alas, carry more weight in Kuching's hotel ballrooms than they do in a longhouse gallery. I am also suggesting that some of Gawai's media rituals retain pre-modern ritual features (precedence, directionality, efficacy, etc.), but they also signal fundamental changes, most notably the fact that they 'go by the clock'.

Ballroom Gawai

On 31 May 2001 I joined the Gawai celebrations at the Crowne Plaza Riverside, an upmarket hotel in Kuching. At around 6.45 p.m. the main organising committee arrived in the spacious ballroom reserved for the occasion. Over the next ninety minutes, flanked by Dayaks in ceremonial costume and press photographers, the guests arrived. As is common practice at official events, their arrival was timed in reverse hierarchical order, with undistinguished guests and VIPs welcomed at 7.00 p.m., the deputy chief minister at 7.30–7.45 p.m., the chief minister at 8.00 p.m. and Malaysia's head of state at 8.15 p.m. Dinner was served soon after the head of state's arrival. This was

Figure 9.2. An elderly Orang Ulu man (second from the left) holding an 'Excellence award to model parents producing the most number of graduates'. In the centre, a smiling Chief Minister of Sarawak.

Source: courtesy Samuel W.F. Onn.

followed by a speech by the deputy chief minister, a Saribas Iban Christian, in which he assured his Muslim superiors that the Dayaks were making steadfast progress along the road to prosperity. There followed the presentation of an 'Excellence award to model [Dayak] parents producing the most number of graduates'.[5] The parents were chosen to represent all three Dayak 'communities': Iban, Bidayuh and Orang Ulu.

The next item caused some embarrassment amongst its participants. It was a procession of Dayak 'intellectuals' who, prompted by the master of ceremonies, came on stage to receive a round of applause for having completed their university degrees. The idea came, I was told by one of them, from 'a high place'. The chief minister of Sarawak then delivered a pre-electoral speech in which he supported Malaysia's prime minister's Vision 2020, his plan to transform Malaysia into a developed country with a national culture by 2020 (see chapter 4). There followed a choreographed dance charting the progress of the Dayak people from the Stone Age to the Computer Age. The piece ended with the dance troupe reverentially wheeling in a computer and sitting on stage to watch a Vision 2020 video on a giant screen. This year's Gawai slogan read: 'Towards a Transformation of Vision 2020 Family'.[6]

Figure 9.3. Choreographed dance charting the progress of the Dayak people from the Stone Age to the Computer Age. Halfway through the dance, Dayak schoolchildren listen intently to a teacher while a woman restrains a warrior who opposes modern education.

Source: courtesy Samuel W.F. Onn.

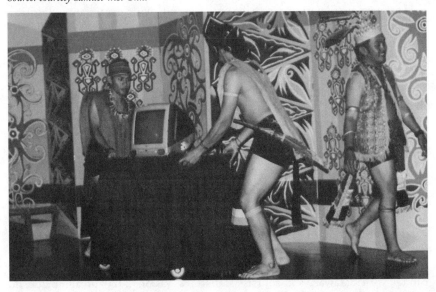

Figure 9.4. Near the end of the performance, two Dayak dancers wheel in a computer monitor to represent the dawn of the Computer Age.

Source: courtesy Samuel W.F. Onn.

Figure 9.5. The monitor projects official propaganda onto a giant screen, including the 2001 Dayak Festival slogan 'Towards a Transformation of Vision 2020 Family'.
Source: courtesy Samuel W.F. Onn.

The next presentation was a beauty pageant, with contestants classified, like the model parents, by subethnicity. At midnight there was a collective countup to the official start of Gawai followed by the Gawai Dayak toast, proposed by the head of state, and the exchange of greetings and handshakes. This was a sober, calm transition to the festive season. Unlike the longhouse Gawai I will describe shortly, there was no heavy drinking or 'disco' dancing involved. Instead, the results of the beauty contest were announced, followed by the awards ceremony, with the winners surrounded by an army of press photographers. Soon afterwards, leaders and followers departed, inverting the order of precedence observed upon their arrival earlier in the evening. The following day, the deputy chief minister held an open house[7] to wish all Dayaks and visitors of other races a Happy Gawai.

This episode shows that the hierarchy of cultural diffusion outlined earlier stretches all the way to Putrajaya, Malaysia's new federal capital. Gawai propaganda spreads not only from Kuching to the longhouses, but also from Putrajaya *to* Kuching. The Kuching political and cultural elites act as mediators in the largely one-way traffic of images and slogans linking the federal capital with Sarawak. Of course, Mahathir's Vision 2020 dream made no reference to Gawai, but mass producers of Gawai propaganda in Kuching are adept at weaving elements of that vision into their programmes. In doing so, they are symbolically assimilating the Dayaks into a calendar-time goal dreamed up in the federal capital. Thus some of the slogans used over the years have included

1992 CULTURE: THE PILLAR OF UNITY AND DEVELOPMENT

1993 ADAT AND TECHNOLOGY FOR NATIONAL PROGRESS

1994 CULTURAL CONFLUENCE AS A BASIS FOR DEVELOPMENT TOWARDS VISION 2020

Another feature of this public event is that it was a uniquely Malaysian 'meta-script' made up of a sequence of modular, mostly imported, social scripts. A social script is a culturally shared mental schema for performing actions in a structured manner. For instance, Europeans dining at a restaurant know that a waiter or waitress will show them to their table, bring them a menu, take their orders, etc. Any abnormal deviation from this sequence would cause surprise and possibly embarrassment (Whitehouse 2001, Rapport and Over-ing 2000: 51–57). In the ballroom Gawai script, the sub-scripts included the arrival and departure of guests, the beauty pageant[8], the unusual – and embarrassing – honouring of intellectuals, the midnight countup, and the greetings and handshakes. The modularity of modern states has been remarked upon by Anderson. Once the modern nation was imaginatively created, it became

Figure 9.6. The overall winner of the 2001 Kumang Gawai beauty contest (an Iban), flanked by her Bidayuh and Orang Ulu co-winners, pose for the cameras.

Source: courtesy Samuel W.F. Onn.

Figure 9.7. The local press photographing the new beauty queens.
Source: courtesy Samuel W.F. Onn.

'modular', that is 'capable of being transplanted … to a great variety of social terrains, to merge and be merged with a correspondingly wide variety of political and ideological constellations' (Anderson 1991: 4, quoted in Foster 2002: 10). Here I wish to point out that this modularity reaches down to a nation's public events. Moreover, it rests upon the taken-for-granted, prior adoption of clock-and-calendar time (CCT). The modularity of public events rests on the CCT notion of 'programme'. The seemingly banal countup script is central to the Gawai programme. It is undoubtedly the climax of the evening, the ritual phase charged with the most symbolic significance. Gawai is more than a 'rite of modernisation' (Peacock 1968); it is a rite of modern time, a celebration *of* and *through* CCT.

Although ostensibly the Dayaks are celebrating their culture and traditions, the underlying message is their cultural parity with the Malays and Chinese. By occupying a hitherto vacant 'slot' in the official calendar, the Dayaks can symbolically claim a parity that is denied them in all other spheres of life – in the economy, administration, media, etc. Given that Gawai is a CCT festival, perfect timing is essential to its successful re-enactment year after year. Thus the arrival and departure of guests is carefully timed, and so is the countup rite, where the margin for error must be minimised. Clock timing marks out the distinguished from the undistinguished guests, just as it distinguishes Gawai's Eve from Gawai proper. The suspense of the countup is a result of its linking tiny fractions of time (seconds) with large fractions of time (months). Rappaport (1999) has stressed the 'digital' nature of rites of passage. These rites turn natural continua into sharp breaks, creating a before-and-after effect. Had he considered the ritual uses of modern time devices, he may have added that CCT enhances the digital quality of rites of passage.

Longhouse Gawai

We may expect precise timing to be adhered to solely during official elite functions in urban areas of Sarawak, but this is not at all the case. Gawai Dayak is as much of a timed festival in rural areas as it is in Kuching. To understand this, we can revisit the longhouse celebration I attended in 1997. As in the ballroom episode, we shall see that clock timing was of the essence in the smooth running of the various media rituals.

On the evening of 25 May, a group of children had gathered at the headman's section of the gallery. Some were studying that year's programme (M. *Aturcara*) posted outside the headman's front door. Others were emulating their favourite martial artists. Soon the gallery was transformed into a manner of television studio. A dozen children aged between 9 and 12 were divided into three teams. The quiz hostess was a young unmarried woman we

Figure 9.8. An advertising banner in a Saribas longhouse gallery (*ruai*) welcoming visitors to the local Dayak Festival.

Source: courtesy Martin Pohlmann.

shall call Suri; her cousin Tom was the time-keeper. He was holding a giant wristwatch of the kind popular on rural Sarawak living-room walls.[9] There were two older judges sat on a woven mat (*tikai*) behind a low table. A small crowd had gathered around the contestants, with some mothers closely behind their offspring. The evening opened with a Malay-language quiz on school knowledge – the first-ever quiz night at Entanak. The woman behind this innovative media ritual was the headman's sister, a Christian modernist in her 40s. A former primary school teacher in the remote interior, she currently held a highly regarded clerical job with the local police. The idea occurred to her while watching a quiz show on television. Her aim was to reward the more studious children in the longhouse to impress the importance of school knowledge upon all youngsters. There followed a quiz on Iban lore, a Malay-language reading contest and a game of Pictionary, also in the national language. Although there was some jovial parental squabbling over the rules of the games, they all had one thing in common: their strict timing.

On 27 May a women's quiz night was held, another 1997 novelty. Contestants had to answer questions on Iban mythology and solve obscure riddles (*entelah*). This was, however, no conventional television studio, as there were no chairs, and contestants sat on woven mats in three files, each representing a team. The atmosphere throughout the contest was decidedly festive, with a fair deal of patting, slapping, pushing, screaming and rolling over with laughter amongst the participants, particularly when a fellow team member blurted out the wrong answer. This happened all too often, for this proletarianised, Christian longhouse is virtually bereft of knowledgeable elders. Much of the 'old knowledge' (*penemu lama*) still held by its residents is likely to have come from Radio Sarawak and RTM programmes aimed at salvaging the Iban heritage (see chapter 3). The second game was an Iban version of Pictionary. These two games were again strictly timed. The evening reached a roaring climax with a mime contest and a *ngajat* (traditional dance) competition.

On 31 May, not long before dawn, a crowd had gathered at the headman's. They were there in time to escort the carved Hornbill (*Burong Kenyalang*) to its Gawai perch: the top of a 'remembrance pole' (*tiang pengingat*). As is customary with rituals associated with birth and fertility, the procession exited the longhouse through its upriver end. It then described a circle to reach the pole, erected in front of the longhouse. Finding a precarious balance upon a follower's shoulders, the headman nailed the Hornbill to the pole illuminated by torches and the flashes of cameras. Safely back on the ground, he was given a round of applause and a cockerel. Waving the cockerel seven times he prayed for the well-being of the longhouse. Being new to the office, he felt unsure and asked an elder whether he wished to add (*nampong*) any further formulae. As the elder had nothing to add, the headman proceeded to sacrifice the fowl. This was followed by a collective, Christian-like exchange of handshakes and well-wishing. It was time to consume the food and drinks. Well into the

Figure 9.9. The front cover of a Dayak Festival karaoke DVD.

Source: courtesy Tiew Brothers Company, Sibu.

feast, someone noticed two items missing from the remembrance pole: the flags of Sarawak and Malaysia. They were promptly fetched and nailed to either side of the Hornbill.

Gawai's Eve was launched that evening with the native chief and headman ceremonially cutting the Gawai ribbon. This done, the drum and gong ensemble (*gendang*) went through a brief warm-up while the master of ceremonies, the native chief's urban-based son, tested his microphone. As the *gendang* began to play, a procession of ten girls and two boys in traditional attire marched out of a family room (*bilek*) and into the gallery. They described a propitious circle around the dance floor and exited the gallery again. Prompted by the MC, the audience gave them a round of applause. Back in the *bilek* the performers found a crowd of men and boys gathered around the television set watching the football. It was a decisive match for Sarawak in their struggle to wrestle the national league title from Sabah. Oblivious to the mesmerised supporters, a group of dancers posed for the parental cameras at the other end of the spacious *bilek*.

But the show had to go on. For the next hour all twelve contestants took it in turns to dance in the gallery to the beat of the *gendang* and the click of cameras. One by one the MC read out their names, ages, hobbies and career dreams (cf. school essays in chapter 5). There followed a beauty pageant featuring the same teenage girls, all vying for the title of Kumang, a mythical figure and paragon of Iban female beauty (Boulanger 2000: 51). At around 9.30 p.m. the official speeches began. The headman thanked the native chief, the organising committee, the *gendang* ensemble and the entire longhouse for the smooth running of the present year's greatly expanded programme. He also thanked the sponsors as well as the elder who mended the wooden Hornbill. He concluded by praying to the Iban Supreme Deity (*Petara*) that those in the government service be promoted, that farmers reap plentiful harvests and that labourers earn high wages. The native chief's speech centred on the presence of a white student of Iban culture from London University who had followed in the footsteps of Robert Pringle, the eminent historian, and chosen Entanak for his study. Finally I, the white guest, delivered a potvaliant Iban speech to thank my hosts.

Having thanked all three speakers, the MC announced the prize-giving ceremony. The winners of the various Gawai contests were called forth to the now playful, suspense-laden beat of the *gendang*. After this ceremony, recorded Iban pop replaced the gongs and drums and a few courageous souls took to the dance floor. Before we had had a chance to warm up, the countup rite described in the opening to this chapter began.

The best part of the following day was spent *bilek*-crawling (*belanggar*) in the propitious manner. That is, the revellers left the longhouse through its upriver end, described a circle by visiting four outlying houses, and re-entered the longhouse once again through its downriver end. Each *bilek*-family laid out its finest woven mats and served potent beverages to the visitors under the deafening blast of vernacular pop. Back in the longhouse gallery, the elder who restored the Hornbill to its former glory took a break to teach me proper Iban ritual. The previous day he was unhappy to see the Hornbill not being adequately fed at the pole while we humans enjoyed a succulent meal. The deity was not even given the roasted rice (*letup*) it would need for its long journey. Not wishing to single out anyone for criticism, he added that the Hornbill had not been properly praised (*dipuji*) or given the right charms (*ubat*). We were sitting close to the elder's section of the gallery, presently taken over by a group of loud Iban karaoke singers. Since we could hardly hope to defeat them, we decided to join them.

It took me two or three days to recuperate from the Gawai excesses. It was around this time that the headman's brother, who worked at a Shell petrol station in Kuching, arrived in the longhouse. This year he had not been given Gawai leave. He was bitterly disappointed to have missed the festival and tried to recreate some of the Gawai ambiance by inviting us to drink and be merry. But CCT waits for no man, and none of us felt like joining him.

Media and Ritual

In modern Western countries we often hear or read about people's daily 'rituals', such as reading the newspaper over a cup of coffee, or watching a soap opera. This deeply engrained identification of ritual with media goes back at least to Hegel. The philosopher, who was born in 1770, already spoke of newspapers as modern man's ersatz for morning prayers (Anderson 1991: 35). Prominent media researchers working in a variety of countries have followed suit. Some use the term 'ritual' interchangeably with 'custom'. Thus according to Nordenstreng (1972), for Finnish viewers watching the news on television is 'a ritual, a custom serving to maintain a feeling of security'. Others take ritual to be a national tradition. For Scannell (1988) the FA Cup, the Last Night of the Proms and other live events broadcast in Britain have become 'traditions, rituals, part of national life'. Hartley (1987: 123–124), following Anderson (1991 [1983]) following Hegel, associates the term with a daily pseudo-religious 'ceremony'. He argues that newspapers are 'the ultimate fiction' for 'they construct the imagined community, and the basis of a mass ritual or ceremony that millions engage in every day'. Others call television viewing a 'rite of passage' or mechanical 'ritual'. Thus according to Silverstone (1988: 26) 'news-watching is a ritual, both in its mechanical repetitiveness and ... more importantly, in its presentation of the familiar and the strange, the reassuring and the threatening'. Still others use ritual in its domestic, everyday sense: Johnson (1981: 167), as we said in chapter 8, considers radio to have been at first an intrusive guest in Australia, for it 'timetabled family activities and challenged domestic rituals'. Finally, there are those who link mediated rituals with capitalism. According to Hobart (1995: 10), media specialists such as Fiske (1989) 'concur that quiz shows are the rituals of late capitalism: they reenact the workings of knowledge, power and success'.[10]

The first four quotes above are taken from the influential media scholar David Morley (1992: 251–270) who uses them at various points of his essay to argue for the importance of detailed ethnographic research into the domestic uses of media. Unfortunately Morley leaves the various contradictory usages of the term 'ritual' unexamined, as is often the case in media studies.[11] In this section I will define the terms 'ritual' and 'media ritual'. First, it is important to agree on what kinds of practices are *not* rituals. For the time

183

being, let us concur that watching television on a daily basis is not, in itself, a ritual practice. David Parkin's (1992) anthropological work on East African rituals is of use here. Parkin (1992: 18) argues, following Turner (1982: 24) who in turn followed Van Gennep (1960 [1909]), that directionality is fundamental to the ritual process. Rituals often take the form of a journey or passage 'undertaken and/or marked by participants standing in spatial relations to each other'. They are based on what Parkin calls 'formulaic spatiality', that is 'the capacity to create and act through idioms of passage, movement, including exchange, journey, axis, concentrism, and up-and-down directions' (1992: 18).

This description matches perfectly the Iban ethnography. Iban pagan rituals are 'structured as journeys (*jalai*) and meanings are conveyed through images arranged linearly, in space and time, to create an itinerary of travel or movement' (Sather 1993: 65). For instance, birth rituals are symbolic and physical journeys from the family *bilek*, then outwards onto the veranda (*tanju*), followed by a ritual procession from the gallery (*ruai*) to the river where both mother and child will take their first bathing or 'ritual cooling' (*ngasoh chelap*). This is followed by a rite of incorporation into the longhouse community consisting of a second ritual cooling in the gallery. In Iban ritual practice, 'spiritual danger is spatialized' (1993: 87). The longhouse architecture 'supplies coordinates of motion rather than stasis'. It is not a 'fixed, physical matrix' but rather the setting where metaphors of time and space render explicit relationships between the individual *bileks* and the longhouse that in daily life remain implicit.

Freeman's (1960, 1970) influential early work, discussed in chapter 2, privileged the Iban longhouse 'as a built form'. In a famous phrase (1992: 129), he defined it not as 'a communal pavilion, but as a street of privately owned, semi-detached houses'. Sather (1993: 65) puts forth an alternative model: the longhouse as a 'ritually constituted structure' in which ritual orders persons and materials in time and space. If we regard the longhouse 'through a ritual lens', he adds, we first discover 'a plurality of symbolic orders' which are constantly created and recreated in ritual. Subsequently, we come to relocate *bilek*-families in 'an ordered series of part-whole relationships' (1993: 65).

Helliwell (1993), on the basis of Gerai Dayak fieldwork in Indonesian Borneo, has proposed a third model of the longhouse (chapter 2). She found 'an almost unimpeded flow of both sound and light' (1993: 51) connecting all longhouse apartments (*lawang*). In lieu of Freeman's physical longhouse, she posits the Gerai Dayak longhouse as a 'community of voices'. Gerai voices, she adds, 'flow in a longhouse in a most extraordinary fashion; moving up and down its length in seeming monologue, they are in fact in continual dialogue with listeners who may be unseen, but are always present. As such they create, more than does any other facet of longhouse life, a sense of community' (1993: 51). This idea of sensorial community-building complements nicely the two mentioned models of the longhouse.

I wish to propose a fourth model that both integrates and updates those of Freeman, Sandin and Helliwell: the Iban longhouse as a *Malaysian social formation*. The longhouse is (1) a physical structure and organisation whose main daily economic unit is the *bilek*-family (Freeman) as well as (2) an organisation which subordinates the *bilek*-family to the longhouse community during ritual and festive periods (Sather), (3) a community of shared sensorial experiences (Helliwell) *as well as* (4) an organisation increasingly built around the demands of nation building, demands partly met by enacting *media rituals* (see below).

To illustrate this model, let us take one of the Gawai media rituals described earlier, for instance the Hornbill rite. In what sense was it a ritual? First, it was a ritual in terms of Parkin's (1992: 18) criterion of directionality. Whilst Saribas burial processions leave the longhouse through the downriver end – as we saw at the opening of chapter 6 – on this ritual occasion of renewal and joyful celebration the procession left through the opposite end. Second, it was a ritual in its search for efficacious performance. Ritual does things, it has effects on the world, it is 'work that is carried out' (Parkin 1992: 14; Ingold 1994: 341). Indeed the most commonly used Iban words for ritual, *gawa'* and *pengawa'*, can also be translated as 'work' (Richards 1981: 271). Participants may quibble over the details, but they are all agreed that the ritual must follow 'some time-hallowed precedent' (Parkin 1992: 15). This explains the inexperienced headman's hesitation and call for assistance when performing the Hornbill rite. Parkin (1992: 19) maintains that rituals survive through 'agency by default' as rival participants criticise each others' performance to gain control over the ritual process. The elder who took me aside did indeed criticise the organisers over the Hornbill rite, but he did so on the quiet, in the sole company of a powerless outsider, not through a microphone or during the rite.

But in what sense was the Hornbill rite a *media* ritual? Here we need to refer to Nick Couldry's (2003) book *Media Rituals*.[12] Couldry describes his approach as 'post-Durkheimian' and 'anti-functionalist'. His starting point is, like Parkin's, the work of Victor Turner. Couldry shares Turner's understanding of rituals as actions that embody and betoken transcendent values rather than as texts that 'express' cultural ideals (Geertz). Media rituals are actions that reproduce the 'myth' of the media as privileged access points to the centre of society – the 'myth of the mediated centre'. This mythical reproduction takes place through tacit categories (e.g., media vs. non-media person) as well as values that engage and direct our attention. Media rituals 'condense' these implicit categories and values into frames of performative action (Goffman) – or, in my terms, 'social scripts' (see above). For instance, in the presence of a celebrity most ordinary people will act in extraordinary, ritualised ways.

Another example of a media ritual would be clapping when directed by staff at a quiz show, or having pictures of oneself taken when on 'pilgrimage' to a soap opera set. This extensive mesh of rituals helps to sustain the myth of the mediated centre.

Couldry takes issue with Dayan and Katz for subscribing to the myth of the mediated centre in their influential book, *Media Events* (1992). Describing their assumptions as functionalist, he doubts that media events such as the funeral of Princess Diana really enhanced social cohesion in Britain, let alone abroad. Instead he redefines media events as occasions when 'particularly intense' claims about accessing the social centre are being made. He then analyses reality TV as another genre that sustains the myth through its promise of taking audiences 'live' to the social centre with a minimum of fuss.

Couldry's theory takes us part of the way to an understanding of media rituals in the contemporary world order. Yet I have to challenge his thesis that the mediated centre is a myth. My experience in Malaysia, Romania and other developing countries tells me that farmers and other low-income residents are well aware of the concentration of political, economic and cultural resources not in a single 'centre', but rather *in a few urban centres* – a concentration that Couldry himself stresses. Are they deluded in assuming that media professionals have better access to the nation's 'central' organisations, i.e., those which allocate strategic resources? I do not think they are. Since the mediated centre – or better, centres – is no myth, a more enabling definition of media rituals would be *rituals that reproduce the media's privileged access to a country's seats of power and knowledge.*

The Hornbill rite may look like a 'traditional' pagan ritual, but on closer inspection it turns out to be a media ritual, for it reproduces the media's privileged access to Malaysia's seats of power and knowledge. The clues are provided by two media technologies that we often take for granted: wristwatches and photographic cameras. The Hornbill rite was carefully timed; like all other Gawai events, it went by the clock and by the calendar. It was also photographed, binding the figurative indexicality of photography (Peirce 1955) to the abstract indexicality of clocks and calendars. Although the Hornbill rite was once about efficacious intent, in the era of scheduled photography it has gained a new layer of significance. It is now 'part of the show', an essential part of Gawai's 'spectacular logic' (Handelman 1998, Debord 1983 [1968]). By shooting the rite with cameras and watches, the locals were aligning their collective performance with that of countless others across Sarawak. Perfect alignment was ensured when someone noticed the absence of two potent symbols of the nation – the flags of Sarawak and Malaysia – and these were promptly nailed to the Hornbill pole.

Perhaps a clearer instance of a Gawai media ritual was the quiz show. I have explained elsewhere in this book that Iban parents are today very eager to send their children to school. Like parents across the developing world, they feel the joint tyranny of place and history has put their people at a disadvantage in relation to more powerful races, an assessment I share (see also Foster 2002). The longhouse quiz show confronts this tyranny by relocating an urban media ritual to a rural setting. It does so by following carefully, with the right props and cast, a social script 'as seen on television'. Television professionals often warn their viewers with formulae such as 'Don't try this at home!'. In 1997 Entanak residents decided to try a television script at 'home'. In doing so, they were seeking remote access to Malaysia's cultural centres. At the same time, they were tacitly asserting – performing – their subordinate relationship to those centres.

The 1997 Dayak Festival at Entanak was an amalgam of old and new ritual elements. It had retained some pre-state ritual features (hallowed precedence, auspicious directionality, collective efficacy, etc.) but the dominant scripts were undoubtedly the nation-building media rituals.

No Rubber Time

The Malaysian and Indonesian middle classes are keen to point out to visitors that many of their fellow citizens practise *masa* (or *waktu*) *gumi* (rubber time), i.e., that they are yet to internalise the importance of punctuality (e.g., Lee 2004). Yet both re-enactments of Gawai that I have discussed show that the event requires precise timing, not temporal elasticity. The central rite is doubtless the midnight countup, as envisaged by Ejau and other Gawai founding fathers. In the minds and actions of modern nation builders – whether politicians, bureaucrats or villagers – collective simultaneity is of the essence (Anderson 1991). This point goes against recent anthropological writings on ritual, performance, and media in which the notion of simultaneity is used very differently. Some of this work can be found in a 1998 edited volume entitled *Ritual, Performance, Media*. In her introduction, F. Hughes-Freeland engages with the problem of defining ritual. In postmodern fashion, she does so by eschewing 'essential' definitions in favour of an ad-hoc, relational approach. The term ritual becomes 'an odd-job word', one subordinated to the broader category of 'situated social action'. In the editor's view, the ritual process cannot be divided into periods of structure and anti-structure (Turner). Rather it is 'a form of practice, in which agency, creativity, structure and constraint become *simultaneous*, rather than distinguished in time and space, whether real or metaphorical' (1998: 8, my emphasis).

Yet it is precisely the segmentation of social time and social space facilitated by CCT media that allows modern people, including Malaysian Iban, to (a) clearly distinguish between daily life and special occasions, e.g., Gawai or Christmas, (b) plan their use of the social time and space available outside school and working hours, (c) carry out their daily, weekly and annual cycles of activities in coordination with others, and (d) actively reflect on those activities in order to abandon some of them and retain others, effectively 'making history' through a process of cultural selection. I suggested earlier, with reference to Rappaport's (1999) theory of ritual, that CCT enhances the digital quality of rites of passage, i.e., their slicing of nature's continua into arbitrary *dis*-continua. In this sense Gawai Dayak would seem merely a modern, timed version of previous harvest festivals (*gawai*). This illation would, however, be misleading, for replacing parochial farming festivals with a single CCT festival has far-reaching implications.

One major effect of Gawai has been its weakening of old ties of riverine reciprocity. In neighbouring Indonesian Borneo, 'Ibanic' groups have resisted government attempts at setting a fixed date for their harvest celebrations.[13] A common date is seen by the authorities as a way of reducing the 'waste' of local financial resources. Drake (2000) who carried out fieldwork in the Belitang Hulu area in 1978–1979, argues that a fixed date would disrupt local arrangements whereby revellers take it in turns to visit one another's communities. For the Mualang people, a local *gawai* is 'the predominant site of kinship reciprocities beyond the village' (2000: 452). Among Saribas Iban in Sarawak, by contrast, Gawai has long eroded the *sapemakai* (literally, 'those who eat together') system of reciprocity binding neighbouring longhouses.[14] Gawai Dayak de-emphasises local ties while emphasising those linking the longhouse to the wider cultural worlds of Sarawak and Malaysia; it (re)produces *national* – not parochial – loyalties. We saw a vivid example of this at Entanak when the flags of both territories where placed on either side of the Hornbill deity.

Perhaps an even greater contributor to the erosion of *sapemakai* is the realistic expectation that migrants will return to their longhouses for Gawai. The same is expected of Malaysia's other major 'races' during their respective festivals.[15] Recall Peter Kedit's (1993: 136) description (chapter 7) of how urban-based Iban still

> maintain ties with their rural communities and help them solve problems in such activities as farming, funerals or festivals. Their original home is a place of sentimental value with fond memories of childhood. But it also has economic value because land holdings are still owned by their families and they have rights to them.

Finally, the longhouse Gawai sketch presented above illustrates another side-effect of CCT: the proliferation of scheduling clashes. In the early 1980s, when the then prime minister of Malaysia, Mahathir, created a single time-zone for the far-flung country, he could not have envisaged, of course, the 1997 clash between Gawai and the football league. Most men and boys at Entanak chose to watch the broadcast match, literally turning their backs on the local Gawai activities. In common with many other Southeast Asian peoples, the Iban will avoid public confrontation, so no protests were heard from the women. Another clash affected the headman's brother whose labour commitments at the petrol station prevented him from returning to the longhouse. The nation-building benefits of time-zone unification are numerous and cannot be covered here.[16] But both instances of scheduling clashes show how such a unification carries its own 'opportunity costs' (Gell 1992: 322–323), for there are grave physical limits intrinsic to human agency, including the inability to be in two places at once (Giddens 1984: 111). The first clash also suggests that the football league organisers – presumably, non-Dayaks – were either unaware of Gawai or incapable of rescheduling the match around this festival. Both examples indicate a conflict between the long-term, spatially broad strategies of the powerful (here, the football, television and oil industries) and the short-term, local 'tactics' of the less powerful, viz. ordinary Dayaks (see de Certeau 1984).

Conclusion

With reference to gendered media practices in the (British) family, Morley (1992: 162) has stressed the need to determine who is in charge of the television remote control, a tangible instrument of domestic power. In a longhouse Gawai, we have to consider other media technologies. We must identify instead who controls (a) the organisation of festive time-space through the elaboration of a printed programme posted outside the headman's door, and (b) the serialised linking and transcending of local time-space by means of the PA system. In the longhouse in question, the organising committee was led by a woman (Indai Sue) who designed the programme, while only the male leaders and their European guest had access to the PA system's microphone. Together, they set the festival's moral and political agenda and constructed the social time and space upon which the agenda rested. The views of Indai Sue – an educated Christian modernist – are revealing. When I asked her about the pagan meaning (*reti*) of the Hornbill rite she was unsure, but dismissed the rite as yet another example of how their ancestors (*urang kelia*) subdued their young with frightening tales of ghosts and spirits (*antu*). The festival was not, therefore, in honour of the mythical Hornbill. It was a secular celebration in honour of modern time and nation building. The various activities that anticipated and marked the passage from May to June were at the very peak of the festival in terms of media usage and degree of community participation. This was a very special time, an eagerly awaited time, a time of crowds (*rami*); it was abstract clock-and-calendar time collectively transformed into concrete social time.

Gawai diffused swiftly in the 1960s from its urban elite birthplace to localities across Sarawak. Today it contributes to Malaysia's nation building in a number of ways. First, it erodes riverine reciprocity and promotes translocal reciprocity (between migrants and longhouse dwellers) while spreading mass-produced materials (flags, slogans, pop songs, etc.). Second, it undermines pagan ritual while fostering new media rituals (the countup, the quiz shows, the award-giving ceremony, etc.). These rituals allow for a recurrent Dayak 'participation' in the building of the nation, but they also re-enact and aid the uneven distribution of cultural and economic capital. Third, Gawai provides the urban elites with renewable social space-time for their nation-building propaganda. This propaganda is duly reproduced in the longhouses. Finally, the modularity of its local programmes makes Gawai easily intelligible across divides of language, creed, race and even nationality. Indeed Malaysia's Ministries of National Unity and Tourism have had no difficulties in incorporating Gawai – and its equivalent in neighbouring Sabah – into their 'nationwide' calendar of events.[17]

Ethnographic analyses of media and ritual often flounder on the rocks of time and history. By overlooking the worldwide impact of clock-and-calendar time (CCT), they make it difficult to gauge social and cultural change. Case studies from peoples that have only recently adopted CCT festivals are illuminating: they signal a global shift towards a spectacular logic of modular 'programmes'. These programmes contribute to cultural homogenisation both within and across modern state borders.

Notes

1. In Iban ritual practice, counting starts from number one (*satu*) and then proceeds upwards. Perhaps for this reason when the Western New Year's Eve countdown was appropriated by the Dayak elites who invented Gawai, they inverted the original order. Another example of 'countup' is provided below in this chapter in relation to the Hornbill rite.

2. According to the Iban anthropologist Peter Kedit (via email, 28 May 1999), the Gawai Dayak bill was passed in September 1964, 'but the lobbying for Gawai special holidays for the Dayaks, was done in the 1950s: the colonial masters refused to give in to the requests/campaign started by Tra Zehnder in the Council Negri, it was left to the Ningkan government [the first post-colonial state government of Sarawak] to legislate it'.

3. Peter Kedit, personal communication, 28 May 1999.

4. Véronique Béguet, personal communication, 16 November 2000.

5. From the English-language programme *Gawai Dayak Celebrations 2001*.

6. In Malay, the national language: '*Bersatupadu Menbangunkan Keluarga Wawasan 2020*'.

7. The open house is an elite-led Malaysian institution designed to foster interracial and inter-religious harmony (Daniels 2000: 166, Boulanger 2000: 50). In theory, all classes and races are invited to join in the religious or ethnic festival of other groups. Hosts are expected to literally 'open' their houses to all well-wishers and offer them food and drinks. This institution is strongly supported by the Ministry of National Unity. Yet critics maintain that, with the exception of politicians in search of votes, most hosts are far from 'open' as attending the open house of a total stranger would be frowned upon.

8. For a comparative study of beauty pageants, see Cohen et al. (1995)

9. I have also seen such artefacts displayed in Romanian households. Are these clocks both symbols and indexes (Peirce 1955) of modernity for urbanising agrarian populations around the world? (cf. Rantanen 2005).

10. The literature on media and ritual is vast. In recent years, a key influential work has been Dayan and Katz's (1992) *Media Events: The Live Broadcasting of History*. The authors consider events such as sports broadcasts, the Pope's visits, or coronations as 'collective rites of communion' which serve to integrate otherwise fragmented parts of society while legitimising its institutions (see Couldry's 2003 critique). More recently, Liebes and Curran (1998) have edited a volume in which they rethink Katz's legacy. Thus Carey (1998: 42–70) studies 'political rituals' on American television and concludes that media events can also divide people; they can create antagonisms. He exemplifies this point with a discussion of the televised struggles between Democrats and Republicans over the nomination of R. Bork to a seat on the United States Supreme Court in 1987. The judge was eventually 'excommunicated'. An older source of inspiration for theorists of media and ritual is Goffman, in particular his *Interaction Ritual* (1972 [1967]) in which he advocates a 'sociology of occasions'.

11. A thorough survey of this erratic usage can be found in Thomas' (1998) *Medien, Ritual, Religion*.

12. See also my review of Couldry in Postill (2004), from which I have borrowed material for this section.

13. It is not only the provincial government of West Kalimantan, in Indonesian Borneo, who is eager to fix a date. Dayak intellectuals in Pontianak have long celebrated Gawai Dayak (see www.pontianak.go.id/sosbud.html). Drake's Indonesian report contrasts with reports from the Paku-Saribas area of Sarawak from the same historical period, where Gawai had been eagerly adopted and was evolving rapidly in accordance with local interests. For example, in the Paku headwaters local people visited their graveyard the day after Gawai, and the preceding days bathed babies in the river. Downstream, some longhouses had erected monuments in cement to earlier Gawai (Clifford Sather, personal communication, 13 November 2000).

14. This system is still, however, in operation during Gawai Antu, a lavish celebration to honour the ancestors held every one or two generations in each longhouse (Rajit 1971, Sandin 1972, Gerijih n.d.).

15. The Malay phrase commonly used throughout Malaysia, even by ethnic Chinese and Indians, is *balik kampong* (literally, 'return [to the] village').

16. To the journalist and author Rehman Rashid (2004), Mahathir's time-zone unification of Malaysia soon after becoming prime minister in 1981, was an early sign of his nation-building acumen.

17. See, for instance, the Tourism Malaysia website at www.malaysia.tourism-asia.net/malaysia-festivals.html or the Malaysian Tourism Portal at www.virtualmalaysia.com.

10

CONCLUSION

In Anthony D. Smith's influential formula, introduced in chapter 1, a nation is a:

> named human population which shares myths and memories, a mass public culture, a designated homeland, economic unity and equal rights and duties for all members (Smith 1995: 56–57).

This succinct definition captures some of the main nation-building themes running through this book. Let us first apply to Malaysia, via a slight re-ordering of Smith's scheme, the idea of the nation as a 'named human population' with 'a designated homeland'. Malaysia undoubtedly belongs to such a category. It is a UN member state with a high profile as a rapidly developing, stable country with a Muslim majority. Following the secession of Singapore in 1965 and the end to Indonesian and Filipino claims over its Borneo territories, Malaysia presently faces no serious threats to its territorial integrity.

In Sarawak, radio was a medium of critical importance to the survival of Malaysia in the early years of independence. BBC-trained broadcasters used psychological warfare techniques against both the Indonesian army and, later on, domestic guerrillas. Over time, as conditions improved, the propagandists' emphasis shifted from psy-war to socio-economic development. This line of ideological work was reinforced by the spread of state schools and the arrival of television to Sarawak in 1977 (chapters 3 and 4). The result was the development of what I have called 'sustainable propaganda', i.e., an enduring form of propaganda assimilated into the lifeworlds of a population. Thanks to decades of radio, television, school and face-to-face propaganda, Malaysia has become an unquestioned reality amongst the Iban of Sarawak, as taken-for-granted an entity as neighbouring Indonesia. In contrast to Indonesia, however, Malaysia is perceived to be a haven of peace and development. As one Iban woman put it to me: 'Those foreign countries, there are so many wars!' (chapter 5). This is a remarkable achievement for the state propagandists, given the cultural and geographical contiguity of Indonesian Borneo and the physical remoteness of Peninsular Malaysia.

Second, to the idea that nations share 'myths and memories'. The Malaysian myths and memories of Sarawak Iban are heavily mass mediated. They range from the heroic deeds of ancient and colonial heroes – mostly Malayan, but including the Iban warrior Rentap – found in school textbooks, to fond memories of the late Malay singer P. Ramlee, the country's equivalent of America's Elvis Presley. Older longhouse Iban also remember non-Malaysian celebrities such as the young Michael Jackson whose dance routines were keenly emulated in the 1980s. What makes Sarawak Iban myths and memories truly Malaysian is not their lack of foreign materials, but rather the unique *combination* of Malaysian and non-Malaysian elements. This combination can be readily contrasted with analogous hybrid forms found in Indonesia or Singapore whose popular culture industries have followed their own unique trajectories (Lockard 1998, Postill 2002c). In 1977, when the Malaysian authorities allegedly burnt and buried heaps of Iban-language publications (chapter 3), they were hastening the nationalisation of native myths and memories. As a result, young Iban today are far more familiar with Malaysian history than they are with the ethnohistory of Benedict Sandin (chapter 2) and other Borneo Literature Bureau authors (chapter 3).

The Iban of Sarawak (but not so their Iban brethren in Indonesian Borneo), are also active participants in Malaysia's 'mass public culture', which encompasses political rallies, music concerts, football matches, television shows, ethnic festivals, and countless other events and institutions. The men and boys who turned their backs on a longhouse event to watch a televised national football final (chapter 9), were actively partaking of that mass public culture. Undeterred, the women and girls continued to re-enact a local version of the Dayak Festival, a public event that has entered the Malaysian calendar of ethnic festivals. It was an unfortunate clash of mass public culture events. Both events shared the same strip of clock-and-calendar time – a technology of social scheduling that has fully colonised Iban lifeworlds. Malaysia's former prime minister, Mahathir, recognised the centrality of synchronised time to nation building early on in his premiership (cf. Anderson 1991). One of his unsung legacies, yet one of lasting import, was to create a unified time-zone for the entire country (Rashid 2004). This temporal unity is regularly sustained across Malaysia through radio, television, newspapers and school media.

The social anthropologist Laura Rival (1997) has contrasted the 'lived-in worlds' and 'communities of practice' of Huaorani Amazonian Indians with the abstract notions of culture diffused by the Ecuadorian state. To Rival, culture is not a set of abstract meanings that can be transferred from one social context to another. Instead, culture is learned and practised through an engagement with one's immediate surroundings, a view also held by Ingold (2000a) and other anthropologists, as we saw in chapter 1. Yet the evidence produced throughout this book suggests that this sharp distinction between an immediate, lived-in culture and an abstract, decontextualised culture is unwarranted. In a world of state-centric mass cultures, people everywhere routinely use media to extend their cultural engagements well beyond their physical surroundings. Thus, longhouse Iban routinely engage with national and world news through Malaysia's governmental broadcaster, RTM. To a large extent, their worldview is an RTM worldview: while all is well with Malaysia, the rest of the global state order is in chaos. But Malaysia is no imagined community; it is a lived-in world, a mediated community of practice. Some of those longhouse men and boys mesmerised by the football match would later relive its most memorable moments on a nearby, hole-ridden pitch. There, the latest foreign and national football lessons were blended with indigenous notions of endurance (*takal*) and fitness (*tan*). Similarly, abstract knowledge about Malaysia can be concretised through longhouse quiz nights and other media rituals. These rituals are aimed at providing remote access to the country's seats of power and knowledge (chapter 9).

Perhaps the best examples of Malaysia as a community of practice are the national crises of 1997 discussed in chapter 5. During three of those crises (a viral epidemic, forest fires and the collapse of financial markets) the entire country became a manner of mass workshop with millions of small groups, both on the media and face-to-face, working out the implications of each crisis. The widely diverging conclusions reflected and reproduced each group's relative position within the national hierarchy, with opinion leaders 'facilitating' the discussions. Thus, longhouse galleries and farm hut groups generally adopted a 'dominant' position (Hall 1973), i.e., they did not question the official propaganda. In stark contrast, highly educated groups in Kuching adopted either 'negotiated' or 'oppositional' readings, as many of them had access to the internet and/or foreign television channels.

Since its creation in 1963, the Federation of Malaysia has made great strides towards what Smith calls 'economic unity'. This unity includes nationwide fiscal policies, a national bank, a single currency, interlinked stock markets, etc. A few anomalies remain, though. For instance, Sarawak still requires work permits of non-Sarawakians, a 1963 relic aimed at protecting its labour market. This being an anthropological study, I have broached the subject of media and economic unification by means of the Iban system of gift and commodity exchange (chapter 7). The biographical paths of Saribas Iban television sets show that these media artefacts are caught up in a nationwide 'system of commensurate differences' (Gewertz and Errington 1991). This is a system whereby Iban assess one another's market value as they all march along the propagandists' 'path to prosperity'. In the case of television sets – the most valued artefacts in *bilek*-families – price, brand, model and size are all part of the reckoning. Meanwhile school pupils compare one another's career prospects on the basis of their estimated moral worth and mastery of the print media (chapter 5).

Television also supplies Malaysians with contents that feed into this very same system of commensurate differences. For example, it provides longhouse Iban with audiovisual information on the financial (mis)fortunes of urban Malay families through news reports and television dramas (chapter 5). Even when rural viewers reject the affluent lifestyles and corrupt ways of wealthy urbanites, they are still partaking of a ubiquitous, countrywide system of socio-economic 'distinction' (Bourdieu 1984). The system extends to all Iban fields of practice, from popular music, broadcasting and publishing (chapters 3 and 4), religion and farming (chapter 6), academia and politics (chapter 9), to manual labour and the civil service. Contrary to Freeman's (1981) insistence that the Iban remain an egalitarian people, there is strong evidence to suggest that they are becoming as *gila gelaran* (Malay for 'title-mad') as the Malays. For instance, the fact that Dr James Masing, a prominent Iban politician who studied anthropology in Australia under Freeman, is both a wealthy politician and a Ph.D. holder, make him as admired as he is envied across the land. Success and recognition in any given field demands the skilled use of media that were unknown to previous generations of Iban. These media resources are finite, and they are shared with all other Malaysian peoples, a sharing that is integral to the nation-building process.

The one area where many of Malaysia's nation builders would challenge Smith's definition is the question of 'equal rights and duties for all members'. Malaysia's political, military and media apparatus is controlled by the country's dominant ethnic group (*ethnie*), the Malays. This and other 'indigenous' groups (*bumiputera*), including the Iban, enjoy constitutional privileges that set them apart from the Chinese, Indians and other non-indigenes. For example, there are university and civil service quotas reserved for *bumiputera*. These privileges are discreetly questioned (for it is unsafe to do so publicly) by Chinese and Indians, but most of them consider it highly unlikely that they will be removed overnight, if ever. A more accurate definition of the ideal nation sought by the ruling Malay party, UMNO, would end with the phrase 'unequal rights and duties for all members'.

Within this order of priorities, the Iban and other Dayaks are often seen as second-class indigenes (see Jawan 1994). Islam is the great divide. Whilst both UMNO and Sarawak's Melanau Muslim ruling elite would welcome the mass conversion of Dayaks to the Muslim faith, it is by now clear that this will not occur. Attempts at Islamisation by the Sarawak state government in the 1970s were promptly abandoned in view of the strong Dayak resistance. Religion, therefore, remains the insurmountable hurdle for Malaysian nation builders as they promote Vision 2020 – Mahathir's dream of a fully developed Malaysia with a cohesive national culture by 2020 – insofar as Islam is integral to this project. Rural Iban 'ideolects' (parochial dialects of the national ideology) differ from those of Peninsular Malaysian propagandists in their de-emphasising of religion, although Christian ideals and ethnic markers have already taken hold. This discrepancy finds an outlet through a medium neglected by media theorists in the affluent North: public-address systems. In front of a longhouse microphone, away from the mass media gaze, local politicians and community leaders promote a syncretistic version of Christianity, not Islam (chapter 5).

Wider Implications

Moving beyond the specificities of Malaysia and Borneo, what are the implications of these findings for (a) the fledgling research area known as 'media anthropology', and (b) the interdisciplinary study of media and nation building? As far as media anthropology is concerned, the present study has demonstrated, first, the need to consider both the diffusion and appropriation of media forms. By adopting an ethnological line of investigation – i.e., one that follows the fates of peoples (*ethnos*) across historical time and geographical space – I could not gloss over the question of cultural diffusion. To understand how the Iban of Sarawak have become Malaysians in a mere two generations, I had to examine the non-Iban origins of diffused media forms (propaganda, literacy, television and time) as well as their various Iban appropriations. Thus, I have devoted two chapters (3 and 4) to analysing the production of contents disseminated through media that spread into rural Sarawak at different stages, from radio in the 1950s to television and karaoke videos in the 1980s. Similarly, I have described the diffusion of clock-and-calendar media as well as their adoption into Iban longhouses, both on a daily basis and during festive periods (chapters 8 and 9).

This ethnological approach challenges the ethno*graphic* paradigm that prevails in current anthropological and other studies of media. Researchers working within this paradigm privilege the creative appropriation of media forms and contents at the expense of their diffusion (chapter 1). I hope to have shown that the capacity to transform imported media, i.e., the agency of local media users, can vary greatly from one media form and social formation to another. For instance, clock-and-calendar time in Sarawak was adopted wholesale from the Europeans. The sole modification was the use of Iban (i.e., Malay) in lieu of English terms. Otherwise, time-related terms in Iban are directly translatable into English or any other European language – a very shallow indigenisation indeed. By contrast, after one and a half centuries of trial and error, the Catholic Church in Sarawak has learned to alter the contents of its prayer books to address native concerns (chapter 6). Thus, the prominence given to prayers aimed at countering inauspicious dreams or bird sightings would baffle Christians from other parts of the world. Here, the co-agency of Europeans and natives in the production of media contents is undeniable.

Second, in this same ethnological vein, I have insisted that Malaysia and other modern states, both old and new, are best understood not as imagined communities (Anderson 1991) but rather as *culture areas* hosting open networks of social formations (state agencies, private firms, kin groups, etc.), cultural forms (language, media, law, sport, etc.) and exchange systems (see Peterson 2003: 15). A remarkable feature of modern states, as Gellner (1983) noted long ago, is the increased social and geographical mobility that accompanies their formation. In light of the foregoing discussion, we should extend that mobility to media artefacts and contents (Spitulnik 1996, 2000). In the contemporary world, the entwined biographies of people and media forms unfold largely within the spatial and temporal confines of modern states (cf. Giddens 1984, Thompson 1995).

Third, just as we should study national identity in relation to a wider field of identity production that encompasses ethnicity, gender, age, occupation, etc. (Comaroff 1996), it is imperative to study media in relation to one another. This may seem obvious, but all too often media anthropologists (and other media scholars) have studied a single medium in isolation from all other media (see Ginsburg et al. 2002, Askew 2002). A strangely overlooked nexus is that between the ancient medium of writing and twentieth century media such as radio or television. Thus, the study of orality and literacy (Street 1993, 2001) has proceeded independently from that of media 'proper', despite the large theoretical and methodological overlap. In both research areas, most anthropologists have rejected the idea that writing and other media have 'autonomous' effects upon human societies. Their stance is related directly to the mentioned ethnographic paradigm that favours creative human agency. In chapter 6, I sought to bridge the chasm, arguing that we need to study both the intrinsic features of the media themselves (diffusionism) and the varying degrees to which the cultural work of media consumers transforms given media (appropriationism). This study joins previous studies in demonstrating a correlation between television viewers' ability to 'decode' dominant television discourse and their educational attainment (e.g., Morley 1980, Caldarola 1993).

A beneficial by-product of this inter-medial approach is that it allows us to relate specific media to competing identity projects in recent world history. For example, it appears that audio, visual and audiovisual media are more amenable to state-sponsored celebrations of 'tolerable difference' (Rival 1997) than print media. The latter media – especially educational, religious and political texts – are often sites of deadly struggles over the monopoly of legitimate national culture (Gellner 1983), as we saw in the Borneo Literature Bureau example. State ideologues around the world have few quarrels with colourful ethnic dances on television, but they actively discourage the development of ethnic minority school systems (Anderson 1991: 45). While televised dances display tolerable differences, minority books can be perceived as intolerable threats.

Finally, I have retained the notion, rejected by most ethnographers, that media can have observable 'effects' on human populations. This notion has proved useful in seeking to understand the relationship between television and social life in Iban longhouses (chapter 8). Although it is true that 'correlation does not necessarily imply causation', there is no doubt that television viewing has led to a sharp decrease in evening socialising in the longhouse gallery (*ruai*), especially in areas close to urban centres. This view is shared by most Iban, both rural and urban. In other areas of routinised life, a direct effect is more difficult to ascertain, and often one finds a number of contributing causes.

Let me conclude with a brief reflection on the contribution of the present study to the neglected study of media and nation building. First, this study seeks to fill a gap in the literature at a time when much is written and broadcast about America's 'recent encounters with nation-building' (Dempsey and Fontaine 2001). The subject of nation building is dominated by journalistic reports that tend to leave the media dimensions unexamined. While over the past two decades most academic attention has been devoted to the study of nationalism, with some reference to media (notably in Anderson 1991 [1983] and Gellner 1983), much less serious scholarship has been devoted to nation building. The cost of such a concentration on elite ideologues has been borne by Connor's (2004) 'silent masses'. The ethnological approach to media and nation building adopted in the present study tackles this problem by engaging both with elites and masses. In this manner, the 'banalities' (Billig 1995) of everyday media consumption in the longhouse (chapter 8) are accorded as much analytical prominence as the state's destruction of an entire field of indigenous media production (chapter 3). That is to say, an ethnological approach covers both the long-term 'strategies' of the strong and the ad-hoc 'tactics' of the weak (de Certeau 1984, cf. Scott 1985).

Second, this study has neither rejected nor embraced modernisation theory, but rather sought a third way between the over-optimism of America's cold war nation builders and the received anti-modernism of much current social theory. I have argued that we need to take the claims and actions of modernist nation builders very seriously, especially in countries like Malaysia where they have brought about huge social changes. On the other hand, the presuppositions of nation builders have to be critically questioned rather than accepted at face value. For instance, we need to query the common equation of modern media with social change. Take the example of radio in rural Sarawak. From the 1980s onwards, ever since the proliferation of television sets, radio has been socially marginalised. Today, it is mostly the elderly and residents in remote upstream longhouses who listen to Iban storytelling on the radio. They do so in poorly-lit longhouse galleries while smoking tobacco and chewing betel nuts in the company of others. When asked why they listen to these programmes instead of watching television, they reply that radio brings them the voices of the ancestors. So radio, once a white-man novelty, has come to be associated with a traditional customary order (*adat*), not with social change. These rare broadcasts provide a degree of continuity with pre-state Iban culture at a time of swift change (chapter 3).

In conclusion, the relationship between media and nation building is in urgent need of further comparative research. Recent events in Iraq, Afghanistan, East Timor and the former Yugoslavia, to mention but a few countries, testify to this urgency. One pending comparative question in a Southeast Asian context is the seeming failure of Indonesian state propaganda when seen in the light of Malaysia's successes. If nothing else, this study confirms what British colonial rulers and their native successors learned through bitter experience, namely that building a nation takes far more than blood, sweat and tear gas.

REFERENCES

Books and Articles

Abdullah, N. 1983. 'Wanita dalam media massa: siapa kata kami kurang kebolehan'. *Sasaran* 8–9.

Abu-Lughod, L. 1997. 'The Interpretation of Cultures after Television'. *Representations* 59, 109–134.

Adam, B. 1994. 'Perceptions of Time'. In: T. Ingold (ed.), *Companion Encyclopaedia of Anthropology*, London: Routledge.

———. 1995. *Timewatch: the Social Analysis of Time*, Cambridge: Polity Press.

Adnan, Mohd. H. 1988. 'Advertising: the Consumer Movement Perspective'. *Media Asia* 15(4), 202–207.

———. 1990. 'Rural Media in Malaysia: a New Trend'. *Journal of Development Communication* (June), 67–76.

Adra, N. 1993. 'The "Other" as Viewer: Reception of Western and Arab Televised Representations in Rural Yemen'. In: P.I. Crawford and S.B. Hafsteinsson (eds), *The Construction of the Viewer: Proceedings from Nafa 3*, Højbjerg: Intervention Press. pp. 255–269.

Aikman, S. 1999. *Intercultural Education and Literacy: an Ethnographic Study of Indigenous Knowledge and Learning in the Peruvian Amazon,* Amsterdam: Benjamin.

Amir, J. and A.R.A. Jaya. 1996. *Isu-isu Media di Sarawak*, Kuching: Gaya Media.

Andaya, B.W. and L.Y. Andaya. 1982. *A History of Malaysia*, London: Macmillan.

Anderson, B. 1991 [1983]. *Imagined Communities: Reflections on the Origin and Spread of Nationalism*, 2nd edn, London: Verso.

———. 1998. 'From Miracle to Crash'. *London Review of Books,* 16 April 1998.

Ang, I. 1991. *Desperately Seeking the Audience,* London: Routledge.

Anuar, M.K. 2004. 'Muzzled? The Media in Mahathir's Malaysia'. In: B. Welsh (ed.), *Reflections: the Mahathir Years*, Washington, D.C.: Southeast Asian Studies Program, Johns Hopkins University, School of Advanced and International Studies. pp. 486–493.

——— and W.L. Kim. 1996. 'Aspects of Ethnicity and Gender in Malaysian Television'. In: D. French and M. Richards (eds), *Contemporary Television: Eastern Perspectives*, London: Sage. pp. 262–281.

Appadurai, A. 1986. 'Introduction: Commodities and the Politics of Value'. In: A. Appadurai (ed.), *The Social Life of Things: Commodities in Cultural Perspective*, Cambridge: Cambridge University Press.

————. 1990. 'Disjuncture and Difference in the Global Cultural Economy'. In:
M. Featherstone (ed.), *Global Culture: Nationalism, Globalisation and Modernity*,
London: Sage. pp. 295–310.

————. 1996. *Modernity at Large: Cultural Dimensions of Globalization*, Minneapolis:
University of Minnesota Press.

Appell, G.N. 1976a. 'The Cognitive Tactics of Anthropological Inquiry: Comments
on King's Approach to the Concept of the Kindred'. In: G.N. Appell (ed.),
The Societies of Borneo: Explorations in the Theory of Cognatic Social Structure,
Washington, D.C.: AAA. pp. 146–159.

————. 1976b. 'Introduction'. In: G.N. Appell (ed.), *The Societies of Borneo:
Explorations in the Theory of Cognatic Social Structure*, Washington, D.C.: AAA.

———— and T.N. Madan. 1988. 'Derek Freeman: Notes Toward an Intellectual
Biography'. In: G.N. Appell and T.N. Madan (eds), *Choice and Morality in
Anthropological Perspective: Essays in Honor of Derek Freeman*, Albany: State
University of New York Press.

———— and V.H. Sutlive (eds). 1991. *Female and Male in Borneo: Contributions and
Challenges to Gender Studies*, Williamsburg, CA: Borneo Research Council.

Archetti, E. 1994. *Exploring the Written: Anthropology and the Multiplicity of Writing*,
Oslo: Scandinavian University Press.

Asad, T. 1992. 'Conscripts of Western Civilization'. In: C.W. Gailey (ed.), *Dialectical
Anthropology: Essays on Honor of Stanley Diamond*, Vol. 1: *Civilization in Crisis:
Anthropological Perspectives*, Gainesville: University Press of Florida. pp. 333–351.

Askew, K. 2002. 'Introduction'. In: K. Askew and R. Wilk (eds), *The Anthropology of
Media: a Reader*, Oxford: Blackwell.

Askew, K. and R. Wilk. 2002. *The Anthropology of Media: a Reader*, Oxford: Blackwell.

Attali, J. 1982. *L'Histoire du Temps*, Paris: Fayard.

Aunger, R. 2002. *The Electric Meme: a New Theory of How We Think*, New York: The
Free Press.

Austin, R.F. 1977. Iban Migration: Patterns of Mobility and Employment in the 20th
Century. Unpublished Ph.D. dissertation, Department of Geography, University
of Michigan.

Bangit, T. 1995. *Sada Bukit Melanjan*, Kuching: Klasik.

Banks, A.S. 1985. 'Film and Change: the Portrayal of Women in Malay Film'. Paper
presented at the East-West Center Symposium, Honolulu, Hawaii, 16–30
November.

Barfield, T. (ed.) 1997. *The Dictionary of Anthropology*, Oxford: Blackwell.

Barnard, A. 2000. *History and Theory in Anthropology*, Cambridge: Cambridge
University Press.

Barnard, A. and J. Spencer (eds). 1996. *Encyclopedia of Social and Cultural Anthropology*,
London: Routledge.

Barrett, R.J. and R.H. Lucas. 1993. 'The Skulls are Cold, the House is Hot:
Interpreting Depths of Meaning in Iban Therapy'. *Man* (N.S.) 28, 573–596.

Barth, F. 1969. *Ethnic Groups and Boundaries: the Social Organisation of Culture
Difference*, Oslo: Universitetsforlaget.

Barton, D. 1988. *Problems with an Evolutionary Account of Literacy*. Department of
Linguistics, University of Lancaster: Lancaster Papers in Linguistics no. 49.

Barton, D. and N. Hall. 1999. *Letter Writing as a Social Practice*, Amsterdam: Benjamin.

Barton, D. and M. Hamilton. 1998. *Local Literacies: Reading and Writing in One Community*, London: Routledge.

Barton, D., M. Hamilton and R. Ivanic (eds). 1999. *Situated Literacies: Reading and Writing in Context*, London: Routledge.

Basso, K. 1974. 'The Ethnography of Writing'. In: R. Bauman and J. Sherzer (eds), *Explorations in the Ethnography of Speaking*, Cambridge: Cambridge University Press. pp. 425–432.

Bastian, M.L. 1993. 'Bloodhounds Who Have No Friends: Witchcraft, Locality and the Popular Press in Nigeria'. In: J. Comaroff and J.L. Comaroff (eds), *Modernity and Its Malcontents: Ritual and Power in Africa*, Chicago: University of Chicago Press.

Bauman, R. and C.L. Briggs. 1990. 'Poetics and Performance as Critical Perspectives on Language and Social Life'. *Annual Review of Anthropology* 19, 59–88.

Beavitt, P. 1995. 'Selling Tradition – the Pesaka Industry in Sarawak'. *Sarawak Gazette* CXXII, 15–19.

Berma, M. 2000. 'Iban Poverty: a Reflection on Its Causes, Consequences and Policy Implications'. In: M. Leigh (ed.), *Proceedings of the Sixth Biennial Borneo Research Conference*, Kuching: University Malaysia Sarawak.

Bertalanffy, L. 1969. *General System Theory: Foundations, Development, Applications*, New York: Braziller.

Besnier, N. 1993. 'Literacy and Feelings: the Encoding of Affect in Nukulaelae Letters'. In: B. Street (ed.), *Cross-Cultural Approaches to Literacy*, Cambridge: Cambridge University Press.

———. 1995. *Literacy, Emotion and Authority*, Cambridge: Cambridge University Press.

Billig, M. 1995. *Banal Nationalism*, London: Sage.

Bingham, D. 1983. 'The Iban Experience of Religion: as Pagans, as Christians'. *EAPR* 2, 18–28.

Bledsoe, C.H. and K.M. Robey. 1993. 'Arabic Literacy and Secrecy among the Mende of Sierra Leone'. In: B. Street (ed.), *Cross-Cultural Approaches to Literacy*, Cambridge: Cambridge University Press.

Bloch, M. 1993. 'The Uses of Schooling and Literacy in a Zafimaniry Village'. In: B. Street (ed.), *Cross-Cultural Approaches to Literacy*, Cambridge: Cambridge University Press.

———. 1998. *How We Think They Think: Anthropological Approaches to Cognition, Memory, and Literacy.* Boulder, CO: Westview.

———. 2000. 'A Well-disposed Social Anthropologist's Problems with Memes'. In: R. Aunger (ed.), *Darwinizing Culture: the Status of Memetics as a Science*, Oxford/New York: Oxford University Press. pp. 189–203.

———. 2003. 'Literacy: A Reply to John Postill'. *Social Anthropology* 11, 101–102.

Bloch, M. and J. Parry. 1989. 'Introduction: Money and the Morality of Exchange'. In: M. Bloch and J. Parry (eds), *Money and the Morality of Exchange*, Cambridge: Cambridge University Press.

Borges, J.L. 1995. *Ficciones*, Barcelona: Emece Editores.

Born, G. 1997. 'Computer Software as a Medium: Textuality, Orality and Sociality in an Artificial Intelligence Research Culture'. In: M. Banks and H. Morphy (eds), *Rethinking Visual Anthropology*, New Haven/London: Yale University Press.

Boulanger, C.L. 1993. 'Government and Press in Malaysia'. *Journal of Asian and African Studies* XXVIII, 54–66.

———. 1999. 'Making Modern Malaysians in Sarawak'. *Sarawak Museum Journal* LIV, 93–104.

———. 2000. 'On Dayak, Orang Ulu, Bidayuh and Other Imperfect Ethnic Categories in Sarawak'. In: M. Leigh (ed.), *Proceedings of the Sixth Biennial Borneo Research Conference*, Kuching: University Malaysia Sarawak. pp. 44–66.

———. 2002. 'Inventing Tradition, Inventing Modernity: Dayak Identity in Urban Sarawak'. *Asian Ethnicity* 3, 221–231.

Bourdieu, P. 1977. *Outline of a Theory of Practice*, Cambridge: Cambridge University Press.

———. 1984. *Distinction: a Social Critique of the Judgement of Taste*, Cambridge, MA: Harvard University Press.

———. 1993. 'Outline of a Sociological Theory of Art Perception'. In: P. Bourdieu (ed.), *The Field of Cultural Production*, Cambridge: Polity Press. pp. 215–237.

———. 1998. *Practical Reason*, Cambridge: Polity Press.

Bourgois, P. 1986. 'The Miskitu of Nicaragua: Politicized Ethnicity'. *Anthropology Today* 2(2), 4–9.

Boyarin, J. 1993. *The Ethnography of Reading*, Berkeley, CA/Oxford: University of California Press.

Boyer, P. 2000. 'Functional Origins of Religious Concepts: Ontological and Strategic Selection in Evolved Minds'. *Journal of the Royal Anthropological Institute* (N.S.) 6, 195–214.

———. 2001. 'Cultural Inheritance Tracks and Cognitive Predispositions: the Example of Religious Concepts'. In: H. Whitehouse (ed.), *The Debated Mind: Evolutionary Psychology versus Ethnography*, Oxford/New York: Berg.

Caldarola, V.J. 1993. *Reception as a Cultural Experience: Mass Media and Muslim Orthodoxy in Outer Indonesia*, New Brunswick, NJ: Rutgers University Press.

Camitta, M. 1993. Vernacular Writing: Varieties of Literacy among Philadelphia High School Students'. In: B. Street (ed.), *Cross-Cultural Approaches to Literacy*, Cambridge: Cambridge University Press.

Carey, J. 1998. 'Political Ritual on Television: Episodes in the History of Shame, Degradation and Excommunication'. In: T. Liebes and J. Curran (eds), *Media, Ritual and Identity*, London: Routledge. pp. 42–70.

Carrier, J.G. 1992. 'Introduction'. In: J. Carrier (ed.), *History and Tradition in Melanesian Anthropology*, Berkeley, CA: University of California Press.

Certeau, M. 1984. *The Practice of Everyday Life*, Berkeley, CA/London: University of California Press.

Chafe, W.L. and D. Tannen. 1987. 'The Relation between Written and Spoken Language'. *Annual Review of Anthropology* 16, 383–407.

Chartier, R. 1989. 'Leisure and Sociability: Reading Aloud in Early Modern Europe'. In: S. Zimmerman and R.F.E. Weissman (eds), *Urban Life in the Renaissance*, Newark: University of Delaware Press.

Chua, S.L. 1996 [1987]. *English in Action*, 7th edn, Kuala Lumpur: Tropical Press.

Cliff, A.D., P. Haggett, J.K. Ord and G.R. Versey. 1981. *Spatial Diffusion: an Historical Geography of Epidemics in an Island Community*, Cambridge: Cambridge University Press.

Cohen, C.B., R. Wilk and B. Stoeltje (eds). 1995. *Beauty Queens on the Global Stage: Gender, Contests, and Power*, New York: Routledge.

Cole, M. and A. Nicolopoulou. 1992. 'Literacy: Intellectual Consequences'. In: W. Bright (ed.) *International Encyclopaedia of Linguistics, Vol. 2*, New York/Oxford: Oxford University Press.

Collins, J. 1986. 'Differential Treatment and Reading Instruction'. In: J. Cook-Gumperz (ed.), *The Social Construction of Literacy*, Cambridge: Cambridge University Press.

———. 1995. 'Literacy and Literacies'. *Annual Review of Anthropology* 24, 75–93.

———. 1998. *Understanding Tolowa Histories: Western Hegemonies and Native American Response*, New York: Routledge.

Comaroff, J.L. 1996. 'Ethnicity, Nationalism, and the Politics of Difference in an Age of Revolution'. In: E. Wilmsen and P. McAllister (eds), *The Politics of Difference: Ethnic Premises in a World of Power*. Chicago: University of Chicago Press.

Connor, W. 2004. 'The Timelessness of Nations'. *Nations and Nationalism* 10, 35–48.

Cook-Gumperz, J. (ed.), 1986. *The Social Construction of Literacy*, Cambridge: Cambridge University Press.

Couldry, N. 2003. *Media Rituals: a Critical Approach*, London: Routledge.

Cramb, R.A. 1985. 'The Importance of Secondary Crops in Iban Hill Rice Farming'. *Sarawak Museum Journal* XXXIV, 37–46.

———. 1988. 'Shifting Cultivation and Resource Degradation in Sarawak: Perceptions and Policies'. *Review of Indonesian and Malaysian Affairs* 22, 115–149.

——— and I.R. Wills. 1990. 'The Role of Traditional Institutions in Rural Development: Community-based Land Tenure and Government Land Policy in Sarawak, Malaysia'. *World Development* 18, 347–360.

Crump, T. 1988. 'Alternative Meanings of Literacy in Japan and The West'. *Human Organization* 48, 137–145.

Curran, J., M. Gurevitch and J. Woollacott. 1982. 'The Study of the Media: Theoretical Approaches'. In: Gurevitch et al. (eds) *Culture, Society and the Media (Part 1, 'Class, Ideology and the Media')*, London: Methuen.

Curtin, P.D. 1984. *Cross-Cultural Trade in World History*, Cambridge: Cambridge University Press.

Daniels, T.P. 2000. 'Cognitive Convergence and Symbolic Advantage in Melaka and Kuching'. In: *Proceedings of the Sixth Biennial Conference of the Borneo Research Council*, Kuching: University of Malaysia in Sarawak.

Davison, J. and V.H. Sutlive. 1991. 'The Children of Nising: Images of Headhunting and Male Sexuality in Iban Ritual and Oral Literature'. In: V.H. Sutlive (ed.), *Female and Male in Borneo: Contributions and Challenges to Gender Studies*, Williamsburg: Borneo Research Council Monograph Series. pp. 153–230.

Dawkins, R. 1976. *The Selfish Gene*, Oxford: Oxford University Press.

Dayan, D. and E. Katz. 1992. *Media Events: The Live Broadcasting of History*, Cambridge, MA/London: Harvard University Press.

Debord, G. 1983 [1968]. *Society of the Spectacle*, Detroit: Black & Red.

Debray, R. 1996. *Media Manifestos*, London/New York: Verso.

———. 1997. 'A Plague Without Fleabites'. *Times Literary Supplement*, 4 July 1997.

Dempsey, G.T. and R.W. Fontaine. 2001. *Fool's Errands: America's Recent Encounters with Nation Building*, Washington, DC: Cato Institute.

Deutsch, K. 1966. *Nationalism and Social Communications*, 2nd edn, New York: MIT Press.

——— and W. Foltz (eds). 1963. *Nation-Building*, New York: Atherton.

Diamond, J. 1999. *Guns, Germs and Steel: The Fates of Human Societies*, New York/London: W.W. Norton & Co.

Dickey, S. 1997. 'Anthropology and Its Contributions to Studies of Mass Media'. *International Social Science Journal* XLIX 3, 413–427.

Dickson, M. 1995. *Longhouse in Sarawak*, Kuala Lumpur: Abdul Majeed.

Donald, J. 1989. *Ensera Bujang Limbang*, Kuching: Klasik.

———. 1997. 'Traditional Songs'. Paper to the Iban Traditional Music, Dance, Costume and Song Workshop. Sarawak Museum, Kuching, 26 July.

Doronilla, M.L. 1996. *Landscapes of Literacy: an Ethnographic Study of Functional Literacy in Marginal Philippine Communities*, Hamburg: UNESCO Institute for Education.

Douglas, M. 1984. *Purity and Danger: an Analysis of the Concepts of Pollution and Taboo*, London: Ark Paperbacks.

———. 1986. *How Institutions Think*, New York: Syracuse University Press.

Drackle, D. 1999. 'Medienethnologie: eine Option auf die Zukunft'. In: W. Kotot and D. Drackle (eds), *Wozu Ethnologie?*, Berlin: Dietrich Reimer Verlag.

Drake, R.A. 2000. 'The Mualang *Gawai* in the Belitang Hulu'. In: M. Leigh (ed.), *Proceedings of the Sixth Biennial Borneo Research Conference*, Kuching: University Malaysia Sarawak.

Duranti, A. and E. Ochs. 1986. 'Literacy Instruction in a Samoan Village'. In: B. Schieffelin and P. Gilmore (eds), *The Acquisition of Literacy: Ethnographic Perspectives*, Norwood, NJ: Ablex.

Ejau, A. 1964. *Dilah Tanah*, Kuching: Borneo Literature Bureau.

———. 1967. *Madu Midang*, Kuching: Borneo Literature Bureau.

———. 1967. *Sebeginda Bujang*, Kuching: Borneo Literature Bureau.

———. 1968a. *Aji Bulan*, Kuching: Borneo Literature Bureau.

———. 1968b. *Batu Besundang*, Kuching: Borneo Literature Bureau.

———. 1968c. *Paloi Nginti*, Kuching: Borneo Literature Bureau.

———. 1972. *Pelangka Gantong*, Kuching: Borneo Literature Bureau.

———. 1985. *Layang Bintang*, Kuching: Sarawak Publishing House.

Eley, G. and R.G. Suny (eds). 1996. *Becoming National: a Reader*, New York/Oxford: Oxford University Press.

Ellen, R.F. (ed.). 1984. *Ethnographic Research: a Guide to General Conduct*, New York: Academic Press.

Ensiring, J. 1968. *Ngelar Menoa Sarawak*, Kuching: Borneo Literature Bureau.

———. 1991. *Emperan Assam Panas*, Kuching: Klasik.

———. 1992. *Dr Ida*, Kuching: Klasik.

Eriksen, T.H. 1993. *Ethnicity and Nationalism: Anthropological Perspectives*, London: Pluto Press.

————. 2004. 'Place, Kinship and the Case for Non-ethnic Nations'. *Nations and Nationalism* 10, 49–62.

———— and F.S. Nielsen. 2001. *A History of Anthropology*, London: Pluto Press.

Erikson, F. and G. Bekker. 1986. 'On Anthropology'. In: J. Hannaway and
M. Lockheed (eds), *The Contributions of the Social Sciences to Educational Policy and Practice: 1965–1985*, Berkeley, CA: McCutchan.

Evans-Pritchard, E.E. 1940. *The Nuer*, Oxford: Oxford University Press.

Fabian, J. 1983. *Time and the Other: How Anthropology Makes Its Object*, New York: Columbia University Press.

Fardon, R. 1990. 'General Introduction'. In: R. Fardon (ed.), *Localizing Strategies: the Regionalization of Ethnographic Accounts*, Edinburgh: Scottish Academic Press.

Finnegan, R. 1988. *Literacy and Orality: Studies in the Technology of Communication*, Oxford: Blackwell.

Fischer, M. 1997. 'Functionalism'. In: T. Barfield (ed.), *The Dictionary of Anthropology*, Oxford: Blackwell. pp. 209–212.

Fiske, J. 1989. 'Moments of Television: Neither the Text Nor the Audience'. In: E. Seiter, H. Borchers, G. Kreutzner and E.M. Warth (eds), *Remote Control: Television, Audiences and Cultural Power*, London: Routledge.

Fishman, J. 1986. 'Nationality-Nationalism and Nation-Nationism'. In: J. Fishman, C. Ferguson, and J.D. Gupta (eds), *Language Problems of Developing Nations*, New York: John Wiley.

Foster, R.J. (ed.). 1997. *Nation Making: Emergent Identities in Postcolonial Melanesia*, Ann Arbor: The University of Michigan Press.

————. 2002. *Materializing the Nation: Commodities, Consumption and Media in Papua New Guinea*, Bloomington and Indianapolis: Indiana University Press.

Fox, J.J. 1993. 'Comparative Perspectives on Austronesian Houses: an Introductory Essay'. In: J.J. Fox (ed.), *Inside Austronesian Houses: Perspectives on Domestic Designs for Living*, Canberra: Australian National University. pp. 1–29.

————. 2002. 'Tracing Genealogies: Toward an International Multicultural Anthropology', *Antropologi Indonesia* 69, 106–117.

Fox, K. 2004. *Watching the English*, London: Hodder & Stoughton.

Freeman, J.D. 1955. *Iban Agriculture: a Report on the Shifting Cultivation of Hill Rice by the Iban of Sarawak*, London: HMSO.

————. 1960. 'Iban augury'. In: B.S. Smythies (ed.), *The Birds of Borneo*, Edinburgh: Oliver and Boyd. pp. 73–98.

————. 1961. 'On the Concept of the Kindred'. *Journal of the Royal Anthropological Institute* 91, 192–220.

————. 1970. *Report on the Iban of Sarawak*, Kuching: Government Printing Office, reprinted as *Report on the Iban*, London, Athlone Press.

————. 1981. *Some Reflections on the Nature of Iban Society*. Australian National University: Advanced School of Pacific Studies. An Occasional Paper of the Department of Anthropology.

————. 1992. *The Iban of Borneo*, Kuching: Abdul Majeed, First published by Kuching: Government Printing Office, 1955 as Report on the Iban of Sarawak.

————. 1999. *The Fateful Hoaxing of Margaret Mead: a Historical Analysis of Her Samoan Research*, Bounder, CO: Westview Press.

Freire, P. 1987. *The Politics of Education: Culture, Power and Liberation*, London: Macmillan.

Frith, K.T. 1987. 'Advertising and the Consumer Movement in Malaysia'. *Forum Komunikasi* 43–48.

Garai, G. 1993. *Puntan*, Kuching: Klasik.

Geertz, C. 1963. *Agricultural Involution: the Process of Ecological Change in Indonesia*, Berkeley, CA: University of California Press.

———. 1973. *The Interpretation of Cultures*, New York: Basic Books.

———. 1988. *Works and Lives: the Anthropologist as Author*, Stanford: Stanford University Press.

Gell, A. 1986. 'Newcomers to the Worlds of Goods: Consumption among the Muria Gonds'. In: A. Appadurai (ed.), *The Social Life of Things: Commodities in Cultural Perspective*, Cambridge: Cambridge University Press.

———. 1992. *The Anthropology of Time: Cultural Constructions of Temporal Maps and Images*, Oxford: Berg.

———. 1998. *Art and Agency: an Anthropological Theory*, Oxford: Clarendon Press.

Gellner, E. 1983. *Nations and Nationalism*, Oxford: Blackwell.

Gerijih, H. 1962. *Raja Langit*, Kuching: Borneo Literature Bureau.

———. n.d. *Gawai Antu*, unpublished manuscript.

Gewertz, D.B. and F.K. Errington. 1991. *Twisted Histories, Altered Contexts*, Cambridge: Cambridge University Press.

———. 1999. *Emerging Class in Papua New Guinea*, Cambridge: Cambridge University Press.

Giddens, A. 1984. *The Constitution of Society*, Cambridge: Polity Press.

Gieri, W. 1972. *Bunga Nuing Ngamboh*, Kuching: Borneo Literature Bureau.

Gingrich, A. 1994. 'Time, Ritual and Social Experience'. In: K. Hastrup and P. Hervik (eds), *Social Experience and Anthropological Knowledge*, London: Routledge.

Ginsburg, F. 1993. 'Aboriginal Media and the Australian Imaginary'. *Public Culture* 5, 557–578.

———. 1994. 'Culture/Media: A (Mild) Polemic'. *Anthropology Today* 10(2), 5–15.

———, L. Abu-Lughod and B. Larkin. 2002. *Media Worlds: Anthropology on New Terrain*, Berkeley and Los Angeles, CA: University of California Press.

Gledhill, J. 2000. *Power and Its Disguises: Anthropological Perspectives on Politics*, London: Pluto Press.

Goffman, E. 1972. *Interaction Ritual*, London: Penguin.

Gomes, E.H. 1911. *Seventeen Years among the Sea Dyaks of Borneo*, London: Seeley & Co.

Gomez, E.T. 2004a. 'Introduction: Politics, Business and Ethnicity in Malaysia: A State in Transition?' In: E.T. Gomez (ed.), *The State of Malaysia: Ethnicity, Equity and Reform*, London/New York: Routledge. pp. 1–28.

———. 2004b. 'Politics of the Media Business: the Press under Mahathir'. In: B. Welsh (ed.), *Reflections: the Mahathir Years*, Washington, DC: Southeast Asian Studies Program, Johns Hopkins University, School of Advanced and International Studies. pp. 475–485.

——— and K.S. Jomo. 1997. *Malaysia's Political Economy: Politics, Patronage and Profits*, Melbourne: Cambridge University Press.

Goody, J. 1968. *Literacy in Traditional Societies*, Cambridge: Cambridge University Press.

————. 1977. *The Domestication of the Savage Mind*, Cambridge: Cambridge University Press.

————. 1986. *The Logic of Writing and the Organization of Society*, Cambridge: Cambridge University Press.

————. 1987. *The Interface between the Written and the Oral*, Cambridge: Cambridge University Press.

————. 1997. *Representations and Contradictions: Ambivalence towards Images, Theatre, Fiction, Relics and Sexuality*, Oxford: Blackwell.

Graff, H.J. 1987. *The Legacies of Literacy: Continuities and Contradictions in Western Culture and Society*, Bloomington: Indiana University Press.

Grillo, R. and A. Rew. 1985. *Social Anthropology and Development Policy, ASA Monograph 23*, London: Tavistock.

Grjebine, L. 1988. *Reporting on Prostitution: the Media, Women and Prostitution in India, Malaysia and the Philippines*, Paris: UNESCO, Communication and Society Document No. 18.

Grohs, G. 1990. 'Ausdrucksformen kulturellen Protests in Africa Südlich der Sahara'. In: K.H.E. Kohl, W. Müller and I. Strecker (eds), *Vielfalt Der Kultur: Ethnologische Aspekte Von Verwansdschaft, Kunst Und Weltauffassung*, Berlin: Mouton. pp. 501–516.

Guibernau, M. and J. Hutchinson. 2004. 'History and National Destiny', *Nations and Nationalism* 10(1/2), 1–8.

Hall, S. 1973. 'Encoding/Decoding in Television Discourse'. Reprinted in S. Hall et al. (eds) (1981) *Culture, Media, Language: Working Papers in Cultural Studies, 1972–79*, London: Hutchinson. pp. 128–138.

Hamilton, A. 2002. 'The National Picture: Thai Media and Cultural Identity'. In: F.D. Ginsburg, L. Abu-Lughod and B. Larkin (eds), *Media Worlds: Anthropology on New Terrain*, Berkeley and Los Angeles, CA: University of California Press.

Handelman, D. 1998. *Models and Mirrors: towards an Anthropology of Public Events*, Oxford and New York: Berghahn.

Hann, C. 1994. 'The Anthropology of Ethnicity'. *Anthropology Today* 10, 21–22.

Hannerz, U. 1996. *Transnational Connections: Culture, People, Places*, London: Routledge.

Hanson, J. 1979. *Sociocultural Perspectives on Human Learning: an Introduction to Educational Anthropology*. Englewood Cliffs, NJ: Prentice-Hall.

Harris, R. 1986. *The Origin of Writing*, London: Duckworth.

Hartley, J. 1987. 'Invisible Fictions: Television Audiences, Paedocracy, Pleasure'. *Textual Practice* 1, 121–138.

Hashim, R. 1995. 'Television Programming'. In: K.S. Jomo (ed.) *Privatizing Malaysia: Rents, Rhetoric, Realities*, Boulder: Westview Press.

Havelock, E. 1976. *Origins of Western Literacy*, Toronto: Ontario Institute of Education.

Heine-Geldern, R.G. 1956 [1942]. *Conceptions of State and Kingship in Southeast Asia (Southeast Asia Program, Data Paper, No. 18.)*, Ithaca: Department of Asian Studies, Cornell University.

Helliwell, C. 1993. 'Good Walls Make Bad Neighbours: the Dayak Longhouse as a Community of Voices'. In: J.J. Fox (ed.), *Inside Austronesian Houses: Perspectives on Domestic Designs for Living*, Canberra: Australian National University. pp. 44–63.

Hirsch, E. 1994. 'The Long Term and the Short Term of Domestic Consumption: an Ethnographic Case Study'. In: R. Silverstone and E. Hirsch (eds), *Consuming Technologies: Media and Information in Domestic Spaces*, London: Routledge. pp. 208–226.

Hobart, M. 1997. 'The Missing Subject: Balinese Time and the Elimination of History'. *Review of Indonesian and Malaysian Studies* 31(1), 123–172.

———. 1995. 'After Anthropology? A View From Too Near'. Paper to the Anthropology Department Seminar, School of Oriental and African Studies, University of London, 16 October 1995.

Hobbes, T. 1651. *Leviathan: or, the Matter, Forme, and Power of a Common Wealth, Ecclesiastical and Civil*, London: Andrew Crooke.

Hobsbawm, R. and E. Ranger. 1983. *The Invention of Tradition*, Cambridge: Cambridge University Press.

Hornberger, N. (ed.), 1998. *Indigenous Literacies in the Americas: Language Planning From the Bottom Up*, Berlin: Mouton.

Horsman, J. 1989. 'From the Learner's Voice: Women's Experience of Illiteracy'. In: M. Taylor and J. Draper (eds), *Adult Literacy Perspectives*, Toronto: Culture Concepts.

Hoskins, J. 1998. *Biographical Objects: How Things Tell the Stories of People's Lives*, London: Routledge.

Houston, R. 1988. *Literacy in Early Modern Europe: Culture and Education 1500–1800*, London: Longman.

Howell, S. 1997. 'Introduction'. In: Howell, S. (ed.), *The Ethnography of Moralities*, London: Routledge. pp. 1–24.

Hughes-Freeland, F. 1998. 'Introduction'. In: F. Hughes-Freeland (ed.), *Ritual, Performance, Media*, London: Routledge. pp. 1–28.

Ignatieff, M. 2003. *Empire Lite: Nation-building in Bosnia, Kosovo and Afghanistan*, London: Vintage.

Ijau, L.S. 1966. *Salidi seduai Sapatu*, Kuching: Borneo Literature Bureau.

Ingold, T. (ed.). 1994. *Companion Encyclopedia of Anthropology*, London/New York: Routledge.

———. 2000a. *The Perception of the Environment: Essays in Livelihood, Dwelling and Skill*, London/New York: Routledge.

———. 2000b. 'The Poverty of Selectionism'. *Anthropology Today* 16, 1–2.

Jackson, M. 1975. 'Literacy, Communications, and Social Change: a Study of the Meaning and Effect of Literacy in Early Nineteenth Century Maori Society'. In: I.H. Kawheru (ed.), *Conflict and Compromise: Essays on the Maori Since Colonization*, Wellington: A.H. & A.W. Reed.

Jalie, J. 1972. *Pemansang mai Pengerusak*, Kuching: Borneo Literature Bureau.

Jawan J.A. 1993. *The Iban Factor in Sarawak Politics*, Serdang: Universiti Pertanian Malaysia with University of Hull.

———. 1994. *Iban Politics and Economic Development: Their Patterns and Change*, Bangi: Penerbit Universiti Kebangsaan.

Jensen, E. 1966. 'The Sarawak Iban'. *Sarawak Museum Journal* 13, 1–31.

———. 1974. *The Iban and Their Religion*, Oxford: Clarendon Press.

Johnson, L. 1981. 'Radio and everyday life: The Early Years of Broadcasting in Australia, 1922–1945'. *Media, Culture and Society* 3, 167–178.

Jones, M. 2002. *Conflict and Confrontation in South East Asia, 1961–1965: Britain, the United States and the Creation of Malaysia*, Cambridge: Cambridge University Press.

Jowett, G.S. and V. O'Donnell. 1999. *Propaganda and Persuasion*, 3rd edn, Thousand Oaks, CA: Sage.

Kalman, J. 1999. *Writing on the Plaza: Mediated Literacy Practices Among Scribes and Clients in Mexico City*, Cresskill, NJ: Hampton Press.

Karim, M.R.A. and N.M. Khalid. 2003. *E-Government in Malaysia*, Subang Jaya: Pelanduk.

Kassim, M. (ed.). 1996. *Taib: Wira Pembangunan Sarawak*, Kuching: Gaya Media.

Kedit, P.M. 1980a. *Modernization among the Iban of Sarawak*, Kuala Lumpur: Dewan Bahasa dan Pustaka.

———. 1980b. *Tourism Report: a Survey on the Effects of Tourism on Iban Longhouse Communities in the Skrang District, Second Division, Sarawak*, Sarawak Museum Field Report No. 2, Kuching: Sarawak Museum.

———. 1993. *Iban Bejalai*, Kuala Lumpur: Ampang Press.

Khoo, B.T. 1995. *Paradoxes of Mahathirism*, Kuala Lumpur: Oxford University Press.

King, L. 1994. *Roots of Identity: Language and Literacy in Mexico*, Stanford: Stanford University Press.

King, V.T. 1976. 'Conceptual and Analytical Problems in the Study of the Kindred'. In: G.N. Appell (ed.), *The Societies of Borneo: Explorations in the Theory of Cognatic Social Structure*, Washington, D.C.: AAA.

———. 1988. 'Models and Realities: Malaysian National Planning and East Malaysian Development Plans'. *Modern Asia Studies* 22(2), 263–298.

———. 1989. 'What's In a Name? Ethnicity and the Problems it Poses for Anthropologists'. *Sarawak Museum Journal* XL(61) (Special Issue 4), 235–245.

———. 1993. *The Peoples of Borneo*, Oxford: Blackwell.

———. 1994. 'Introduction'. In: V.T. King (ed.), *World Within: the Ethnic Groups of Borneo*, Kuala Lumpur: S. Abdul Majeed.

———. 2001. 'Review of Derek Freeman, *The Fateful Hoaxing of Margaret Mead. A Historical Analysis of Her Samoan Research*'. Boulder, CO and Cumnor Hill, Oxford: Westview Press, 1999. *Aseasuk News* 34–37.

———. n.d. 'Introduction'. In: J.A. Jawan, V.T. King, J.R. Noel and V.H. Sutlive, *A Checklist of Materials on the Iban of Borneo*. Unpublished manuscript, Tun Jugah Foundation, Kuching.

——— and M.J.G. Parnwell. 1999. 'Environmental Change, Local Responses, and the Notion of "Development" in Sarawak'. In: V.T. King (ed.), *Rural Development and Social Science Research: Case Studies From Borneo*, Phillips, USA: Borneo Research Council, Inc. pp. 159–191.

——— and W.D. Wilder. 2003. *The Modern Anthropology of South-East Asia: An Introduction*, London: RoutledgeCurzon.

Kolstø, P. 2000. *Political Construction Sites: Nation-Building in Russia and the Post-Soviet States*. Boulder, CO: Westview.

Kopytoff, I. 1986. 'The Cultural Biography of Things: Commoditization as Process'. In: A. Appadurai (ed.), *The Social Life of Things: Commodities in Cultural Perspective*, Cambridge: Cambridge University Press. pp. 64–94.

Kuklick, H. 1996. 'Diffusionism'. In: A. Barnard and J. Spencer (eds), *Encyclopaedia of Social and Cultural Anthropology*, London/New York: Routledge. pp. 160–162.

Kulick, D. and C. Stroud. 1993. 'Conceptions and Uses of Literacy in a Papua New Guinean Village'. In: B. Street (ed.), *Cross-Cultural Approaches to Literacy*, Cambridge: Cambridge University Press.

Langub, J. 1995. 'Obituary: Tan Sri Datuk Gerunsin Lembat 1924–1995'. *Sarawak Gazette* CXXII, 57–59.

———— and H.C. Belawing, n.d. 'The Significance of Gawai Dayak to the Orang Ulu'. In: Anon. (ed.), *Gawai Dayak Kuala Lumpur 2000*, Kuala Lumpur: National Unity and Community Development Ministry. p. 8.

Larkin, B. 1997. 'Indian Films and Nigerian Lovers: Media and the Creation of Parallel Modernities'. *Africa* 3 (Fall).

Larsen, A.K. 1998. Discourses on Development in Malaysia'. In: S. Abram and J. Waldren (eds), *Anthropological Perspectives on Local Development*, London: Routledge.

Latham, M.E. and J.L. Gaddis. 2000. *Modernization as Ideology: American Social Science and 'Nation-Building' in the Kennedy Era*, Chapel Hill, NC: University of North Carolina Press.

Latour, B. and S. Woolgar. 1979. *Laboratory Life: the Social Construction of Scientific Facts*, Beverly Hills/London: Sage.

Lavery, D., A. Hague and M. Cartwright. 1996. *Deny All Knowledge: Reading the X-Files*. Syracuse, NY: Syracuse University Press.

Leach, E. 1976. *Culture and Communication: the Logic by Which Symbols Are Connected*, Cambridge: Cambridge University Press.

Lee Su Kim 2004. *Malaysian Flavours: Insights into Things Malaysian*, Kelana Jaya: Pelanduk.

Le Goff, J. 1980. *Time, Work and Culture in the Middle Ages*, Chicago: Chicago University Press.

Leigh, M. 1974. *The Rising Moon: Political Change in Sarawak*, Sydney: Sydney University Press.

————. 1983. 'Reflections on Political Change, Sarawak in Malaysia: 1963–1983'. *Sarawak Museum Journal* XXXII(53), 159–166.

————. 1991. 'Money Politics and Dayak Nationalism: the 1987 Sarawak State Election'. In: M.I. Said and J. Saravanamuttu (eds), *Images of Malaysia*, Kuala Lumpur, Persatuan Sains Sosial Malaysia (Malaysian Social Science Association). pp. 180–202.

Lent, J.A. 1979. 'Social Change and the Human Right of Freedom of Expression in Malaysia'. *Universal Human Rights*, July-September, 51–60.

————. 1982. 'Mass Media in East Malaysia and Brunei'. *Gazette: International Journal for Mass Communication Studies* 30, 97–108.

————. 1984a. 'Human Rights in Malaysia'. *Journal of Contemporary Asia* 14, 442–458.

————. 1984b. 'Restructuring of Mass Media in Malaysia and Singapore – Pounding in the Coffin Nails?'. *Bulletin of Concerned Asian Scholars* October-December, 26–35.

————. 1989. 'Human Rights and Freedom of Expression in Malaysia and the Philippines'. *Asian Profile*, June, 137–154.

————. 1991. 'Telematics in Malaysia: Room at the Top for a Selected Few'. In: G. Sussman and J.A. Lent (eds), *Transnational Communications: Wiring the Third World*, Newbury Park, CA: Sage. pp. 165–199.

————. 1994. 'Mass Communications'. In: *Studies in Third World Societies, no. 44*, Virginia, USA: Dept of Anthropology, College of William and Mary.

Lévi-Strauss, C. (1972 [1963]) *Structural Anthropology*, Harmondsworth: Penguin.

Lewis, I.M. 1993. 'Literacy and Cultural Identity in the Horn of Africa: The Somali Case'. In: B. Street (ed.), *Cross-Cultural Approaches to Literacy*, Cambridge: Cambridge University Press.

Liebes T. and J. Curran (eds). 1998. *Media, Ritual and Identity*, London: Routledge.

Linklater, A. 1990. *Wild People*, London: John Murray.

Lockard, C.A. 1998. *Dance of Life: Popular Music and Politics in Southeast Asia*, Honolulu: University of Hawai'i Press.

Lull, J. 1990. *Inside Family Viewing: Ethnographic Research on Television's Audience*, London: Routledge.

————. 1991. *China Turned On: Television, Reform, and Resistance*, London: Routledge.

Lynch, T. 1998. 'The Undertaking'. In: P. Lopate (ed.), *The Anchor Essay Annual*, New York: Doubleday. pp. 9–19.

Lyons, H.D. 1990. 'Television in Contemporary Urban Life: Benin City, Nigeria'. *Visual Anthropology* 3, 411–428.

Mackie, J.A.C. 1974. *Konfrontasi: The Indonesia-Malaysia Dispute 1963–1966*, Kuala Lumpur: Oxford University Press.

Maidin, Z. 1994. *The Other Side of Mahathir*, Kuala Lumpur: Utusan Publications.

Majang, A.A. 1967. *Padi Ribai*, Kuching: Borneo Literature Bureau.

Mandel, R. 2002. 'A Marshall Plan of the Mind: the Political Economy of a Kazakh Soap Opera'. In: F.D. Ginsburg, L. Abu-Lughod and B. Larkin (eds), *Media Worlds: Anthropology on New Terrain*, Berkeley and Los Angeles, CA: University of California Press. pp. 211–228.

Mankekar, P. 1993. 'National Texts and Gendered Lives'. *American Ethnologist* 20, 543–563.

————. 1999. *Screening Culture, Viewing Politics: an Ethnography of Television, Womanhood, and Nation in Postcolonial India*, Durham/London: Duke University Press.

Marcus, D.C. n.d. *Adat Kristian*, Kuching: Lee Ming Press Co.

Marcus, G.E. 1995. 'Ethnography In/Of the World System: the Emergence of Multi-Sited Ethnography', *Annual Review of Anthropology* 24: 95–117.

Marquis, J.P. 2000. 'The Other Warriors: American Social Science and Nation Building in Vietnam'. *Diplomatic History* 24, 79–105.

Marx, K. and F. Engels. 2004 [1848]. *The Communist Manifesto*, London: Penguin.

Masing, J. 1997. *The Coming of the Gods: an Iban Invocatory Chant (Timang Gawai Amat) of the Baleh River Region, Sarawak*, Canberra, Australia: Dept. of Anthropology, Research School of Pacific and Asian Studies, Australian National University.

Maxwell, A.R. 1989. 'A Survey of the Oral Traditions of Sarawak'. *Sarawak Museum Journal* XL(61), 167–208.

McDaniel, D.O. 1994. *Broadcasting in the Malay World: Radio, Television and Video in Brunei, Indonesia, Malaysia and Singapore*, Norwood, NJ: Aplex.

McLuhan, M. 1964. *Understanding Media: the Extensions of Man*, New York: McGraw-Hill.

Mead, M. and R. Métraux. 2000. *The Study of Culture at a Distance*, Oxford/New York: Berghahn.

Meggitt, M. 1968. 'Uses of Literacy in New Guinea and Melanesia'. In: J Goody (ed.), *Literacy in Traditional Societies*, Cambridge: Cambridge University Press.

Mertz, O. and H. Christensen. 1997. 'Land Use and Crop Diversity in Two Iban Communities, Sarawak, Malaysia'. *Danish Journal of Geography* 97, 98–110.

Meyer, B. 2004. '"Praise the Lord." Popular Cinema and Pentecostalite Style in Ghana's New Public Sphere'. *American Ethnologist* 31(1): 92–110.

Michaels, E. 1991. 'A Model of Teleported Texts (with Reference to Aboriginal Television)'. *Visual Anthropology* 4(3/4): 301–323.

Miller, D. 1994. 'Artefacts and the Meanings of Things'. In: T. Ingold (ed.), *Companion Encyclopaedia of Anthropology*, London: Routledge. pp. 396–419.

———. 1998. 'Why Some Things Matter'. In: D. Miller (ed.) *Material Cultures: Why Some Things Matter*, London: UCL Press. pp. 3–24.

———. 2000. 'The Fame of Trinis: Websites as Traps'. *Journal of Material Culture* 5(1), 5–24.

Miyazaki, H. 2000. 'Faith and Its Fulfillment: Agency, Exchange, and the Fijian Aesthetics of Completion'. *American Ethnologist* 27, 31–51.

Moores, S. 1986. 'Review of D. Gregory and J. Urry (eds), *Social Relations and Spatial Structures*, London: Macmillan, 1985'. *Media, Culture and Society* 8, 243–245.

———. 1988. 'The Box on the Dresser: Memories of Early Radio'. *Media, Culture and Society* 10(1), 23–40.

Morley, D. 1980. *The 'Nationwide' Audience: Structure and Decoding*, London: BFI.

———. 1986. *Family Television: Cultural Power and Domestic Leisure*, London: Comedia.

———. 1992. *Television, Audiences and Cultural Studies*, London: Routledge.

——— and R. Silverstone. 1990. 'Domestic Communication – Technologies and Meanings'. *Media, Culture and Society* 12, 31–55.

Morrison, H. 1954. 'Broadcasting Comes to the Sea Dyaks'. *Geographical Magazine* XXVII, 390–393.

Munan, S. 1985. 'Tempalai Jako'. In: A. Ejau, *Layang Bintang*, Kuching: Sarawak Publishing House. pp. 1–2.

Munn, N.D. 1992. 'The Cultural Anthropology of Time: a Critical Essay'. *Annual Review of Anthropology* 21, 93–123.

Murdock, G.P. 1960. *Social Structure in Southeast Asia*, Chicago: Quadrangle.

Musa, M.B. 2004. 'Education: a Blemished Legacy'. In: B. Welsh (ed.), *Reflections: the Mahathir Years*, Washington, DC: Southeast Asian Studies Program, Johns Hopkins University, School of Advanced and International Studies. pp. 450–460.

Nain, Z. 1996. 'The Impact of the International Marketplace on the Organisation of Malaysian Television'. In: D. French and M. Richards (eds), *Contemporary Television: Eastern Perspectives*, London: Sage. pp. 157–180.

Needham, R. 1976. 'Skulls and Causality'. *Man* 11, 71–88.

Ngidang, D. 1993. 'Media Treatment of a Land Rights Movement in Sarawak, East Malaysia'. *Media Asia* 20(2), 93–99.

Nordenstreng, K. 1972. 'Policy for News Transmission'. In: D. McQuail (ed.), *Sociology of Mass Communication*, Harmondsworth: Penguin.

O'Connor, U. 1999. *Celtic Dawn: a Portrait of the Irish Literary Renaissance*, Dublin: Town House and Country House.

O'Leary, B. 1998. 'Gellner's Diagnoses of Nationalism: a Critical Overview of What is Living and What is Dead in Gellner's Philosophy of Nationalism'. In: J.A. Hall (ed.), *The State of the Nation: Ernest Gellner and the Theory of Nationalism*, Cambridge: Cambridge University Press. pp. 40–88.

Olson, D.R. and N. Torrance (eds) 2001. *The Making of Literate Societies*, Oxford: Blackwell.

Ong, W.J. 1982. *Orality and Literacy: the Technologizing of the World*, London: Methuen.

Pace, R. 1993. 'First-time Televiewing in Amazonia: Television Acculturation in Gurupa, Brazil'. *Ethnology* 32, 187–206.

Padoch, C.A. 1982a. *Migration and Its Alternatives among the Ibans of Sarawak*, The Hague: Martinus Nijhoff.

———. 1982b. 'Land Use in New and Old Areas of Iban Settlement'. *Borneo Research Bulletin* 14, 3–13.

———. 1984. 'The Iban of the Engkari: a History of Migration and Settlement'. *Sarawak Museum Journal* XXXIII, 1–14.

Parkin, D. 1992. 'Ritual as Spatial Direction and Bodily Division'. In: D. de Coppet (ed.), *Understanding Rituals*, London: Routledge. pp. 11–25.

Peacock, J. 1968. *Rites of Modernization: Symbolic and Social Aspects of Indonesian Proletariat Drama*, Chicago, IL: University of Chicago Press.

Pedelty, M. 1995. *War Stories: the Culture of Foreign Correspondents*, London.

Peel, J. 1989. 'The Cultural Work of Yoruba Ethnogenesis'. In: E. Tonkin, M. McDonald and M. Chapman (eds), *History and Ethnicity*, London: Routledge.

Peirce, C. 1955. 'Logic as Semiotic: the Theory of Signs'. In: J. Buchler (ed.), *Philosophic Writings of Peirce*, New York: Dover Publications.

Pelzer, K.J. 1945. *Pioneer Settlement in the Asiatic Tropics: Studies in Land Utilization and Agricultural Colonization in Southeastern Asia*, New York: American Geographical Society Special Publication No. 29.

Perrot, M. 1992. 'La radio et la télévision dans les sociétés inuit: Groenland, Canada, Alaska et Tchoukotka'. *Etudes Inuit* 16, 257–289.

Peterson, M.A. 2003. *Anthropology and Mass Communication: Myth and Media in the New Millennium*. Oxford/New York: Berghahn.

Pinker, S. 1997. *How the Mind Works*, New York: WW Norton.

Piyadasa, R. 2002. *Masterpieces from the National Art Gallery of Malaysia*, Kuala Lumpur: National Art Gallery.

Postill, J. 2001. 'The Mediated Production of Ethnicity and Nationalism among the Iban of Sarawak, 1954–1976'. *Borneo Research Bulletin* 32, 146–171.

———. 2002a. 'The Mediated Production of Ethnicity and Nationalism among the Iban of Sarawak (II), 1977–1997'. *Borneo Research Bulletin* 33, 100–126.

———. 2002b. 'Clock and Calendar Time: a Missing Anthropological Problem', *Time & Society*, 11, 251–270.

———. 2002c. 'Nation-states as Culture Areas: a Comparison of Popular Media in Bali and Sarawak'. Paper to the International Institute for Asian Studies IIAS workshop Globalizing Media and Local Society in Indonesia, Leiden, 13–14 September 2002.

———. 2003. 'Knowledge, Literacy, and Media among the Iban of Sarawak: a Reply to Maurice Bloch'. *Social Anthropology* 11(1), 79–100.

———. 2004. 'Running Suburbia: New Media and Local Governance in Subang Jaya'. Paper to the 4th International Malaysian Studies Conferences, UKM, Bangi, Malaysia, 3–5 August 2004, URL (consulted 3 November 2004): http://www.jamesgomeznews.com/ article.php?AID=156.

Poulgrain, G. 1998. *The Genesis of Konfrontasi: Malaysia, Brunei, Indonesia 1945–1965*, London: C. Hurst & Co.

Pringle, R. 1970. *Rajahs and Rebels: the Iban of Sarawak under Brooke Rule, 1841–1941*, London: Macmillan.

Prinsloo, M. and M. Breier. 1996. *The Social Uses of Literacy*, Amsterdam: John Benjamin.

Probst, P. 1993. 'The Letter and the Spirit: Literacy and Religious Authority in the History of the Aladura Movement in Western Nigeria'. In: B. Street (ed.), *Cross-Cultural Approaches to Literacy*, Cambridge: Cambridge University Press.

Provencher, R. 1994. 'Anthropology in the Malayan Peninsula and North Borneo: Orientalist, Nationalist and Theoretical Perspectives'. *Studies in Third World Societies* 54: 45–70.

Radway, J.A. 1984. *Reading the Romance: Women, Patriarchy, and Popular Literature*, Chapel Hill: The University of North Carolina Press.

Rajit, F. 1969. *Sabak Kenang*, Kuching: Borneo Literature Bureau.

———. 1971. *Rintai Gawai Antu*, Kuching: Borneo Literature Bureau.

Ramakrishna, K. 2002. *Emergency Propaganda: the Winning of Malayan Hearts and Minds, 1948–1958*, Richmond, UK: Curzon.

Rantanen, T. 2005. *The Media and Globalization*, London: Sage.

Rappaport, R. 1999. *Ritual and Religion in the Making of Humanity*, Cambridge: Cambridge University Press.

Rapport, N. and J. Overing. 2000. *Social and Cultural Anthropology: the Key Concepts*, London/New York: Routledge.

Rashid, R. 2004. 'Destinies Delayed but Not Denied', *Malaysiakini*, 15 January 2004. URL (consulted 10 November 2004): http://www.malaysiakini.com/opinionsfeatures/ 200401150041504.php

Raslan, K. 2004. 'Hardware without Software? Malaysian Contemporary Art in the Mahathir Era'. In: B. Welsh (ed.), *Reflections: the Mahathir Years*, Washington, DC: Southeast Asian Studies Program, Johns Hopkins University, School of Advanced and International Studies. pp. 494–504.

Reder, S. and K.R. Wikelund. 1993. 'Literacy Development and Ethnicity: an Alaskan Example'. In: B. Street (ed.), *Cross-Cultural Approaches to Literacy*, Cambridge: Cambridge University Press.

Reece, R.H.W. 1981. 'The First Malay Newspaper in Sarawak'. *Sarawak Gazette* April 1981, 9–11.

———. 1998. *Masa Jepun: Sarawak under the Japanese 1941–1945*, Kuching: Sarawak Literary Society.

Rhum, M. 1997. 'Cognatic Descent'. In: T. Barfield (ed.), *The Dictionary of Anthropology*, Oxford: Blackwell. p. 67.

Richards, A. 1961. *Rita Tujoh Malam*, Kuching: Borneo Literature Bureau.

———. 1981. *An Iban-English Dictionary*, London: Clarendon Press.

Ritchie, J. 1993. *A Political Saga: Sarawak 1981–1993*, Singapore: Summer Times.

Rival, L. 1997. 'Modernity and the Politics of Identity in an Amazonian Society'. *Bulletin of Latin American Research* 16, 137–151.

Robinson-Pant, A. 2001. *'Why Eat Cucumbers at the Time of Dying?': Women's Literacy and Development in Nepal*, Hamburg: UNESCO Institute for Education.

Rodgers, S. 1995. *Telling Lives, Telling History: Autobiography and Historical Imagination in Modern Indonesia* (With an English Translation of *Aku Dan Toba* by P. Pospos and *Semasa Kecil Di Kampung* by M. Radjab), Berkeley and Los Angeles, CA: University of California Press.

Rodrigues, W.A. 1983–1984. *The Image of Women in Television Advertisements*, Kuala Lumpur: University of Malaya Department of Anthropology and Sociology.

Rofel, L. 1994. 'Yearnings: Televisual Love and Melodramatic Politics in Contemporary China'. *American Ethnologist* 21, 700–722.

Rogers, E.M. 1995. *Diffusion of Innovations*, 4th edn, New York: Free Press.

Rorty, R. 1991. *Objectivity, Relativism, and Truth*, New York: Cambridge University Press.

Rothenbuhler, E.W. and M. Coman (eds) 2005. *Media Anthropology*, London: Sage.

Rousseau, J. 1980. 'Iban Inequalities'. *Bijdragen tot de Taal-, Land- en Volkenkunde* 136, 52–63.

Said, S. 1994. 'Better Late than Never: Sarawak's Oral Tradition Project, 1991–1992'. *Sarawak Museum Journal* XLVII, 57–83.

Sandin, B. 1962. *Duabelas Bengkah Mimpi Tuai Dayak-Iban*, Kuching: Borneo Literature Bureau.

———. 1964. *Raja Durong*, Kuching: Borneo Literature Bureau.

———. 1967. 'Apai Salui Sleeps with a Corpse: an Iban Folk Story'. *Sarawak Museum Journal* XV, 223–227.

———. 1968. *Leka Sabak*, Kuching: Borneo Literature Bureau.

———. 1970. *Peturun Iban*, Kuching: Borneo Literature Bureau.

———. 1972. *Gawai Antu*, Kuching: Borneo Literature Bureau.

———. 1980. *Iban Adat and Augury*, Penang: Penerbit Universiti Sains Malaysia.

———. 1994. 'Sources of Iban Traditional History'. *Sarawak Museum Journal* (N.S.) XLVI(67), Special Monograph no. 7.

Sather, C. 1981. 'Benedict Sandin, 1918–1982: a Biographical Memoir'. *The Sarawak Museum Journal* XXIX, 101–136.

———. 1984. *Apai Aloi Goes Hunting and Other Stories*, Kuching: Persatuan Kesusasteraan Sarawak.

———. 1990. 'Trees and Tree Tenure in Paku Iban Society: the Management of Secondary Forest Resources in a Long-established Iban Community'. *Borneo Review* 1, 16–40.

———. 1992. 'The Rites of Manggol: Work and Ritual in Paku Iban Agriculture'. *Sarawak Museum Journal* XLIII, 107–137.

———. 1993. 'Posts, Hearths and Thresholds: The Iban Longhouse as a Ritual Structure'. In: J.J. Fox (ed.), *Inside Austronesian Houses: Perspectives on Domestic Designs for Living*, Canberra: Australian National University. pp. 64–115.

———. 1994. 'Introduction to B. Sandin "Sources of Iban Traditional History"'. *Sarawak Museum Journal* (N.S.) XLVI(67), Special Monograph no. 7, 1–78.

———. 1996. 'All Threads are White: Iban Egalitarianism Reconsidered'. In: J.J. Fox and C. Sather (eds), *Origins, Ancestry and Alliance: Explorations in Austronesian Ethnography*, Canberra: The Australian National University.

———. 2001. *Apai Alui Becomes a Shaman and Other Iban Comic Tales. Apai Alui Nyadi Manang Enggau Ensera Iban Bukai*, Kota Samarahan: Universiti Malaysia Sarawak.

Scannell, P. 1988. 'Radio Times: the Temporal Arrangements of Broadcasting in the Modern World'. In: P. Drummond and R. Paterson (eds), *Television and Its Audience*, London: British Film Institute. pp. 15–29.

——— and D. Cardiff. 1991. *A Social History of British Broadcasting*, Oxford: Basil Blackwell.

Schieffelin, B. and P. Gilmore (eds). 1986. *The Acquisition of Literacy: Ethnographic Perspectives*, Norwood, NJ: Ablex.

Schmidt, P.W. 1910. *Grundlinien einer Vergleichung der Religionen und Mythologien der austronesischen Völker*, Vienna: Alfred Hölden.

Scott, A.J. 2000. *The Cultural Economy of Cities: Essays on the Geography of Image-Producing Industries*, London: Sage.

Scott, J.C. 1985. *Weapons of the Weak: the Everyday Forms of Peasant Resistance*, New Haven/London: Yale University Press.

Seymour, J.M. 1974. 'The Rural School as an Acculturating Institution: the Iban of Malaysia'. *Human Organization* 333, 277–290.

———. 1977. 'Urbanization, Schooling and Adaptation: Iban Students of Sarawak, Malaysia'. *Sarawak Museum Journal* XXV, 177–200.

Seymour-Smith, C. 1986. *Macmillan Dictionary of Anthropology*, London: Macmillan.

Sheridan, D., B. Street and D. Bloome. 1999. *Ordinary People Writing: Literacy Practices and Identity in the Mass-Observation Project*, Cresskill, NJ: Hampton Press.

Shuman, A. 1986. *Storytelling Rights: the Uses of Oral and Written Texts by Urban Adolescents*, Cambridge: Cambridge University Press.

Siebert, F.S., T. Peterson and W. Schramm. 1963. *Four Theories of the Press*, Urbana: University of Illinois Press.

Sillitoe, P. 2000. *Social Change in Melanesia: Development and History*, Cambridge: Cambridge University Press.

Silverstone, R. 1988. 'Television, Myth and Culture'. In: J.W. Carey (ed.), *Media, Myths, and Narratives*, Newbury Park, CA: Sage. pp. 20–47.

———, E. Hirsch and D. Morley. 1994. 'Information and Communication Technologies and the Moral Economy of the Household'. In: R. Silverstone and E. Hirsch (eds), *Consuming Technologies: Media and Information in Domestic Spaces*, London: Routledge.

Skuse, A. 1999. Negotiated Outcomes: an Ethnography of the Production and Consumption of a BBC World Service Soap Opera for Afghanistan. Unpublished Ph.D. thesis, University of London.

Slater, D. 1998. 'Trading Sexpics on IRC: Embodiment and Authenticity on the Internet'. *Body and Society* 4(4), 91–117.

Smalley, W.A., C.K. Vang and G.Y. Yang. 1990. *Mother of Writing: the Origin and Development of a Hmong Messianic Script*, Chicago: University of Chicago Press.

Smith, A.D. 1986. *The Ethnic Origins of Nations*, Oxford: Blackwell.
———. 1994. 'The Crisis of Dual Legitimation'. In: J. Hutchinson and A.D. Smith (eds), *Nationalism*, Oxford: Oxford University Press.
———. 1995. *Nations and Nationalism in a Global Era*, Cambridge: Polity Press.
———. 2001. *Nationalism: Theory, Ideology, History*, Cambridge: Polity Press.
———. 2004. 'History and National Destiny: Responses and Clarifications'. *Nations and Nationalism* 10, 195–209.
Sperber, D. 1996. *Explaining Culture: A Naturalistic Approach*, Oxford: Blackwell.
———. 2000. 'An Objection to the Memetic Approach to Culture'. In: R. Aunger (ed.), *Darwinizing Culture*, Oxford: Oxford University Press.
Spindler, G. 1974. *Educational and Cultural Process: Toward an Anthropology of Education*, New York: Holt, Rinehart & Winston.
Spitulnik, D. 1993. 'Anthropology and Mass Media'. *Annual Review of Anthropology* 22, 293–315.
———. 1996. 'The Social Circulation of Media Discourse and the Mediation of Communities'. *Journal of Linguistic Anthropology* 62, 161–187.
———. 2000. 'Documenting Radio Culture as Lived Experience: Reception Studies and the Mobile Machine in Zambia'. In: R. Fardon and G. Furniss (eds), *African Broadcast Cultures: Radio in Transition*, Oxford: James Currey.
Spolsky, B., G. Engelbrecht and L. Ortiz. 1983. 'Religious, Political, and Educational Factors in the Development of Biliteracy in the Kingdom of Tonga'. *Journal of Multilingual and Multicultural Development* 4: 459–469.
Steinmayer, O. 1990. 'The Borneo Literature Bureau: Publications in Iban and Other Bornean Languages'. *Borneo Research Bulletin* 22, 114–129.
———. 1999. *Jalai Jako Iban*, Kuching: Klasik.
Stetter, C. 1997. *Schrift und Sprache*, Frankfurt: Suhrkamp.
Stirratt, J. 1989. 'Attitudes to Money among Catholic Fishing Communities in Sri Lanka'. In: M. Bloch and J. Parry (eds), *Money and the Morality of Exchange*, Cambridge: Cambridge University Press.
Strathern, M. 2000. *Audit Cultures: Anthropological Studies in Accountability, Ethics and the Academy*, London: Routledge.
Street, B. 1984. *Literacy in Theory and Practice*, Cambridge: Cambridge University Press.
———. 1993. *Cross-Cultural Approaches to Literacy*, Cambridge: Cambridge University Press.
———. 2001. *Literacy and Development: Ethnographic Perspectives*, London: Routledge.
Sullivan, N. 1993. 'Film and Television Production in Papua New Guinea: How Media Becomes the Message'. *Public Culture* 5, 533–555.
Sutlive, V.H. 1972. From Longhouse to Pasar: Urbanization in Sarawak, East Malaysia. Unpublished Ph.D. dissertation, Pittsburgh University.
———. 1977. 'The Many Faces of Kumang: Iban Women in Fiction and Fact'. *Sarawak Museum Journal* XV, 157–164.
———. 1978. *The Iban of Sarawak*, Arlington Heights, IL: AHM Publishing Corporation.
———. 1985. 'Urban Migration into Sibu, Sarawak'. *Borneo Research Bulletin* 17(2), 85–95.
———. 1989. 'The Iban in Historical Perspective'. *Sarawak Museum Journal* XL, 33–44.

————. 1992. *Tun Jugah of Sarawak: Colonialism and Iban Response*, Kuala Lumpur: Penerbit Fajar Bakti.

———— and J. Sutlive. 1994. *Dictionary of Iban and English*, Kuching: Tun Jugah Foundation.

Sweeney, A. 1987. *A Full Hearing: Orality and Literacy in the Malay World*, Berkeley, CA: University of California Press.

Swzed, J.F. 1981. 'The Ethnography of Literacy'. In: M.F. Whiteman (ed.), *Writing: the Nature, Development, and Teaching of Written Communication, Vol. 1*, Hillsdale, NJ: Lawrence Erlbaum.

Tacchi, J. 1998. 'Radio Texture: Between Self and Others'. In: D. Miller (ed.), *Material Cultures: Why Some Things Matter*, London: UCL Press. pp. 25–46.

Tarling, N. 1998. *Nations and States in Southeast Asia*, Cambridge: Cambridge University Press.

Tawai, J. 1989. *Kelimbak Darah*, Kuching: Star Company.

————. 1997. 'Masalah dan masa depan yang dihadapi di dalam pendidikan bahasa ibunda bagi bahasa Iban di Malaysia: suatu laporan ringkas'. Paper to the seminar Pendidikan bahasa ibunda bagi etnik minoriti di Malaysia: masalah dan masa depan. DJZ High Learning Centre, Kajang, Selangor, 1 November 1997.

Thomas, G. 1998. *Medien, Ritual, Religion*, Frankfurt: Suhrkamp.

Thompson, E.P. 1967. 'Time, Work-discipline, and Industrial Capitalism', *Past and Present* 38, 56–97.

Thompson, J.B. 1995. *The Media and Modernity: a Social Theory of the Media*, Cambridge: Polity Press.

Tong Y.S. 2004. '*Malaysiakini*: Treading a Tightrope of Political Pressure and Market Factors'. In: S. Gan, J. Gomez and U. Johannen (eds), *Asian Cyberactivism: Freedom of Expression and Media Censorship*, Bangkok: Friedrich Naumann Foundation.

Tønnesson, S. 2004. 'Globalising Nation States'. *Nations and Nationalism* 10(1/2), 179–194.

Turner, T. 1992. 'Defiant Images: the Kayapo Appropriation of Video'. *Anthropology Today* 8, 5–16.

Turner, V.W. 1982. *From Ritual to Theatre*, New York: Performing Arts Journal Publications.

Tuzin, D.F. 2001. *Social Complexity in the Making: a Case Study among the Arapesh of New Guinea*, London: Routledge.

Uchibori, M. 1988. 'Transformations of Iban Social Consciousness'. In: J.G. Taylor and A. Turton (eds), *Southeast Asia*, London: Macmillan. pp. 250–258.

Uimonen, P. 2003. 'Mediated Management of Meaning: On-line Nation Building in Malaysia'. *Global Networks* 3(3), 299–314.

Undau, D.M. 2001. 'A Brief History of Gawai Dayak'. In: *Gawai Dayak Celebrations 2001*, Kuching: Lee Ming Press. pp. 28–29.

Untie E. 1998. 'Penabur Radio Sekula'. Paper to the Workshop on the Current Situation and Future of Iban language Broadcasting. Stambak Park, Kuching, 4 April.

Van Gennep, A. 1960. *The Rites of Passage*, Chicago: University of Chicago Press.

Van Groenendael, M.C. 1985. *The Dalang Behind the Wayang: the Role of the Surakarta and the Yogyakarta Dalang in Indonesian-Javanese Society*, Dordrecht: Foris.

Varenne, H. and R. McDermott, 1986. 'Why Sheila Can Read: Structure and Indeterminacy in the Reproduction of Familial Literacy'. In: B. Schieffelin and P. Gilmore (eds), *The Acquisition of Literacy: Ethnographic Perspectives*, Norwood, NJ: Ablex.

Wadley, R. 1999b. 'Disrespecting the Dead and the Living: Iban Ancestor Worship and the Violation of Mourning Taboos'. *Journal of the Royal Anthropological Institute* 5, 595–610.

Wagner, D.A. (ed.). 1983. *Literacy and Ethnicity (International Journal of the Sociology of Language 42)*, Berlin: Mouton.

———. 1993. *Literacy, Culture and Development: Becoming Literate in Morocco*, Cambridge: Cambridge University Press.

Wagner, R. 1981. *The Invention of Culture*, Chicago: The University of Chicago Press.

Walker, W. 1993. 'Native American Writing Systems'. In: C.A. Ferguson and S.B. Heath (eds), *Language in the USA*, Cambridge: Cambridge University Press.

Whitehouse, H. 2001. 'Conclusion: Towards a Reconciliation'. In: H. Whitehouse (ed.), *The Debated Mind:Evolutionary Psychology versus Ethnography*, Oxford/New York: Berg.

Whorf, B.L. 1956. *Language, Thought, and Reality*, Cambridge, MA: MIT Press.

Wibisono, S. 1975. 'The Wayang as a Medium of Communication'. *Prisma* 1(2), 44–63.

Willis P. 1977. *Learning to Labor: How Working Class Kids Get Working Class Jobs*, New York: Columbia University Press.

Wilson, J.K. 1969. *Budu, or, Twenty Years in Sarawak*, North Berwick, Scotland: Tantallon Press.

Winzeler, R.L. (ed.) 1997. *Indigenous Peoples and the State: Politics, Land and Ethnicity in the Malayan Peninsula and Borneo*, New Haven: Yale University Press.

Wolf, E. 1997. *Europe and the People without History*, Berkeley, CA: University of California Press.

Woolard, K. 1989. *Double Talk: Bilingualism and the Politics of Ethnicity in Catalonia*, Stanford, CA: Stanford University Press.

Yates, R. 1994. Gender and Literacy in Ghana. Unpublished Ph.D. thesis, University of Sussex, UK.

Yong, J.S.L. 2003. 'Malaysia: Advancing Public Administration into the Information Age'. In: J.S.L. Yong (ed.), *E-Government in Asia: Enabling Public Service Innovation in the 21st Century*, Singapore: Times.

Zeppel, H. 1994. Authenticity and the Iban: Cultural Tourism at Iban Longhouses in Sarawak, East Malaysia. Unpublished Ph.D. thesis, James Cook University of North Queensland, Townsville.

Zerubavel, E. 2003. *Time Maps: Collective Memory and the Social Shape of the Past*, Chicago: University of Chicago Press.

Zulficly, Z.A. 1989. 'Language and Oral Tradition: the Role of Dewan Bahasa dan Pustaka'. *Sarawak Museum Journal* XL, Special Issue 4, 159–165.

INDEX

T
Tacchi, J., 141
Taib Mahmud, 85, 92
Tarling, N., 1, 9, 17
television, 3, 9–10, 14, 134–51
    arrival in Sarawak, 17
    'double articulation' in culture and
        economy, 144
    effects on Iban sociality, 19, 158–59, 198
    in Malaysia, 81–85
    in Papua New Guinea, 74
    sets and Iban exchange system, 18–19,
        134–51, 194
    visuality, 145
territory, 1–4, 15, 17
Third World, 5, 7, 107, 141
    lack of electricity, 36, 129, 137, 141, 160,
        166
Thompson, E.P., 152–53
Thompson, J., 17, 103, 144, 197
Tiew Brothers Company (Sibu), 79–81
time. *See* clock-and-calendar time
tribes, 1, 9, 17
Tun Jugah of Sarawak, 45
Turner, T., 9, 18, 74
Turner, V., 172, 184–85
TV3 (Malaysia), 82–83

U
United Malays National Organisation
    (UMNO), 82, 195
United Nations (UN), 1, 3, 106, 192
United States (US), 1, 5, 76, 123, 126, 151n.
    5, 154–55, 191n. 10.
    foreign policy, 5, 7, 62–63n. 8., 155, 198
    government, 5
    multinational companies, 48, 83–84, 126
    popular music influence of, 48

scholars, 5, 7, 10
television exports to Malaysia, 83–84
uses research, 7
utilitarianism, 137–38, 140

V
value, 137–38
Van Gennep, A., 184
Vietnam, 5
Vision 2020 (*Wawasan 2020*), 5, 91–92, 95,
    100, 111, 167–68, 174, 195

W
West, the (North Atlantic), 3, 125, 128,
    132, 137–38, 141, 147, 153–54, 156,
    158–59
    media/social theory in, 5, 141, 183
Wilder, W.D., 12, 15, 22, 27–28, 43, 44, 86
Wilk, R., 7, 20n. 2.
Williams, R., 8, 93
Wilson, J.K., 50–51, 57, 62n. 1., 63n. 11.,
    169n. 4.
Winzeler, R.L., 42, 43, 45n. 4., 56–57
Wolf, E., 155
world history, 12–13, 152, 154–55, 197
writing. *See* literacy

Y
Yakub, A.R., 32, 58
Yemen, 155
Yoruba people (Nigeria), 61
Yugoslavia, 1, 199

Z
Zambia, 13–14, 128
    as culture area, 16